IMAGES
of America

BATAVIA

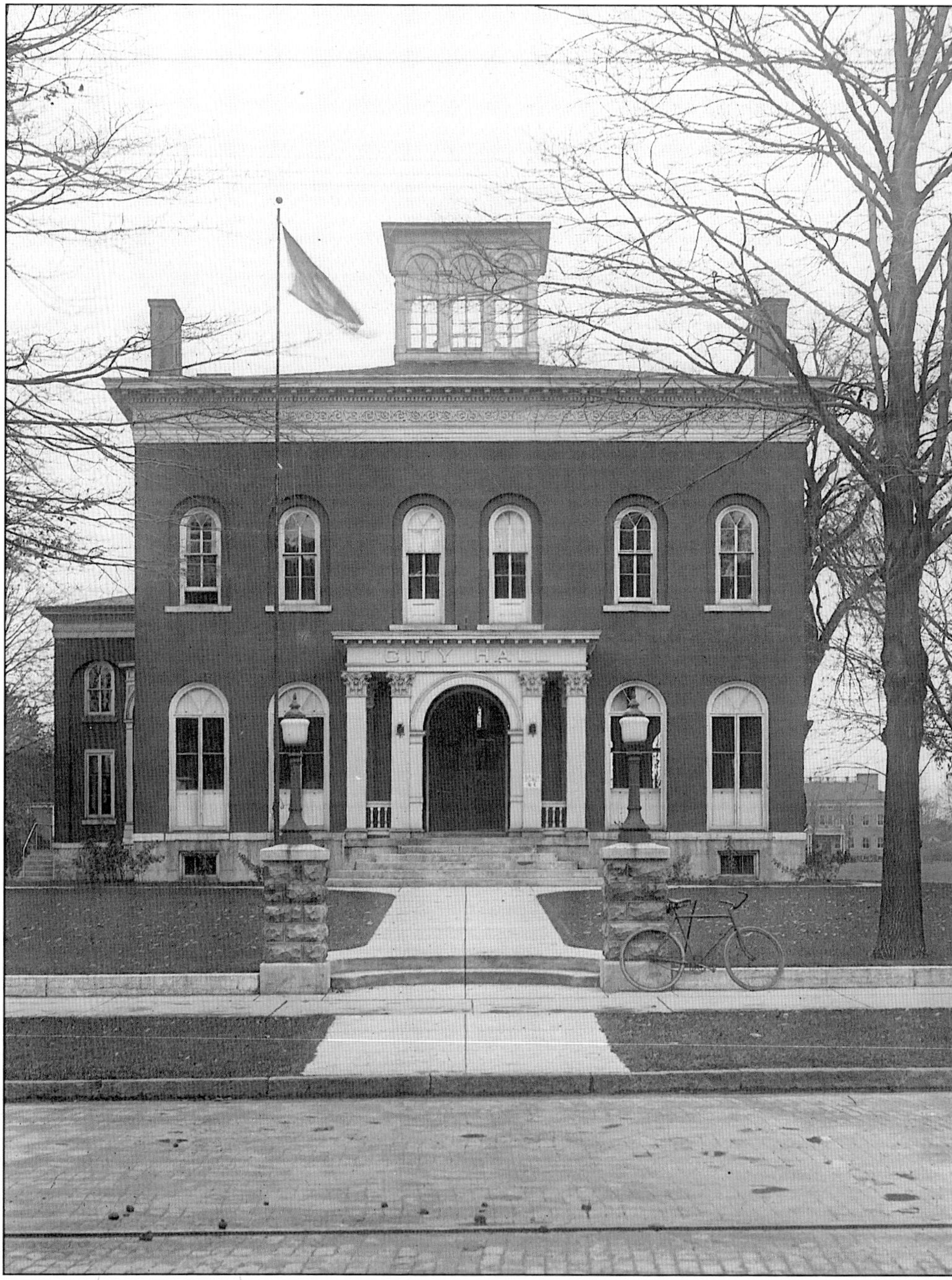

This photograph shows Batavia City Hall. At one time, the building was the Brisbane home. Later, it was remodeled and became city hall.

IMAGES
of America

BATAVIA

Barbara Ann Toal

ARCADIA
PUBLISHING

ISBN 978-0-7385-0467-4

Published by Arcadia Publishing
Charleston, South Carolina

Printed in the United States of America

Library of Congress Catalog Card Number: 00104056

For all general information contact Arcadia Publishing at:
Telephone 843-853-2070
Fax 843-853-0044
E-mail sales@arcadiapublishing.com
For customer service and orders:
Toll-Free 1-888-313-2665

Visit us on the Internet at www.arcadiapublishing.com

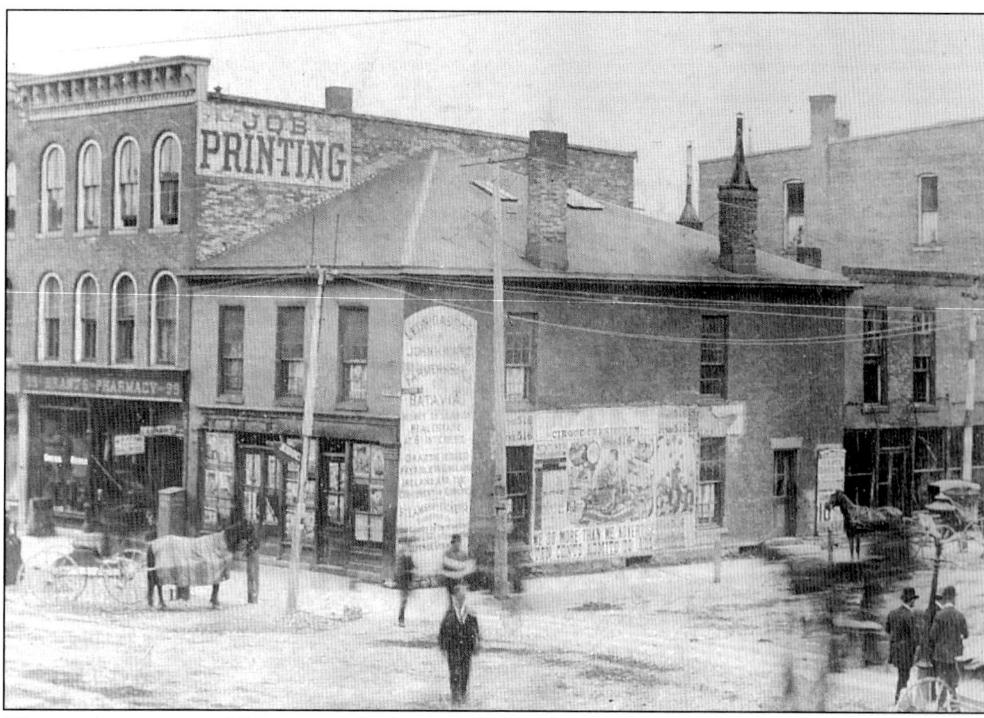

This is the corner of Main and Jackson Streets, the location that is at the center of the city's activities.

Contents

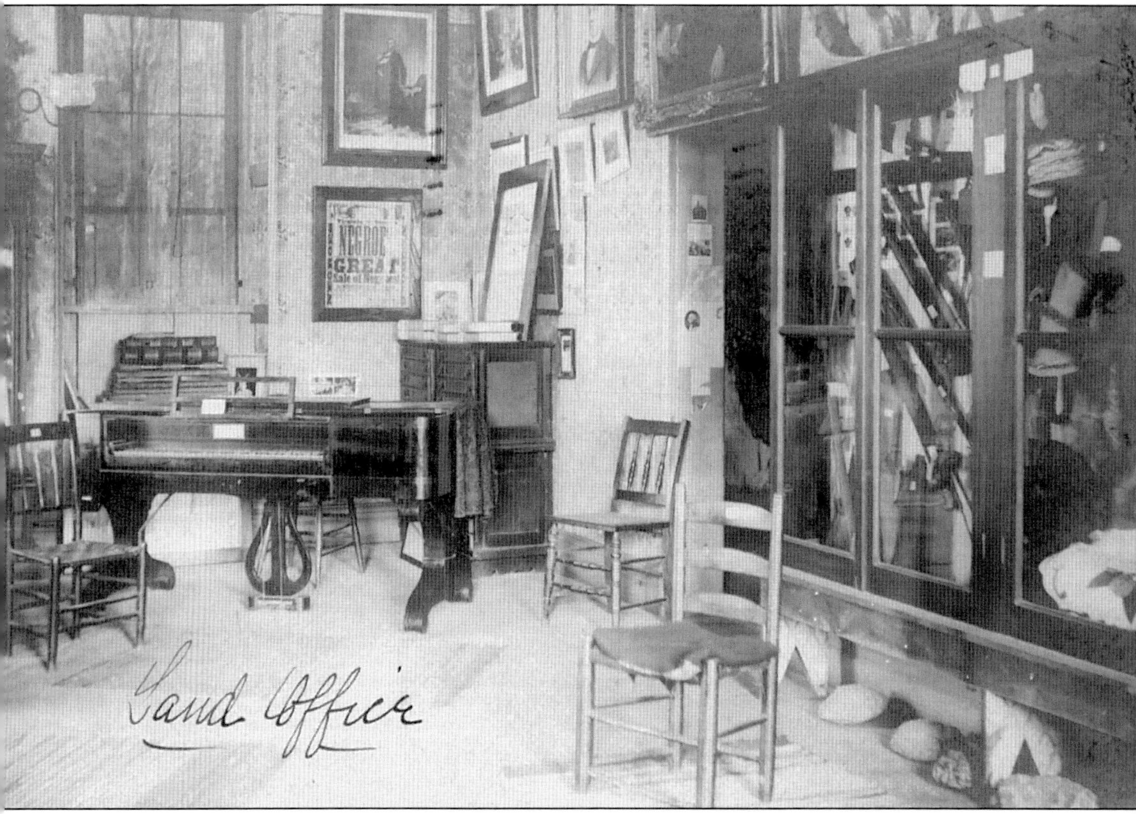

This room inside the Holland Land Office was the first place that the founders of Batavia gathered and met to discuss the surveying of the lands that later became Batavia.

Introduction

This pictorial journey blends photographs, postcards, and drawings to recount Batavia's history from the early 1700s, when Indian trails converged at the Great Meeting Place, to the vibrant city that Batavia is today.

The area was important hundreds of years before Columbus arrived in America. Over the centuries it has been called by at least six different names. Among its earlier names were *Jo-a-ki*, meaning "raccoon," *Ton-nor-aun-to*, meaning "swift running water," *Je-ne-an-da-sase-geh*, meaning "mosquito," and *Deo-on-go-wa*, or "the Great Meeting Place," so called because it was the junction of two great Indian trails, one leading from Lake Erie to the Hudson River and the other from Lake Erie to the Susquehanna River.

When the Europeans came, they called the place "the Great Bend of the *Ton-ne-wan-ta*. The current name, Batavia, was chosen by Joseph Ellicott, local agent of the Holland Land Company; it was once the name of the Netherlands. Batavia would have been named "Bustiville," after Paolo Busti, the general agent of the Holland Land Company. Busti, however, refused to allow the place to be named in his honor.

In the chapters that follow, are glimpses of the American Revolution, the War of 1812, the Great Depression, and the two world wars. Also inside are economic growth that came with the railroad, the impact of the automobile, and the responses of the community to the growth in population.

The railroad brought Batavia industries to their peak in the early 1900s, as all trains stopped here to load and unload. As highways improved, the city's central location between Rochester and Buffalo became key. Today, the city has an abundance of parks and recreational opportunities, and stands at the junction of Routes 5, 33, 63 and 98—all meeting at the Holland Land Office and the bend of the Tonawanda Creek.

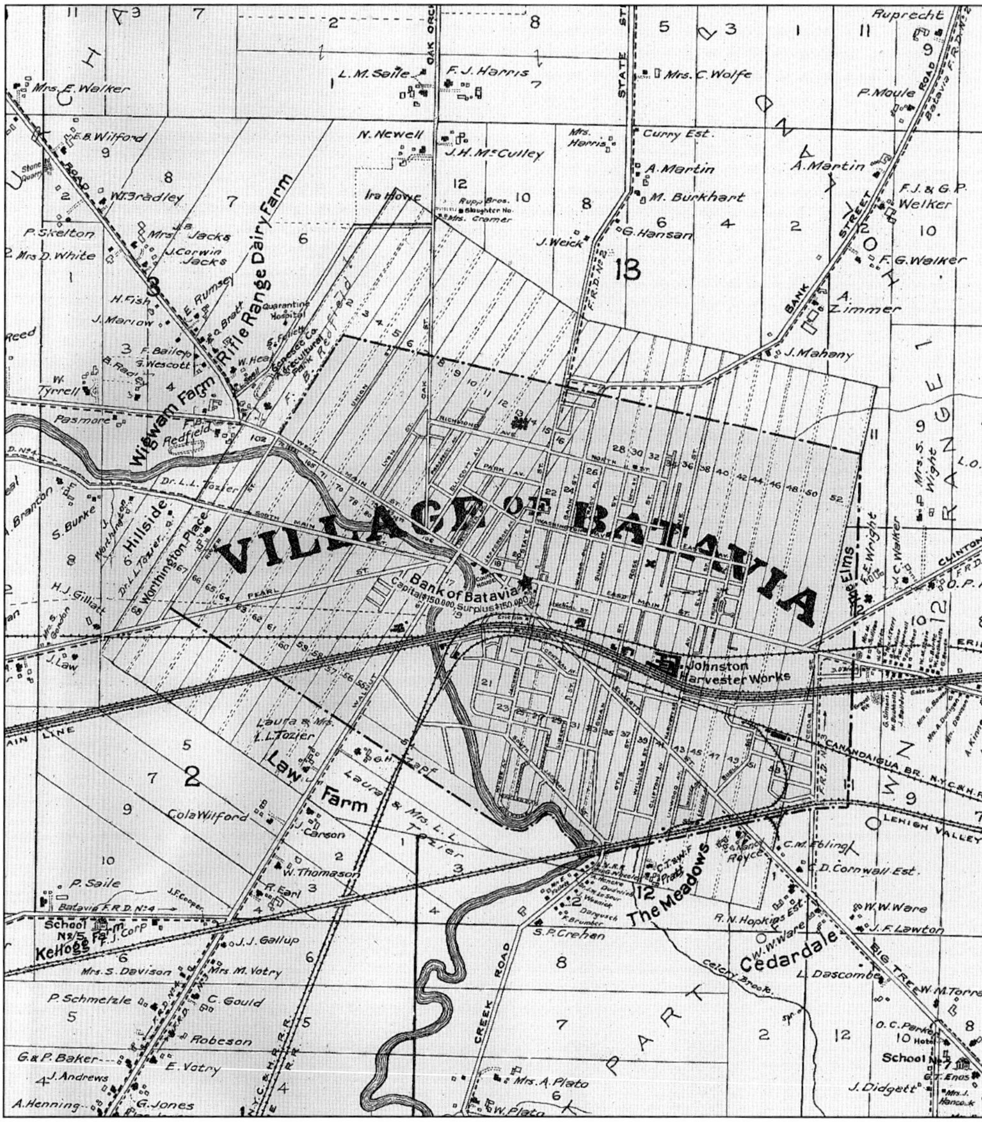

This map shows the central area of Batavia.

One

Early Inhabitants, Early Development

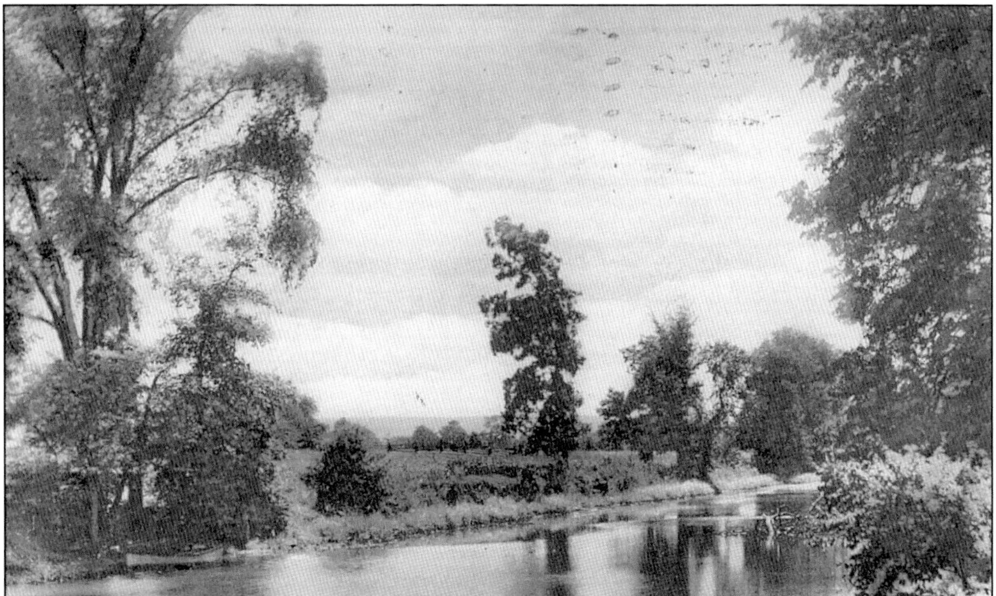

The Tonawanda Creek is the historical focal point of Batavia. This was where Joseph Ellicott, the founder of Batavia, decided to start surveying lands. Another name for the creek was *Tonnewanta*, which means "the bend." Oddly enough, the name Tonawanda signifies "swiftly running water," even though for most of its course the stream is a sluggish one.

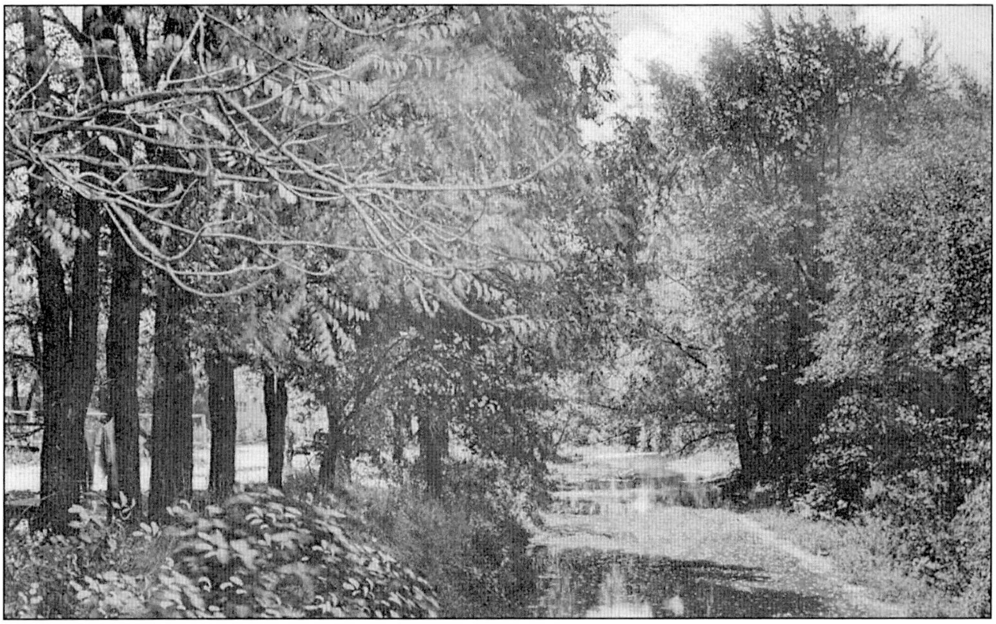

The Iroquois trails ran alongside the creek, providing access to not only fresh water but also fresh fish. The trails were used by a number of different tribes who traveled here from their villages, which were scattered throughout this area. The region was heavily wooded and, therefore, offered ideal hunting grounds with a plentiful supply of food.

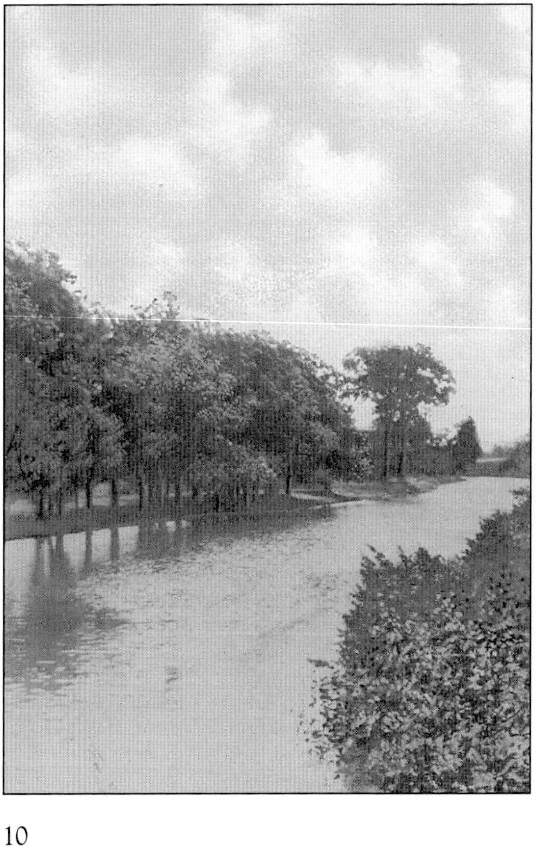

This is the famous bend in the Tonawanda Creek. According to Indian folklore, at the great bend stood an ancient town called *Deo-on-go-wa*, meaning "the Great Meeting Place." The Tonawanda Creek rises in Wyoming County. It enters the town of Alexander from the south and flows in a northeasterly direction through the town of Batavia and through the village of Batavia. There, it turns and flows in a westerly and then a northwesterly direction through the town of Pembroke and then through the town of Alabama, leaving the latter town at a point trifle north of the center of its western boundary. The course of the Tonawanda Creek is treacherous but, for the most part, its waters flow in a very sluggish manner.

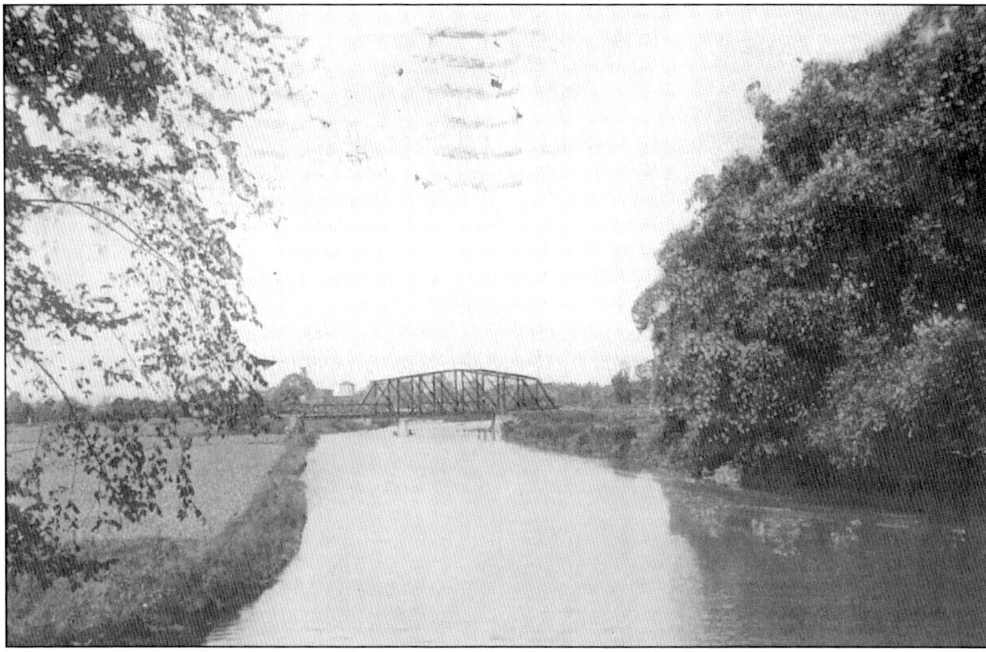

The Tonawanda Creek flows from east to west through Batavia. The River Street Bridge, above, crosses the Tonawanda Creek at the most westerly point in the city of Batavia. The Walnut Street Bridge, below, stands just west of the dam, beyond the bend in the Tonawanda Creek.

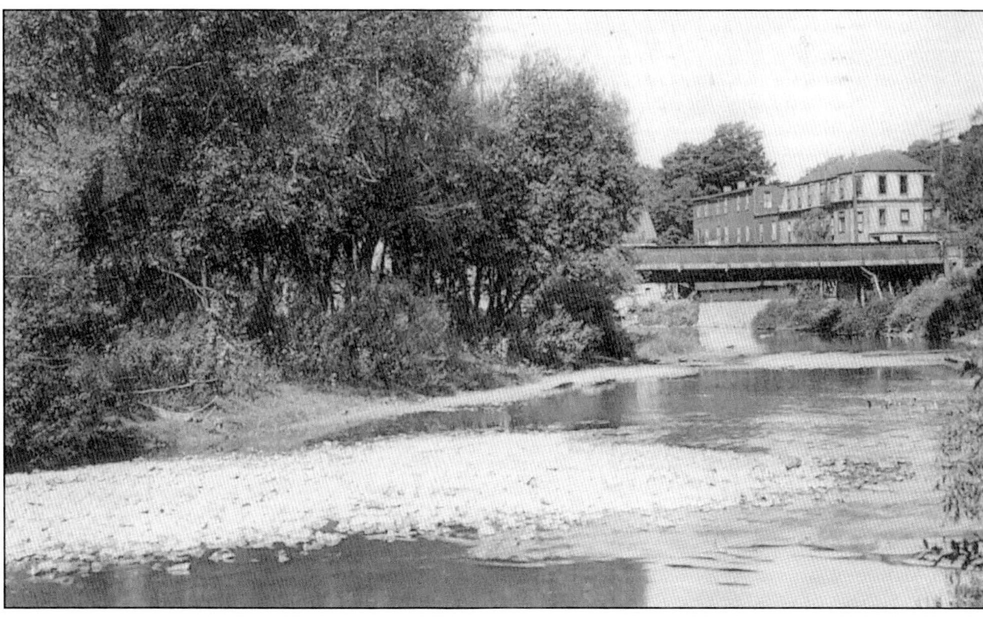

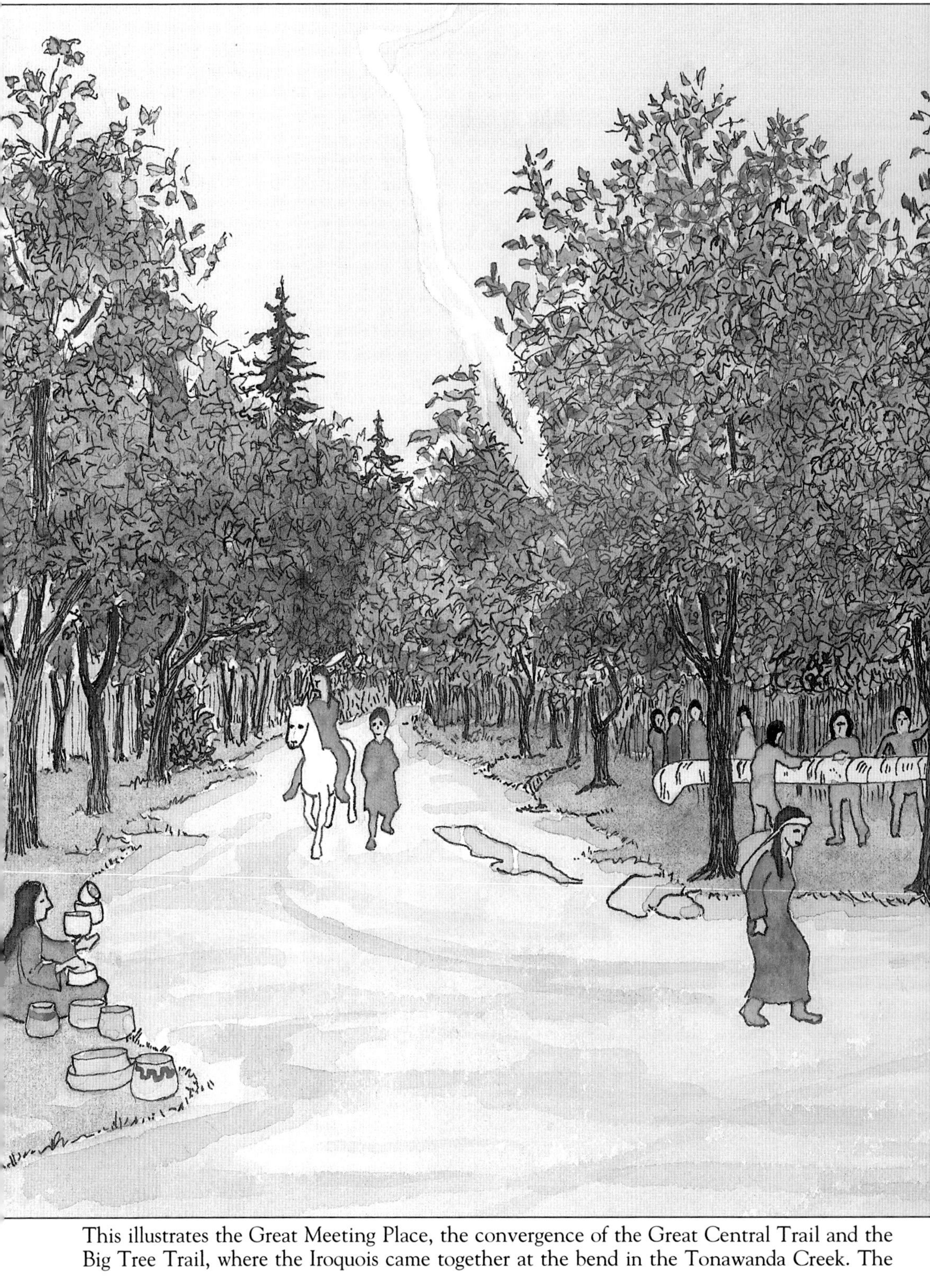

This illustrates the Great Meeting Place, the convergence of the Great Central Trail and the Big Tree Trail, where the Iroquois came together at the bend in the Tonawanda Creek. The

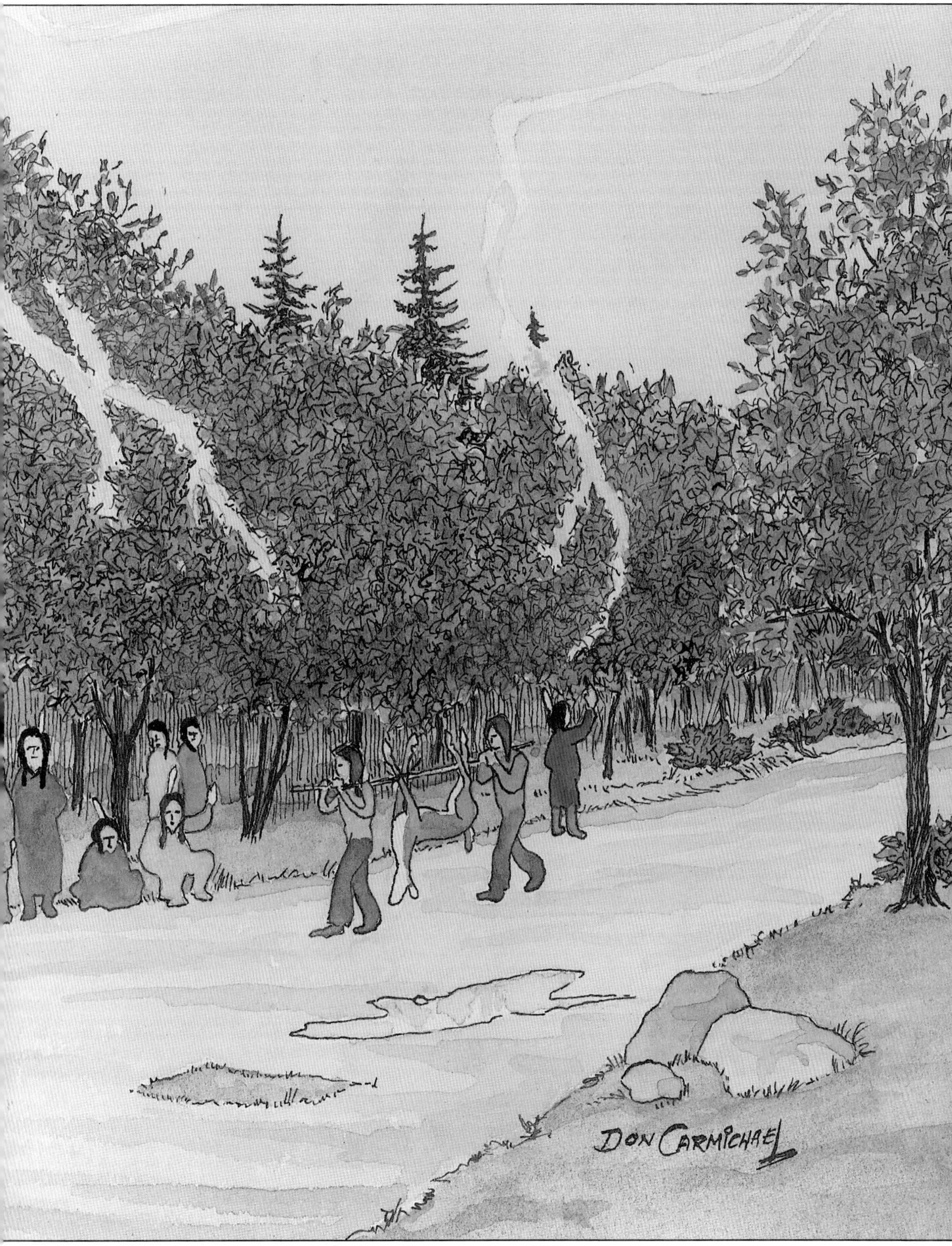

artist depicts a meeting as it might have happened c. 1720.

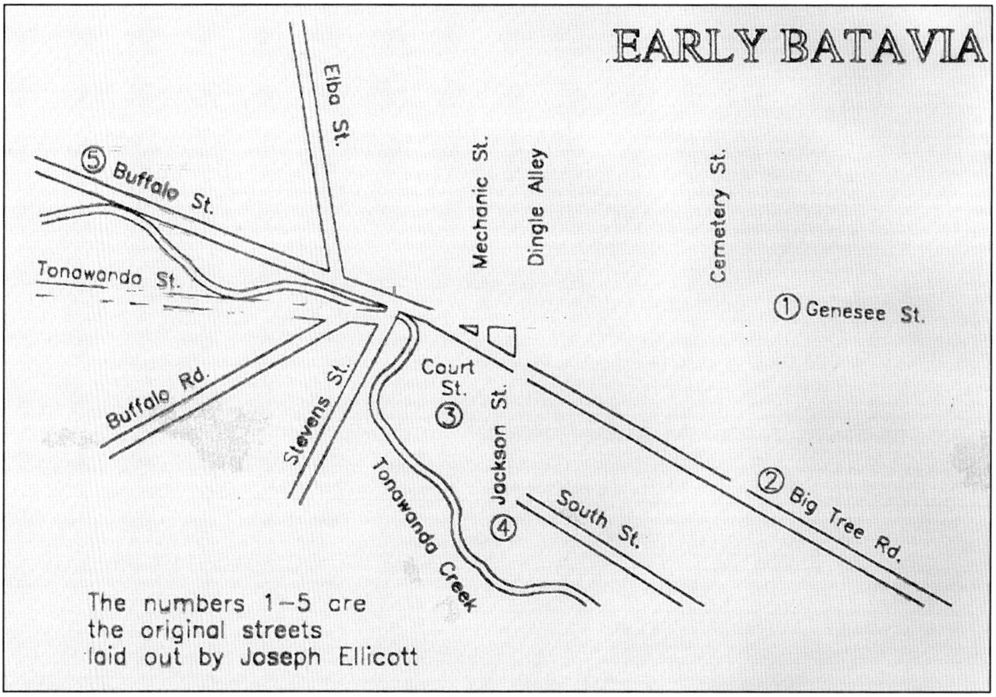

One of the other reasons that the Indians chose to make their meeting place at the bend of the creek was because of the fresh water supply that sustained them. The source was Indian Springs.

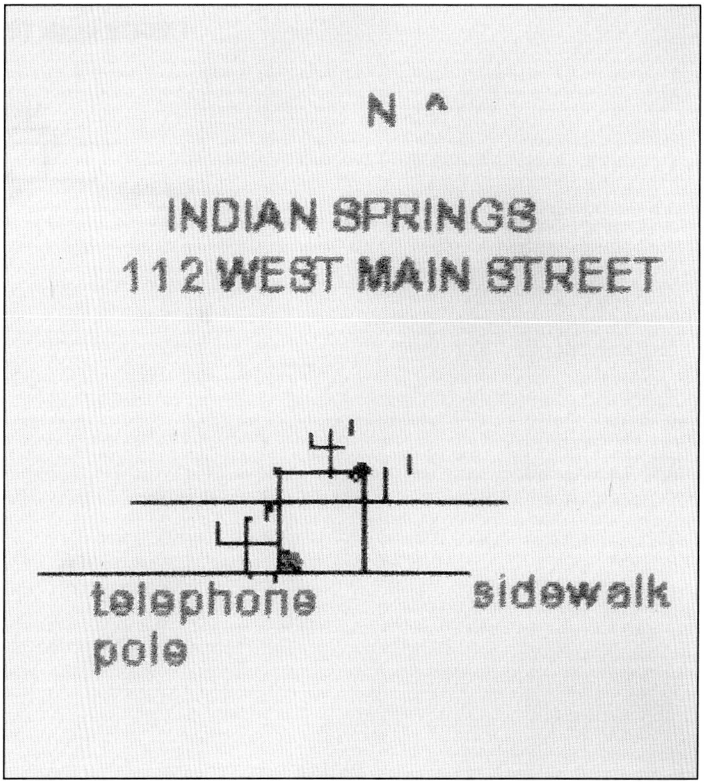

The actual location of Indian Springs is where the buildings at 112–126 West Main Street stand today.

Red Jacket (1758–1830) was a chief of the Seneca, best known for his talents as an orator and statesman. His Indian name was *Sa-go-ye-wath-a*, which means "he that keeps them awake." Reared in traditional Seneca fashion, he was given the name *Otetiani*, meaning "always ready," at the age of 10. By the time of the Revolutionary War, he possessed unusual intelligence and was recognized by the British, who employed him as a messenger. One of the British officers presented him with an embroidered scarlet jacket, which he proudly wore and from which came the name Red Jacket.

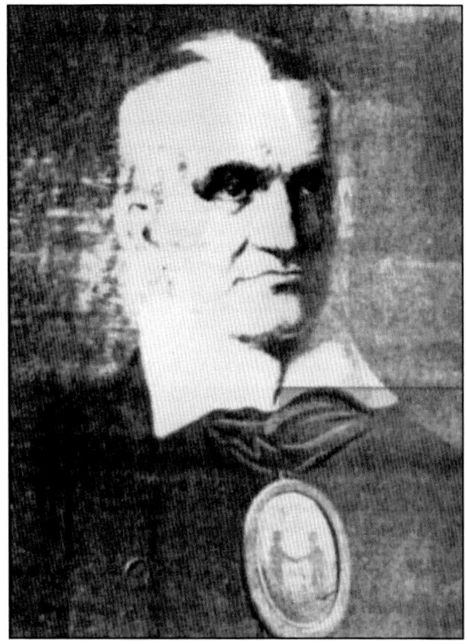

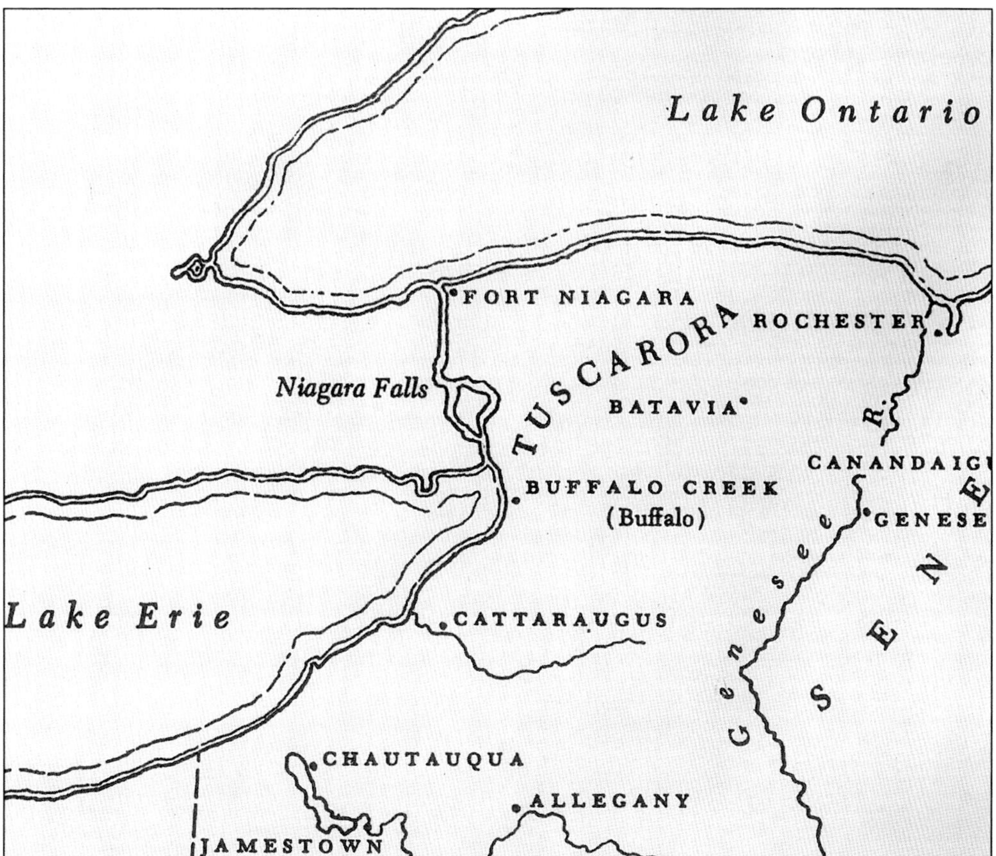

This map shows the lands of the Iroquois in the days of Red Jacket.

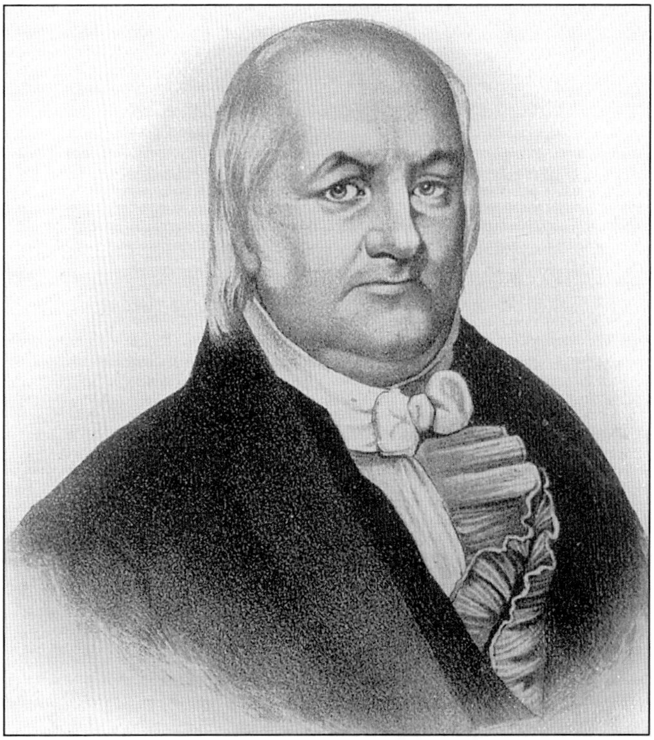

Joseph Ellicott (1760–1826) came to Batavia as the principal surveyor of the Holland Land Company in western New York; he was engaged to survey 3.3 million acres of land. At 6 feet 3 inches tall, he was a man of commanding presence who possessed a splendid constitution and great powers of endurance. He accumulated a large estate, which by special bequest, was divided among his surviving relatives. A monument was erected in his memory.

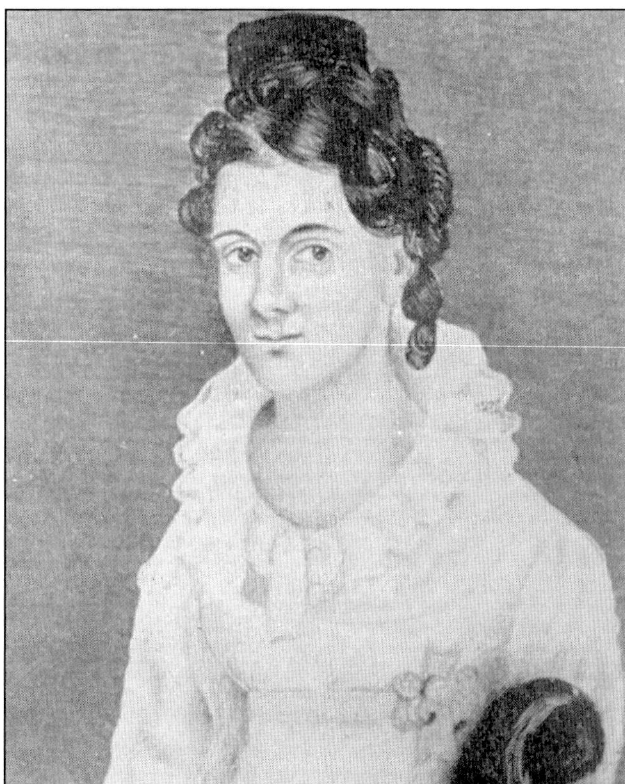

Ann Ellicott was the cousin and close companion of Joseph Ellicott. It is said that Joseph Ellicott was "a most agreeable companion," as well as being "methodical, prompt, and faithful."

Robert Morris was a patriot whose great contribution to the American Revolution has been largely ignored—except in Batavia. Morris, who came into possession of the Holland Land Purchase c. 1771, procured the money that virtually saved the Revolution. A practical man, he had accumulated a large fortune of $8 million. He saw that the Revolutionary forces were struggling and needed money. Thus, he negotiated several loans in Holland and backed all of his transactions with his own personal credit. The founding of Batavia was part of that great transaction. As a result, the Revolution was saved but Morris ended up in debtors' prison and died in abject poverty.

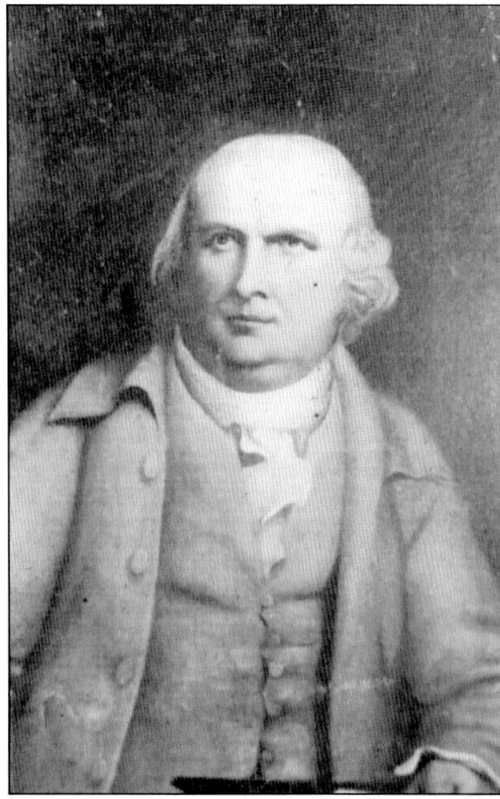

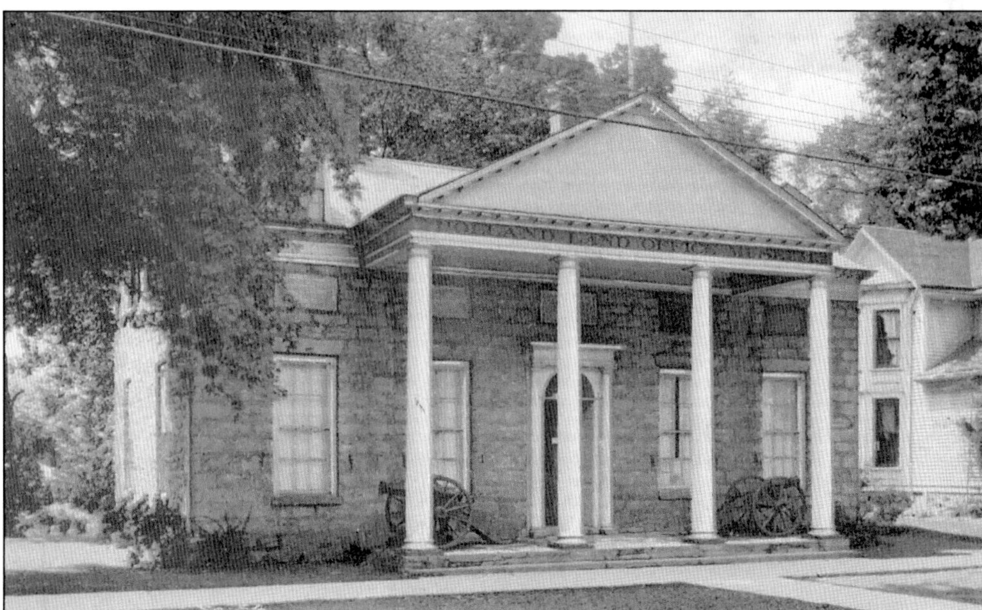

This is the Holland Land Office. In 1798, Joseph Ellicott and Benjamin Ellicott and James Brisbane were recorded inhabitants of the village of Batavia. The survey of the Holland Purchase began. The first improvement of the Indian trails for wagon passage was accomplished by Joseph Ellicott, who employed hands to clear the East Transit Line to Buffalo Creek.

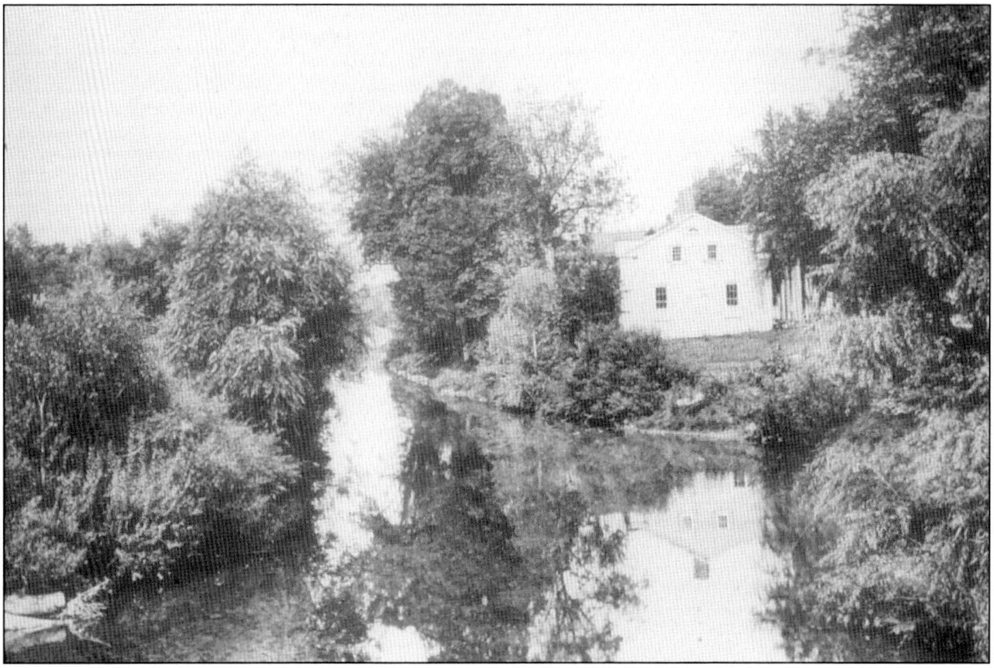

Joseph Ellicott approved his brother Benjamin Ellicott's selection of a site for the Holland Land Office at the big bend of the Tonawanda Creek and the great plan for a town that he was surveying there *c.* 1800. The majority of the settlers were from New England, and they gave tone to the manners and habits of the people. The town was laid out in lots with 20 rods of frontage and one mile of depth, which originally sold for $5 per acre.

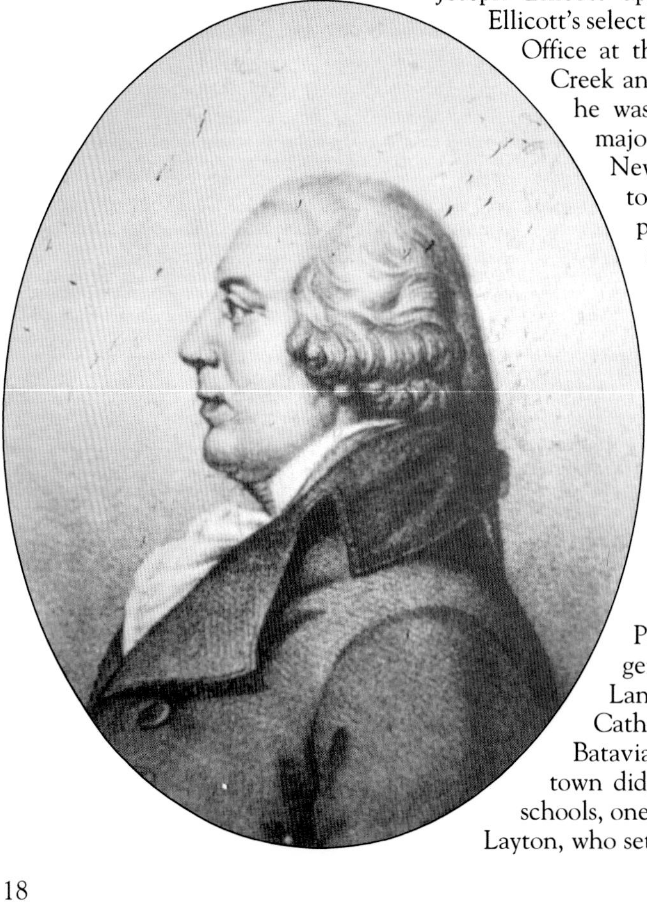

Paolo Busti was appointed general agent of the Holland Land Company *c.* 1799. A devout Catholic, he was startled to learn that Batavia had no church building. The town did, however, have several private schools, one of which was taught by Thomas Layton, who settled in Batavia in 1801.

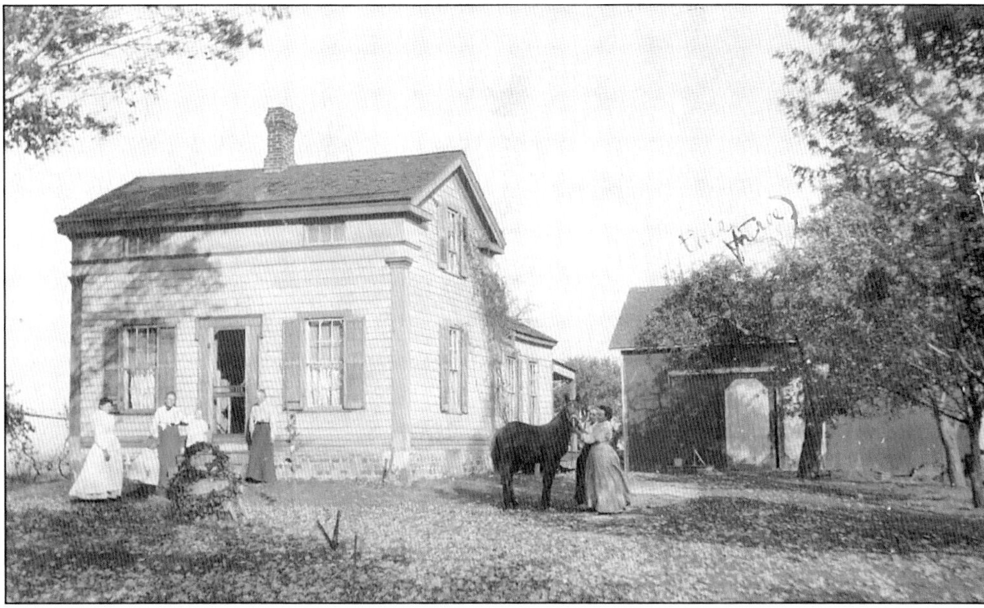

A man by the name of Abel Rowe purchased the first lot of land in the village *c.* 1801. This was the house that Rowe built.

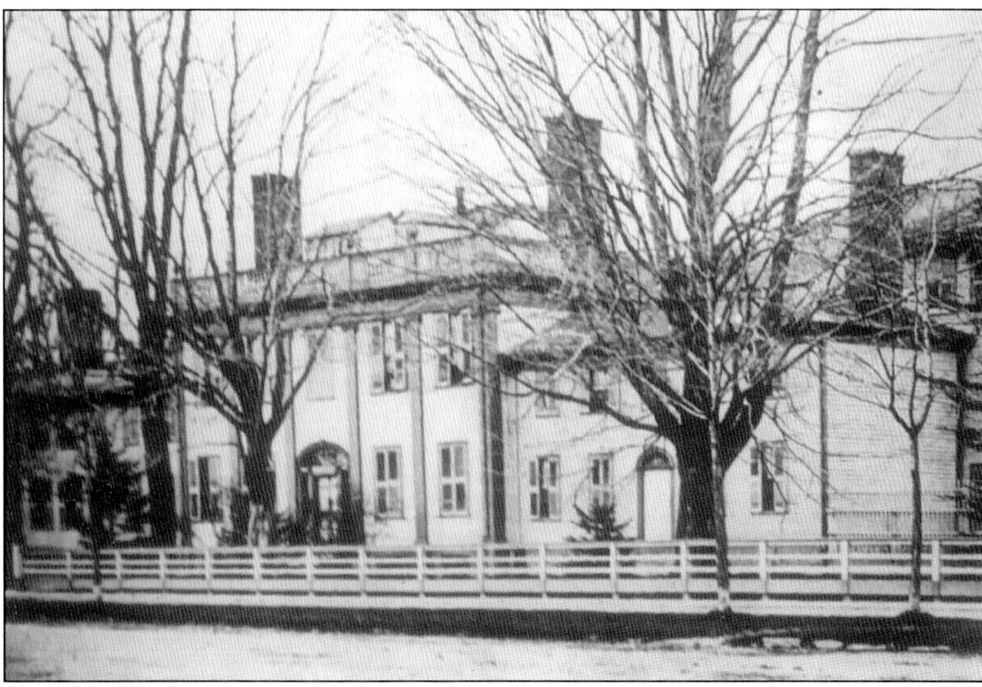

Joseph Ellicott's house was built *c.* 1800 on the north side of Main Street. During the War of 1812, it was used as military headquarters. The Holland Land Office was housed here for a time, while the two-story log structure was being replaced with a stone house. After Ellicott's death, the building was owned by nephew David Ellicott Evans. In 1850, it housed the Bryan Seminary for Young Ladies. In 1887, the building was razed to make way for Dellinger Avenue. The east wing was moved to a site behind 128 West Main Street.

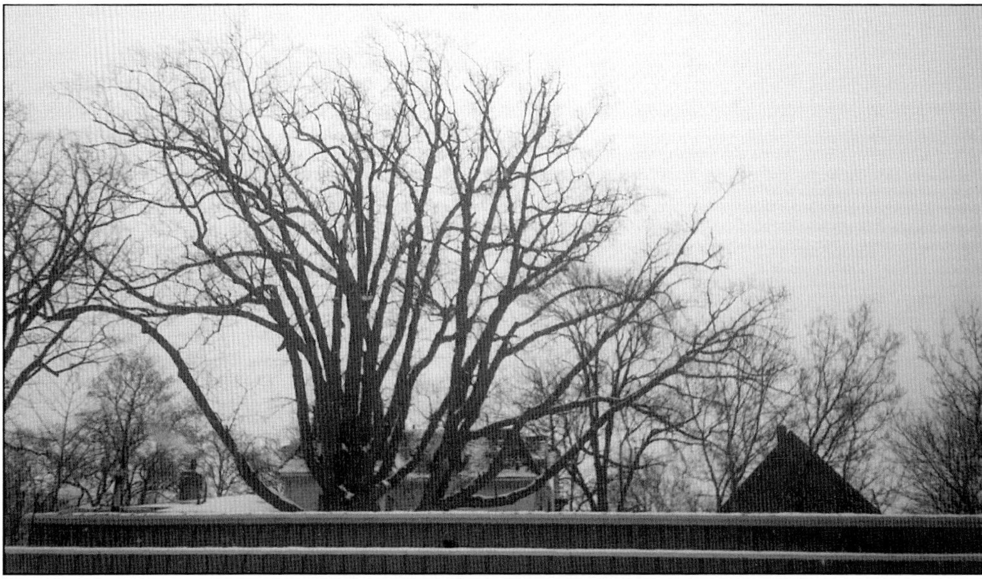

The oldest tree in the village stands in the backyard at 3 Thomas Avenue.

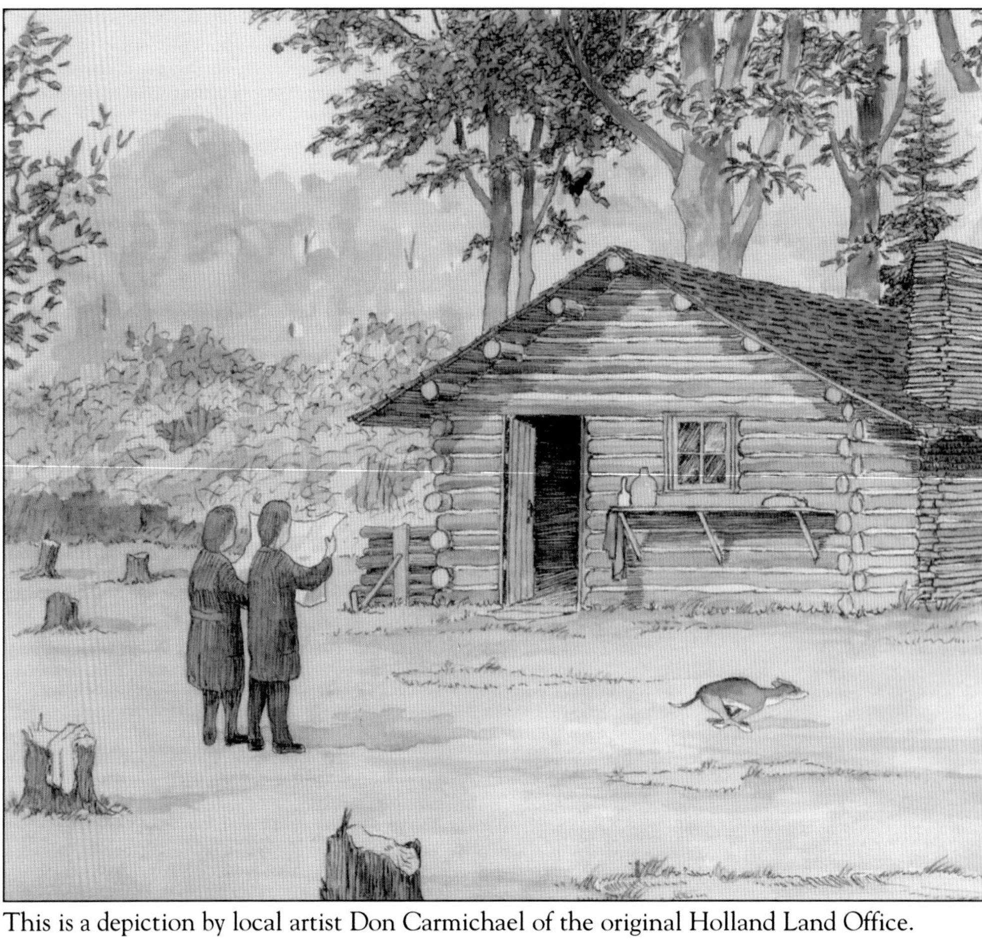

This is a depiction by local artist Don Carmichael of the original Holland Land Office.

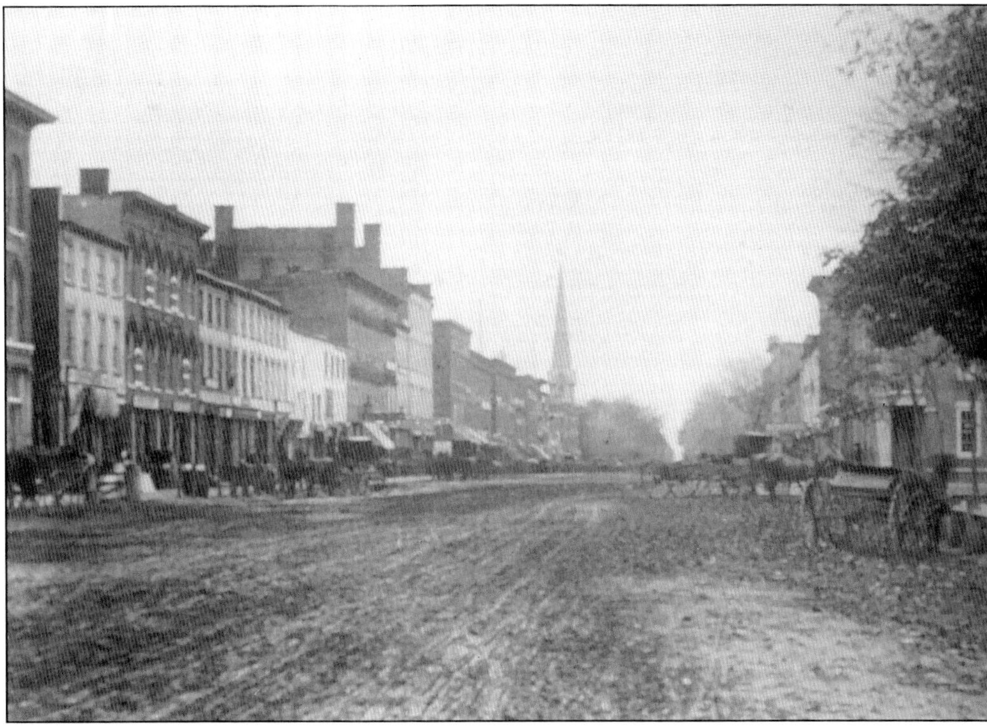

In 1800, mail delivery was scheduled only once every two weeks. It was carried sometimes on foot and sometimes on horseback over the Indian trails from Canandaigua to Batavia, Lewiston, and Fort Niagara. The post office was opposite the site of the current post office, across the corner of Main and Jefferson Streets in the store owned and operated by James Brisbane, the village's first postmaster.

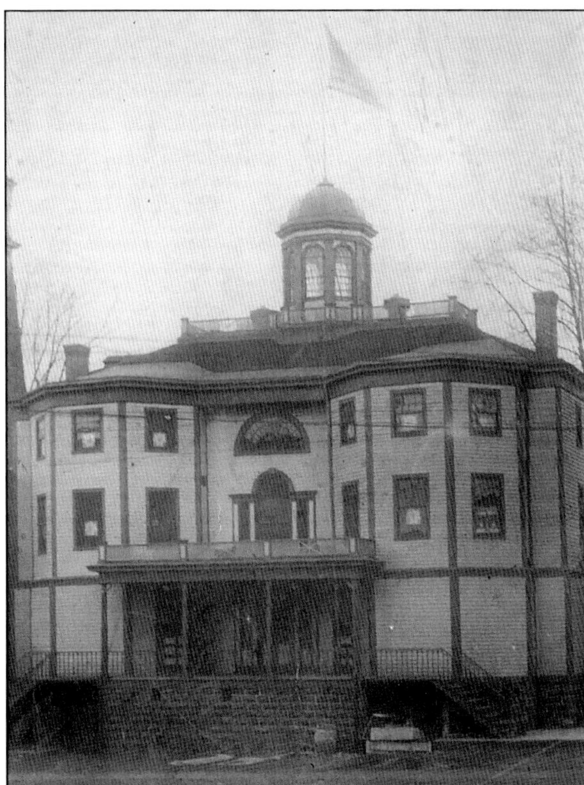

Ellicott Hall was located at the junction of the two great Indian trails, the Via Appia and Via Media of the Seneca Indians, right in the lap of the most ancient and memorable spot in the valley of the Genesee. A city was born, and Ellicott Hall became Batavia's first courthouse.

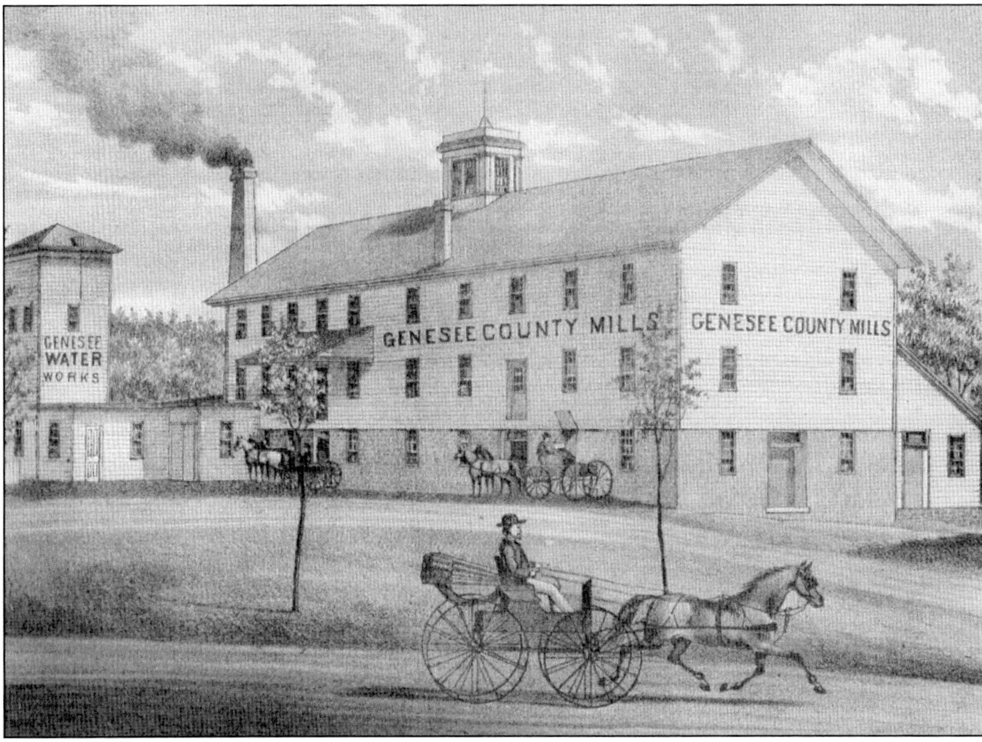

This sawmill, the Genesee County Mills, was constructed on the bank of the Tonawanda Creek.

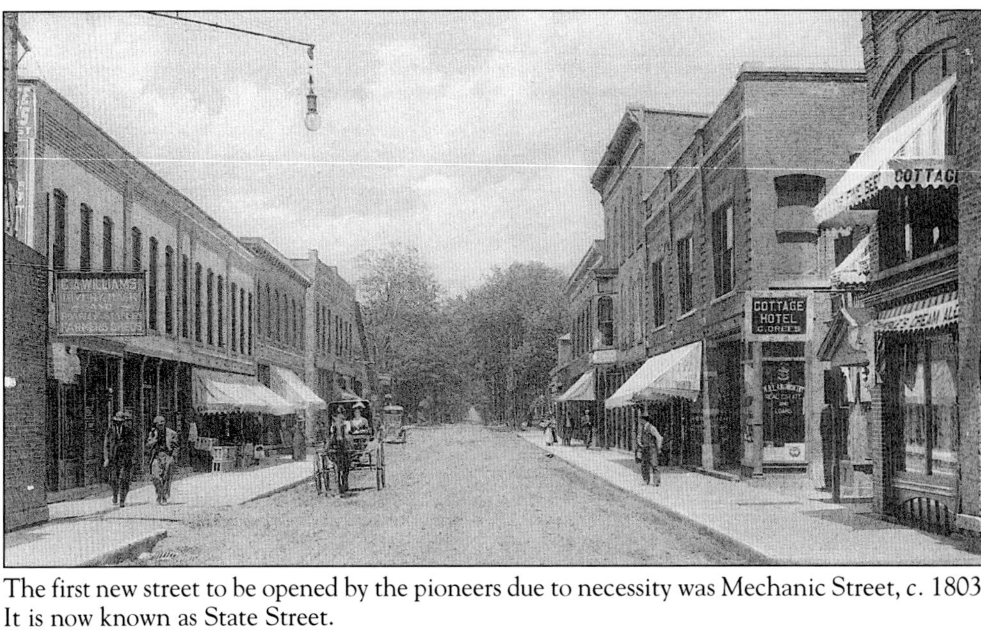

The first new street to be opened by the pioneers due to necessity was Mechanic Street, *c.* 1803. It is now known as State Street.

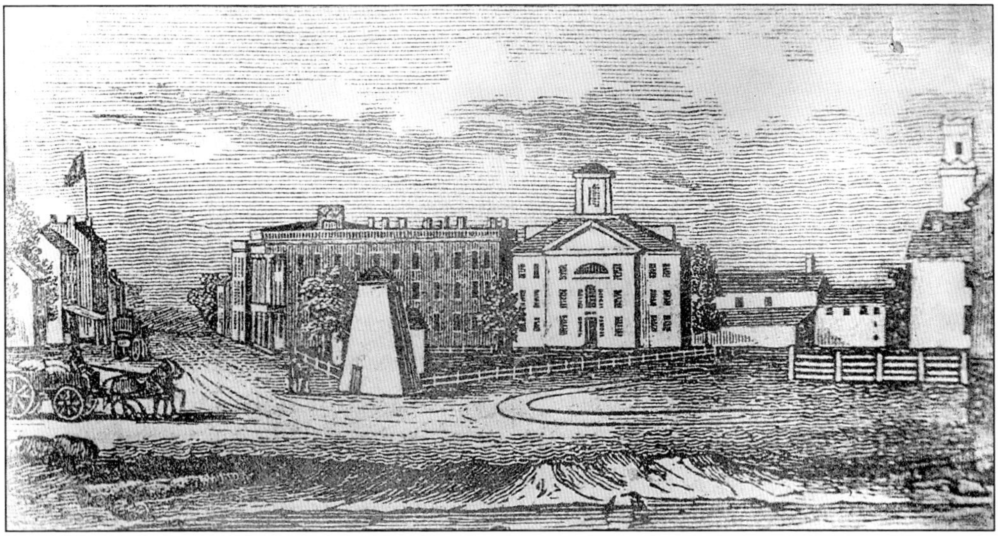

This early woodcut shows the junction of Main and Ellicott Streets as it appeared in 1804. The black lines in the roadway at the right represent the tracks of the old wooden railroad that came from Rochester to Batavia and had its terminal at the bank of the Tonawanda Creek, where it took on wood and water. The buildings, from left to right, are an old church that stood at Church (Jefferson) and Main Streets, the old Murderers' Row, named for housing five rowdy saloons in a row, and Tisdale's Tavern, a hotel. In the center is the fire tower. Immediately behind the tower is the Eagle Tavern, and behind the tavern is the Farmers Hotel. The large building with the tower is Ellicott Hall, and behind it is the Genesee County Jail. The large building with the steeple is St. James Church, and the corner of the building shown at the extreme right is that of the Genesee Flour Mills.

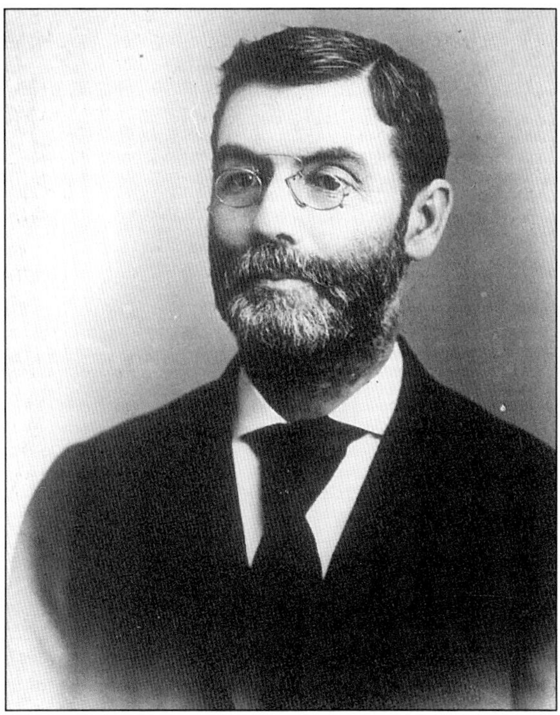

This gentleman, Prof. John Kennedy, once remarked that "Batavia was started by college men and patriots—the very clearing in these woods was braced by the highest society in America."

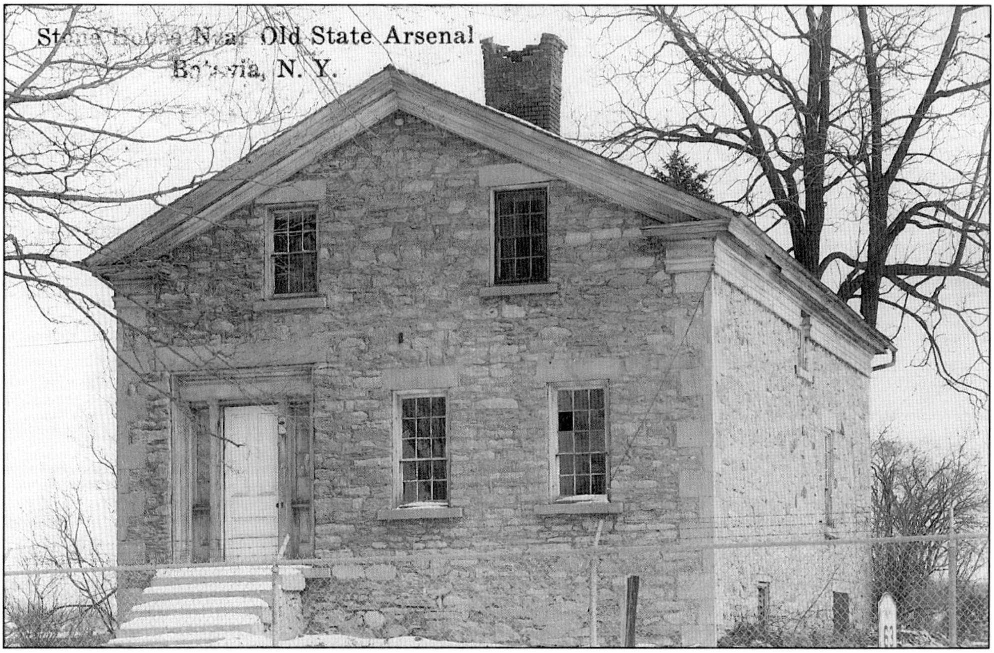

The Arsenal was erected *c.* 1812 at the Genesee Road, with the forks that lead to Buffalo and to Queenston. The building was known as "the guardian of the frontier."

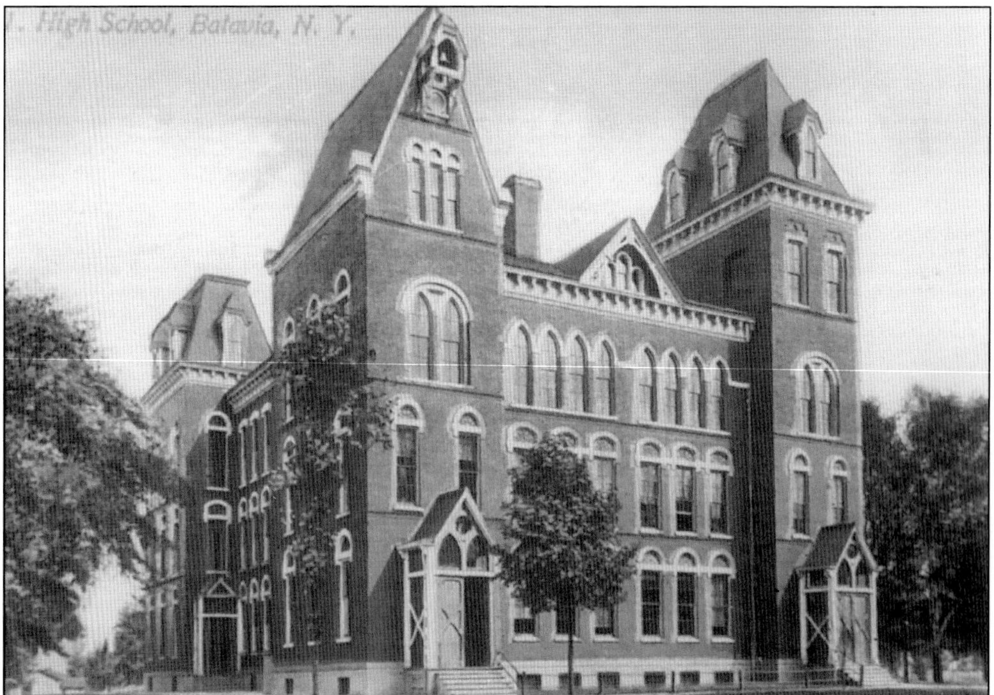

The exact date of the establishment of the earliest school in Batavia cannot be determined from the records. There were many private schools established in the village and it is believed that the first public school of record was Union School District No. 2. Batavians put up $85,000 for this brick high school building, one of the finest examples of school architecture in the state.

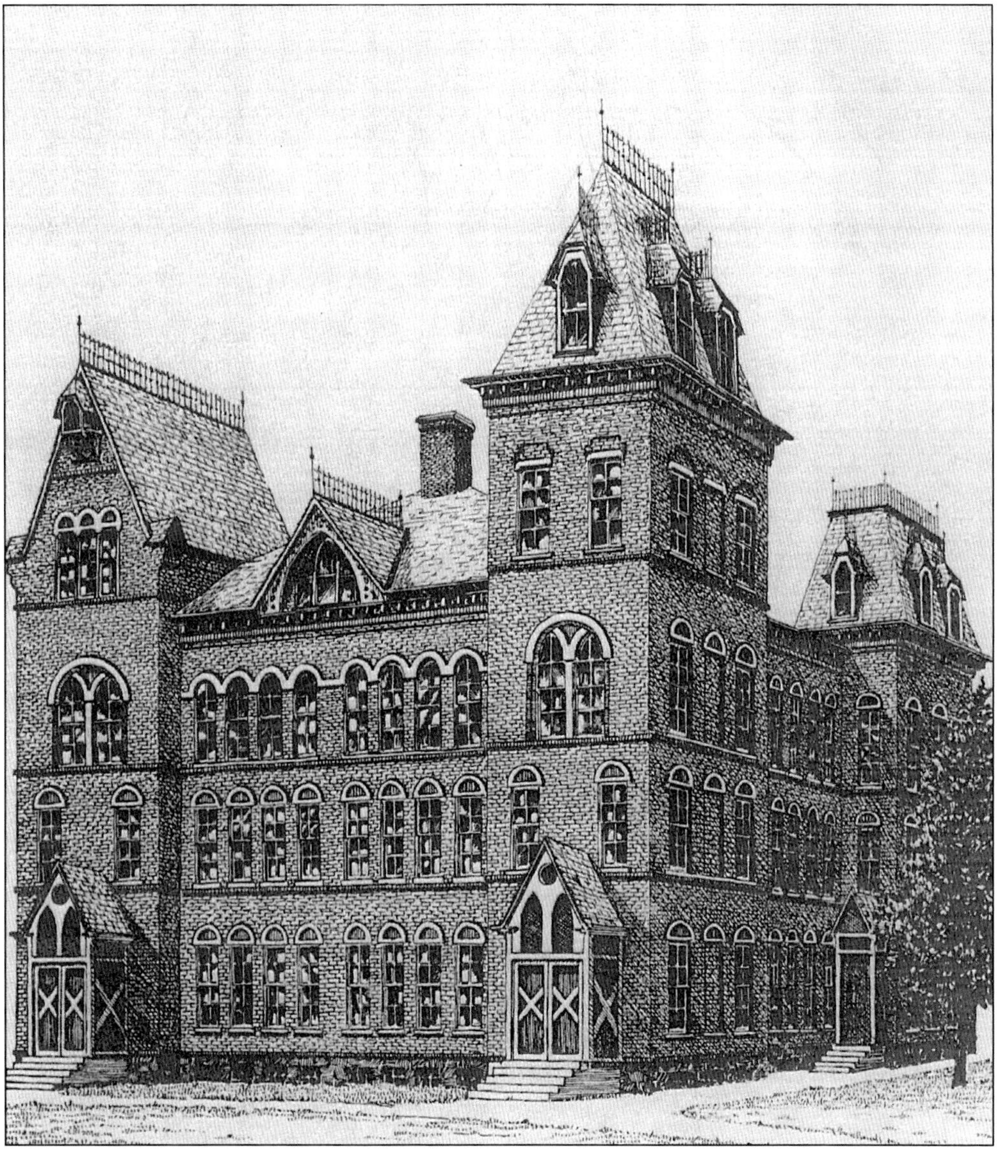

This school stood east of where the Batavia Middle School now stands. It encompassed the entire block from Main Street to Ross Street.

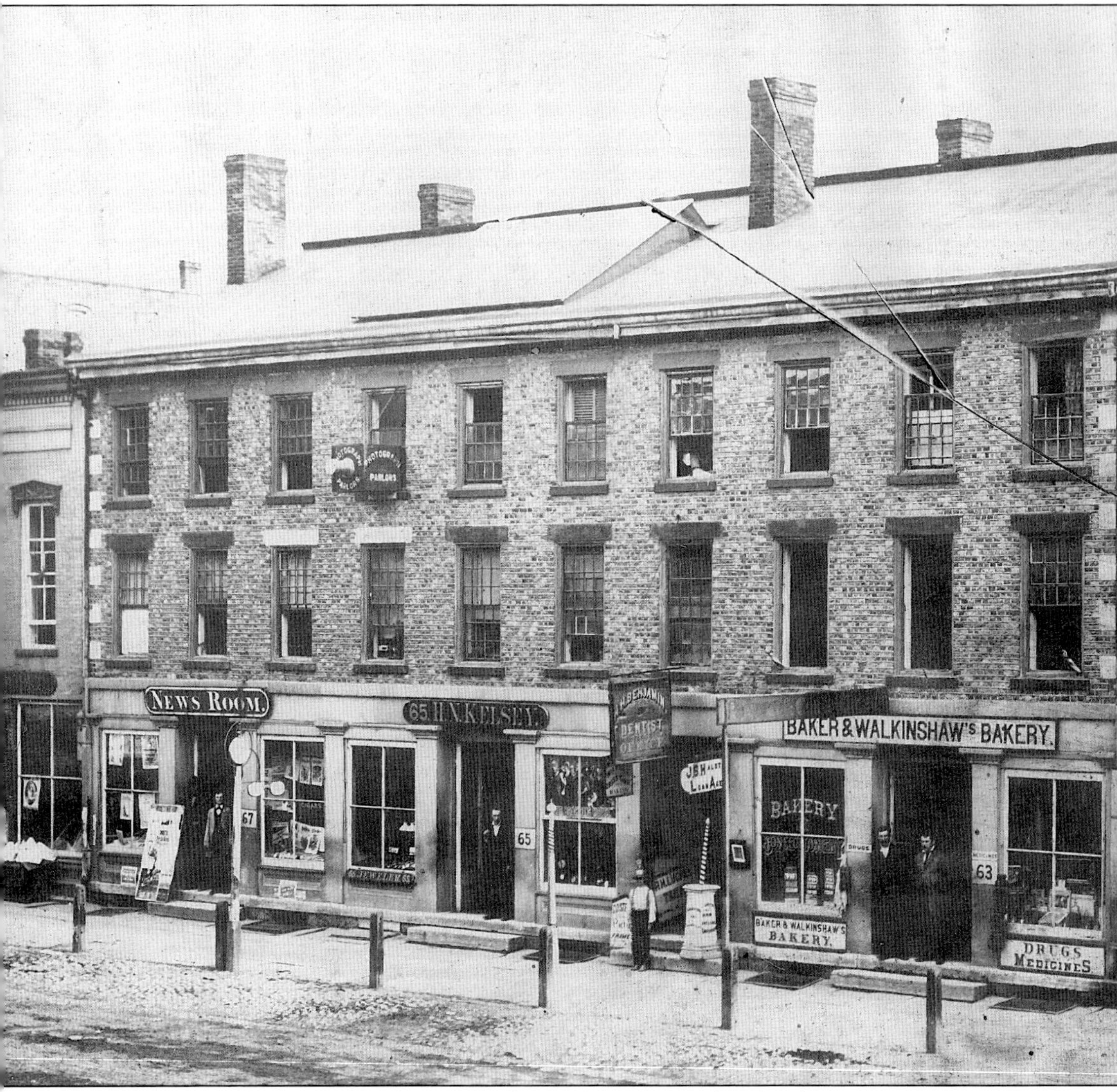

This is the Cobblestone Block, *c.* 1825, located on the south side of Main Street.

Two

Establishing Community Living

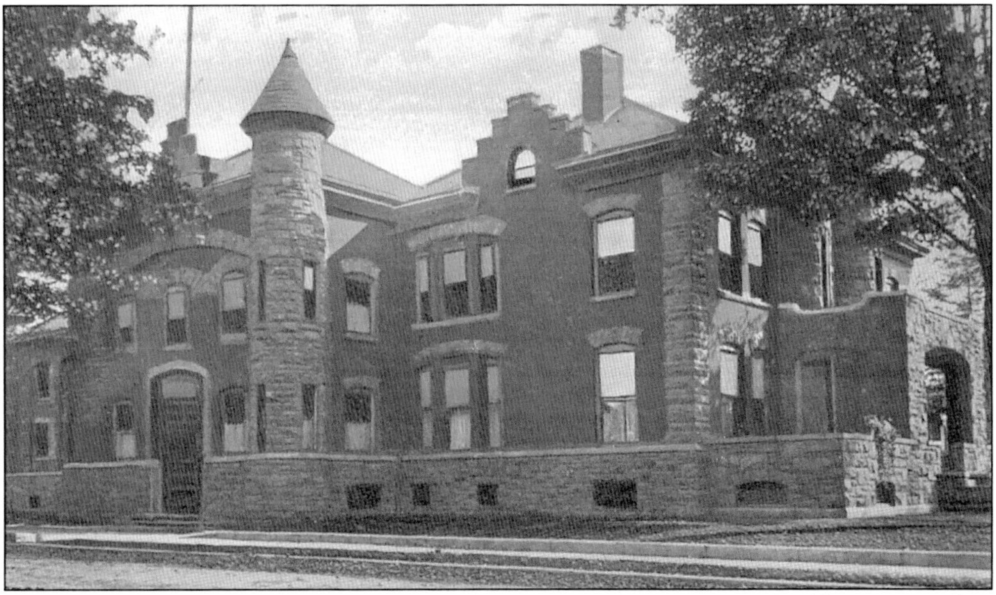

A jail was built c. 1826 on the south side of Main and Oak Streets. The building remained in use until it was razed in 1951. A second jail was built in 1901. Known today as the Genesee County Jail, it is located at the corner of Main Street and Porter Avenue.

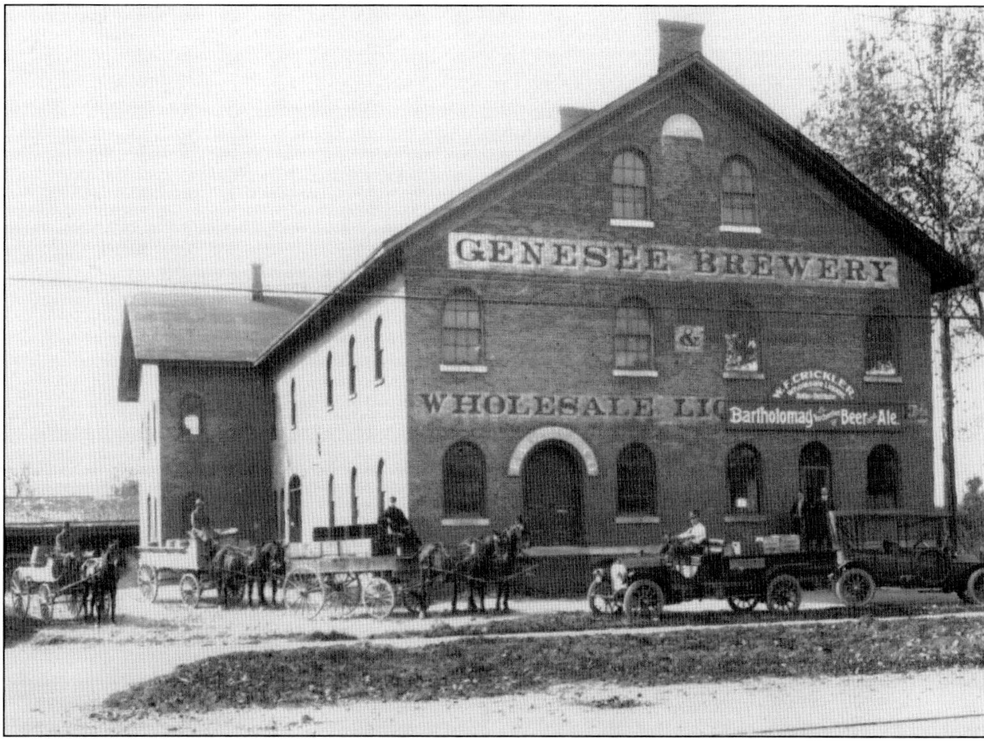

The brewing industry in Batavia had its inception in a brewery and malt house established *c.* 1827 by Libbeus Fish. By 1880, this establishment had changed hands several times and was in the possession of William Gamble when it burned in 1887. It was rebuilt in the eastern part of the village as the Batavia Brewing Company, with Gamble as superintendent. Today, this business is the R.R. Gamble Distributing Company, located in the Batavia Industrial Park.

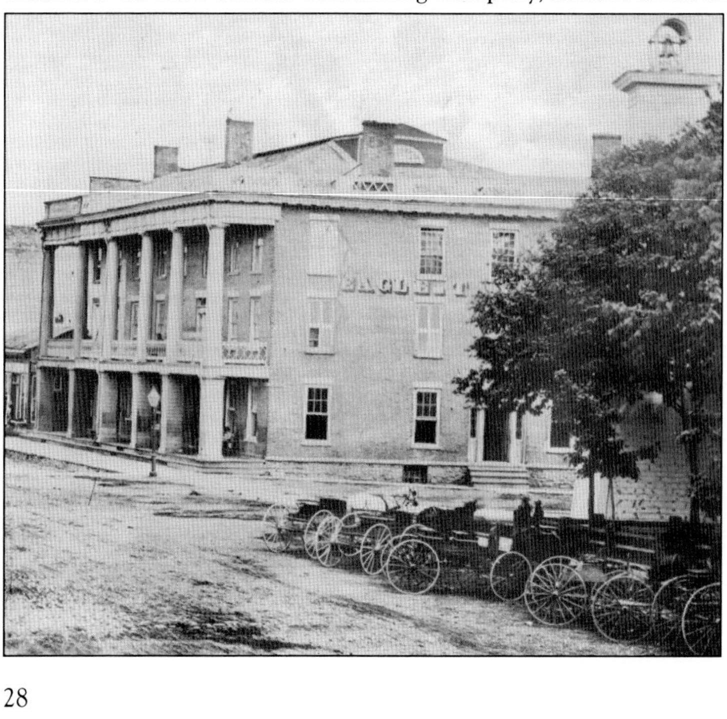

After the first one was destroyed by fire, a second Eagle Tavern was built *c.* 1834.

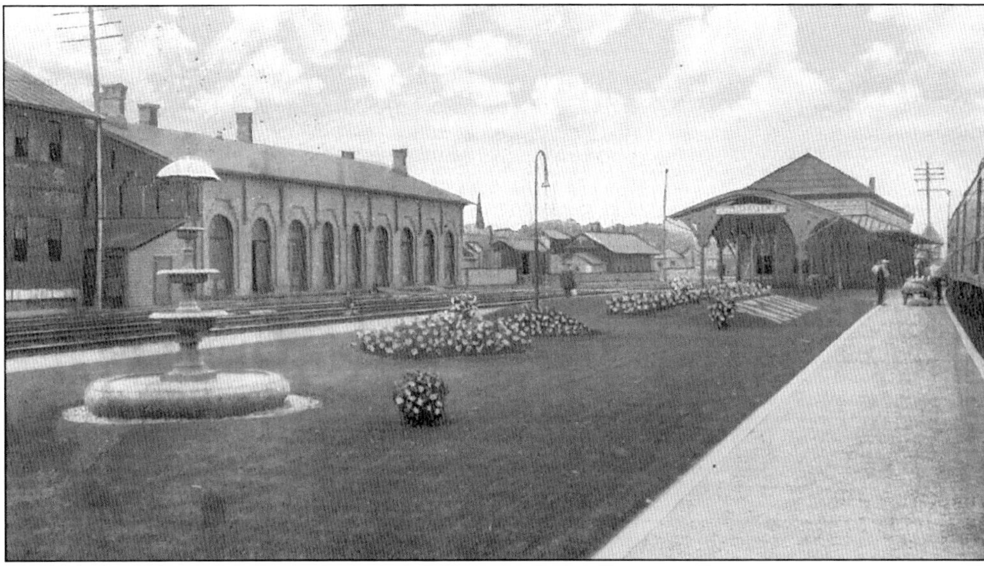

The Buffalo, New York, and Erie Railroads arrived in Batavia *c.* 1837. The engines were run into a turntable, where they were turned around for the eastern trip. The turntable is believed to have been in the Mill Street area. Some years later, after Buffalo had become the western terminus of the rail line, Dean Richmond became president of the New York Central. He required all trains to stop at Batavia. The strong competition of rival roads had forced the consolidation of seven distinct companies into the New York Central. Richmond was foremost in the struggle and his perseverance alone carried the measure in the state legislature.

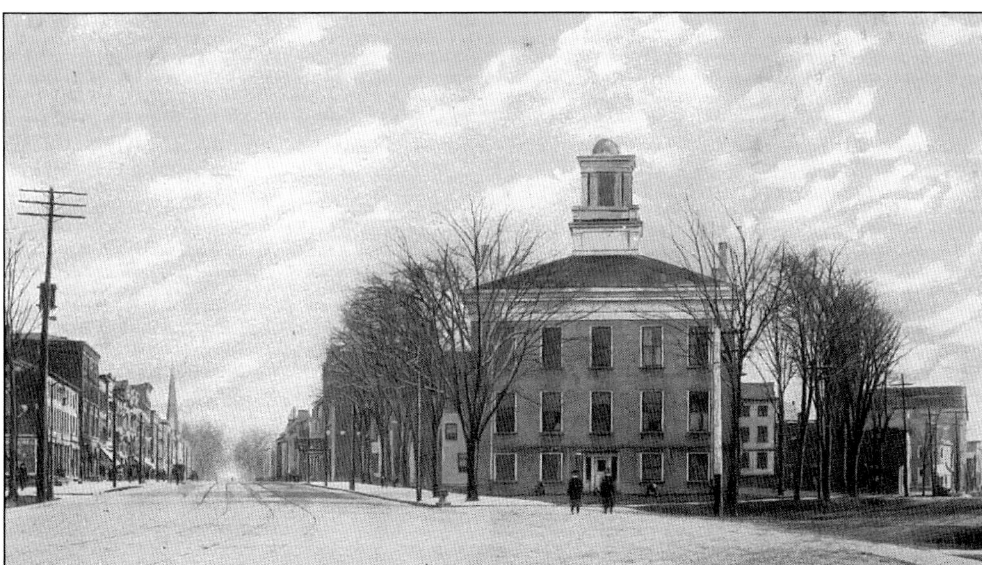

The courthouse at Main and Ellicott Streets was completed in 1843 at a cost of $17,000.

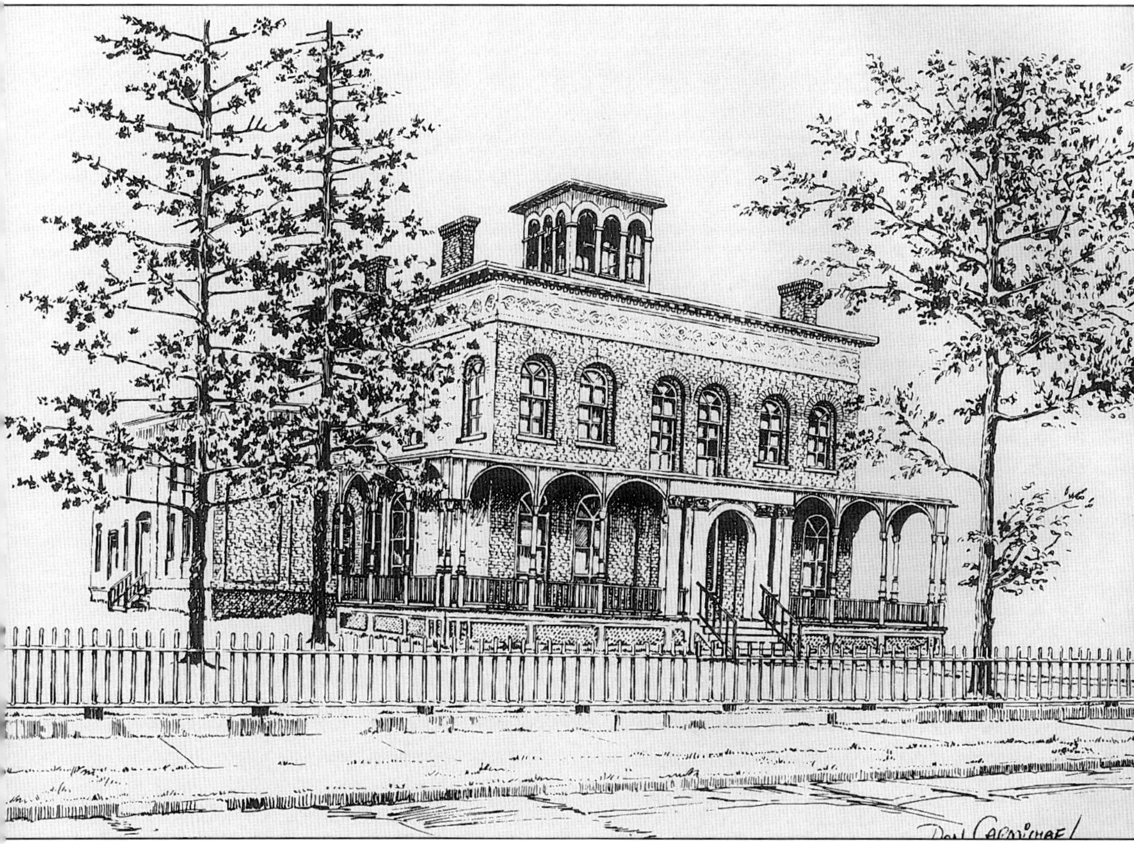

James Brisbane built his home *c.* 1852. Some 65 years later, that building became the Batavia City Hall. In 1911, the village took an option to buy the property from the Brisbane Estate, a parcel of land bordered by Washington Avenue, Jefferson Avenue, and West Main Street. The Brisbane House was a large brick structure that faced West Main Street.

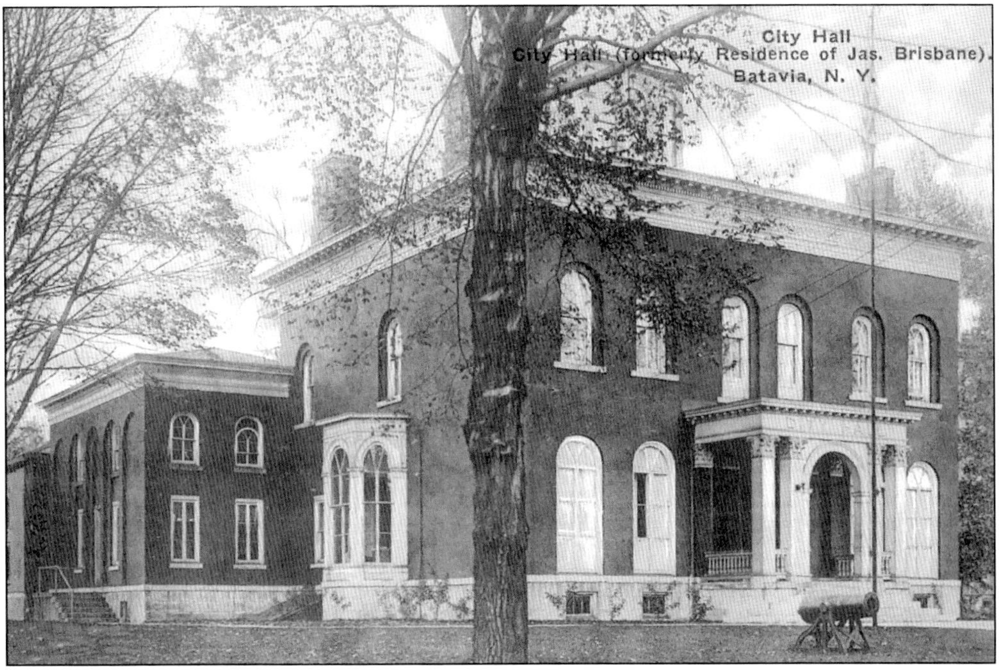

Although not used as a year-round residence for many years, this house served as the summer home of Sarah Brisbane until 1909. The city purchased the Brisbane property in 1912 for $50,000, and Frank Homelius remodeled the Brisbane House into the present city hall in 1917. In 1931, part of the Brisbane property became Austin Park.

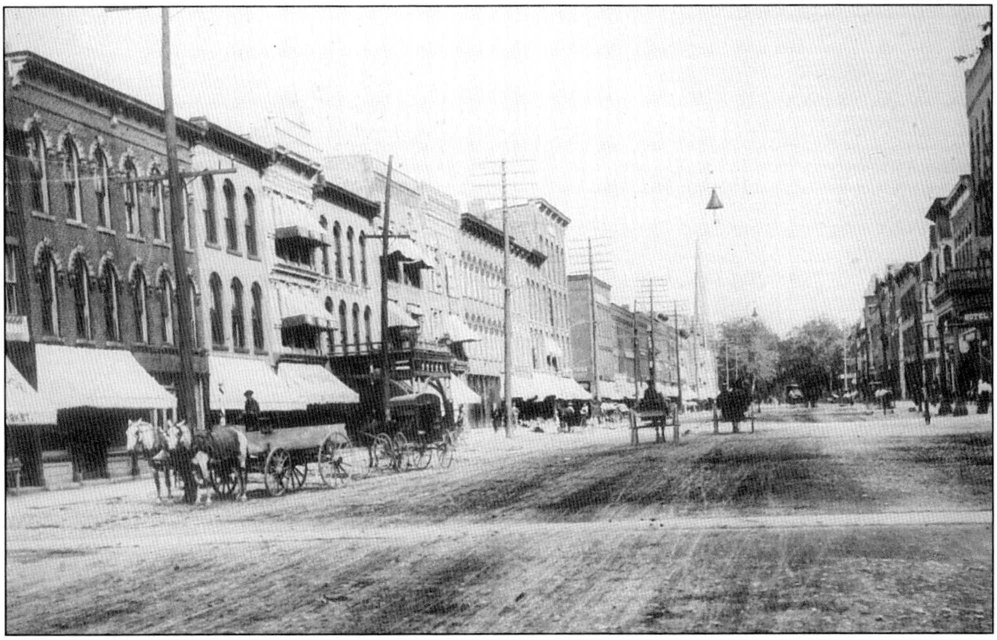

Batavia's streets became gaslit *c.* 1855. Gas for the lights was stored in buildings called gas holders. Two of these buildings were located in Batavia. A dozen or so of these structures still survive in upstate New York and New England.

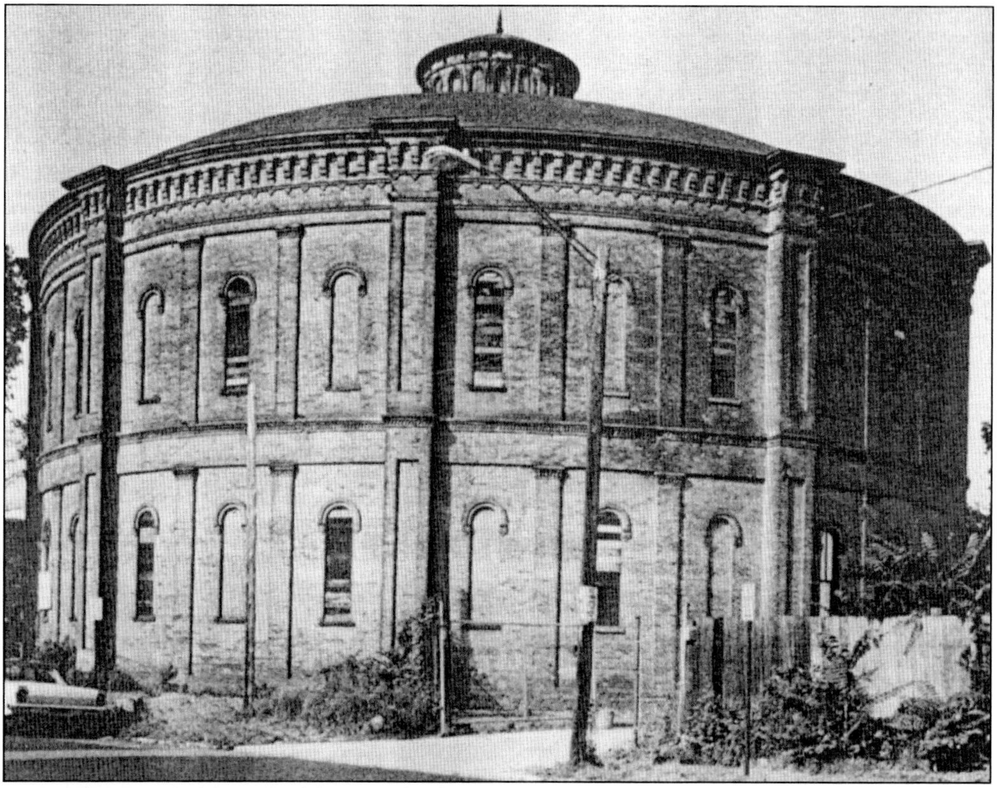

Pictured is a gas holder, a building in which gas for city lighting was stored. Two such structures were located in Batavia.

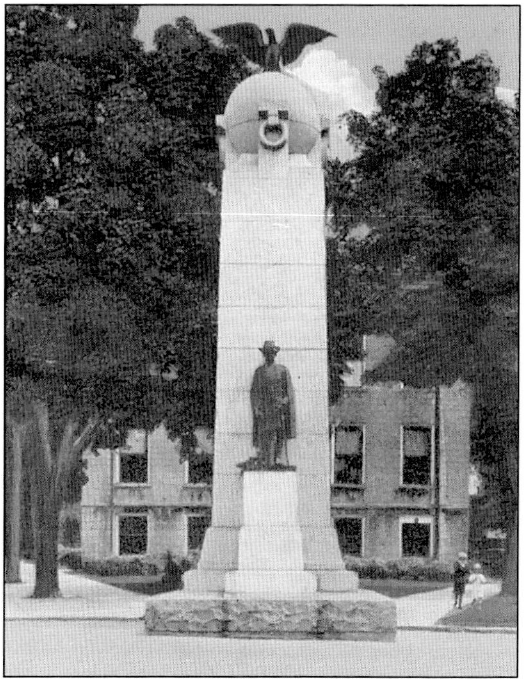

In April 1861, the Civil War was under way and Batavia businesses closed. The first Union soldier to enlist in the Civil War was from Batavia. Emery Upton was a native Batavian who attended West Point Academy, served with distinction in the Civil War, and was promoted to general at age 25. He lost both legs in the war. He is said to be represented by the bronze figure that stands on the base of the Upton Monument, also known as the Soldiers and Sailors Monument The monument was dedicated on August 15, 1919. Three bronze tablets are attached to its granite base. The one facing the north lists the engagements in the Civil War in which Genesee County men took part. The one facing south lists World War I engagements. In 1984, a plaque was placed on the eastern side of the base in honor of the local men who served in World War II, Korea, and Vietnam.

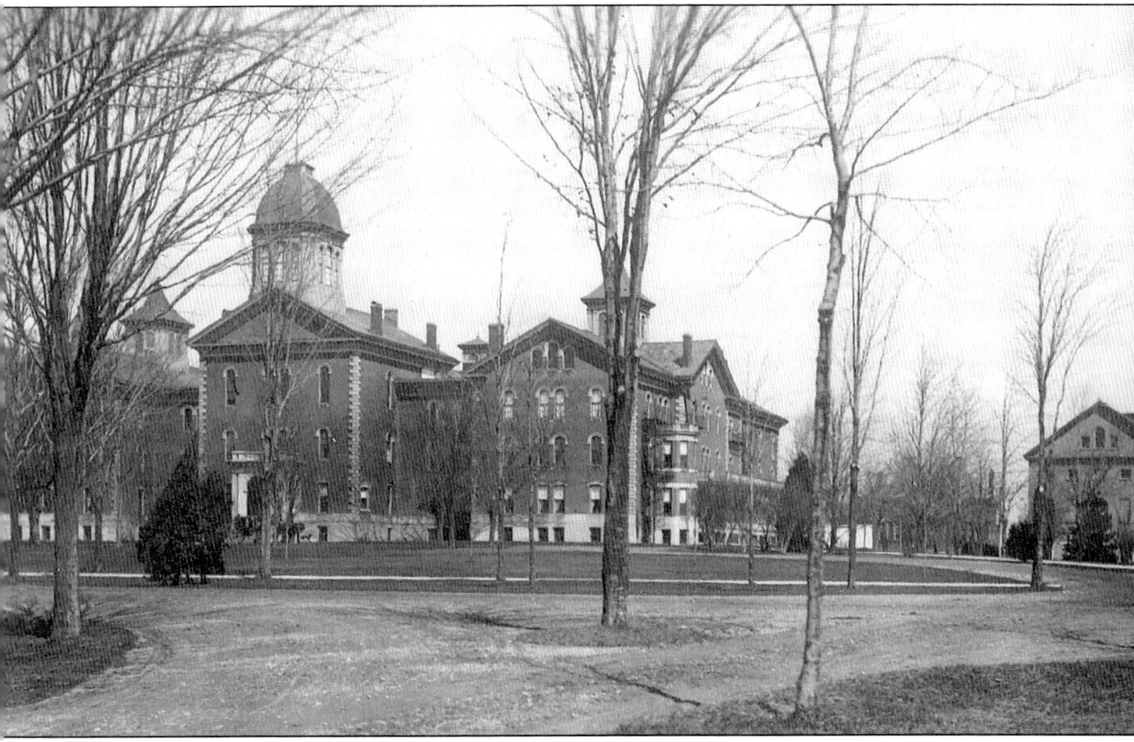

The New York School for the Blind opened in 1868. In its first year, it had 40 pupils enrolled and 64 residents. At the opening ceremonies, the school's superintendent, Dr. Asa Lord, received a national award in connection with his 12 years as superintendent of the Ohio institution for the Blind at Columbus.

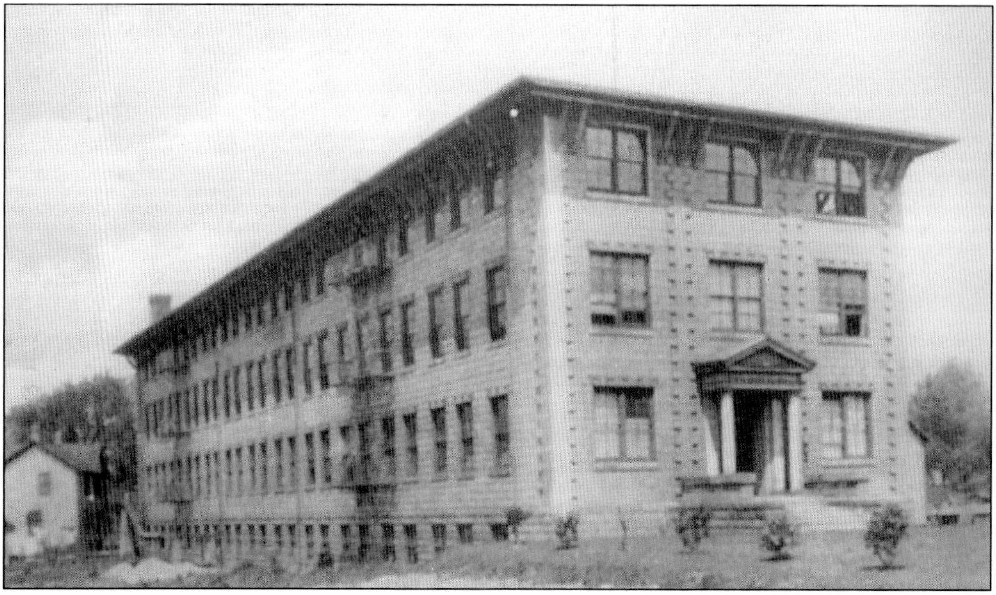

P.W. Minor Shoes was founded at Interlake in Seneca County *c.* 1867. The company moved into the old E.N. Rowell factory in Batavia in 1891. Seven years later the company built a factory on State Street; in 1921, the factory was enlarged with an addition. When urban renewal changed the north side of Main Street, the shoe company built a new plant in the Industrial Park at 1 Treadeasy Drive and began production there in 1972. Today, the plant employs 250 people and is set up to manufacture 1,050 pairs of shoes per day.

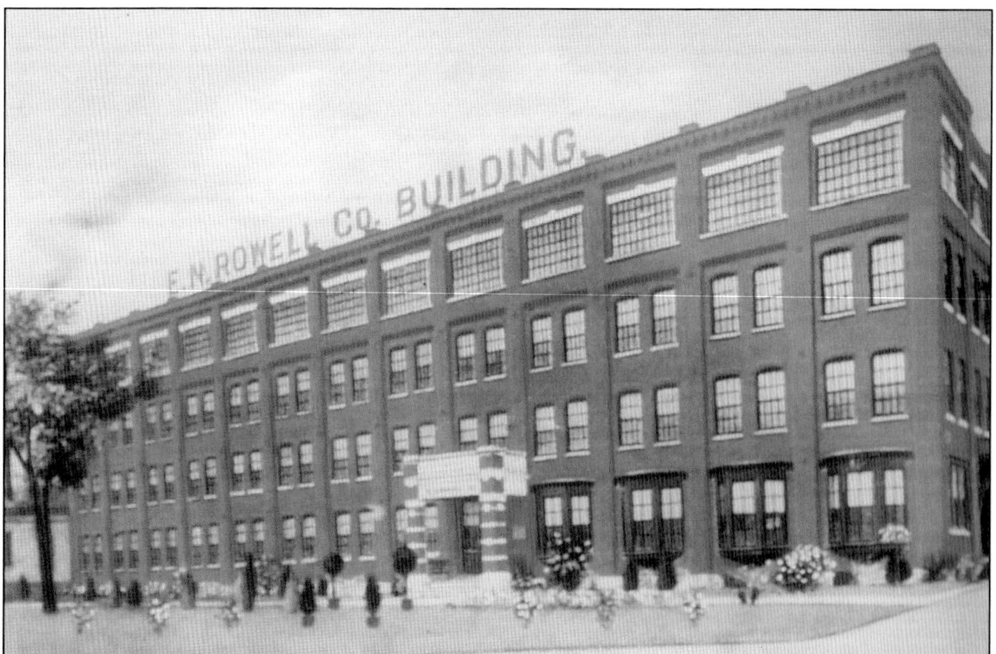

This view shows the E.N. Rowell Company box factory in the late 1800s. Edwin Newton Rowell came to Batavia in 1888, opened the factory, and operated the successful box-manufacturing business until he died in 1929.

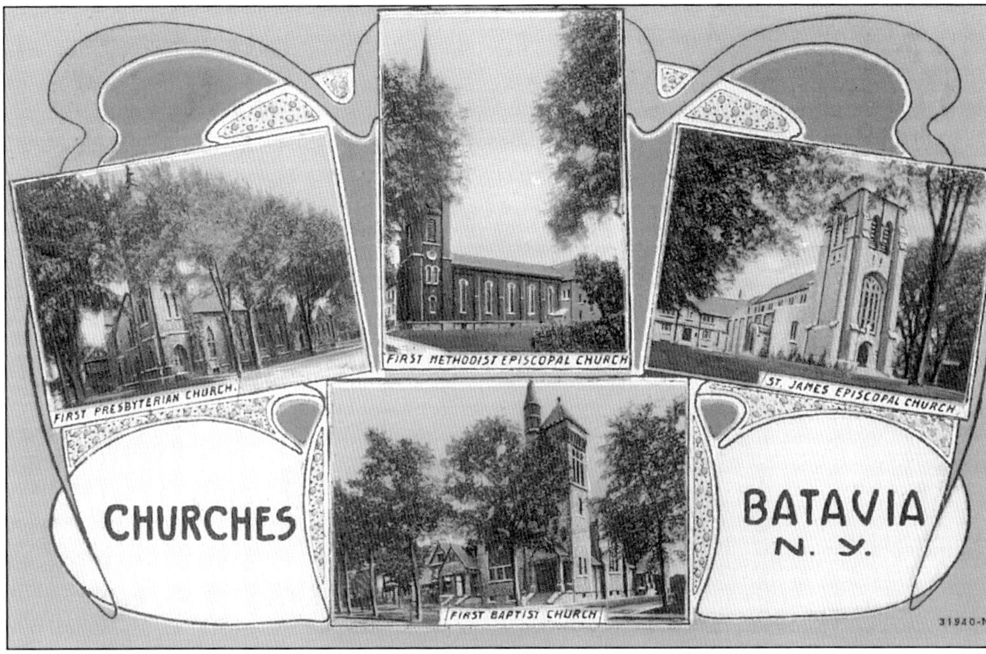

The United Methodist Church was organized in Batavia c. 1869. This postcard shows some of the churches in Batavia—clockwise from left, the First Presbyterian Church, the First Methodist Episcopal Church, St. James Episcopal Church, and the First Baptist Church.

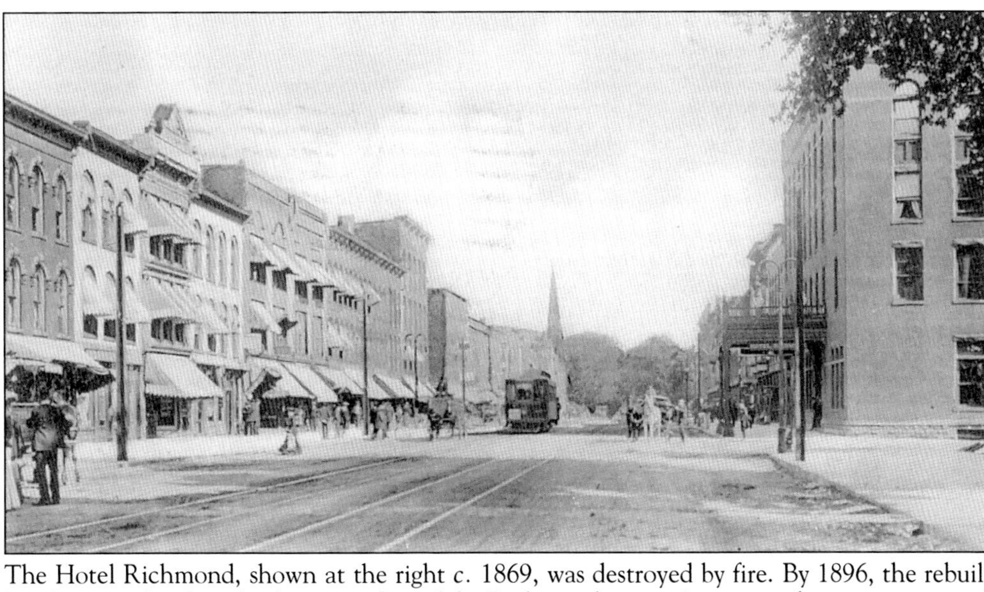

The Hotel Richmond, shown at the right c. 1869, was destroyed by fire. By 1896, the rebuilt hotel was under the sole the ownership of the Richmond estate. It remained in operation until it was razed in 1958, during the first stage of Batavia's urban renewal.

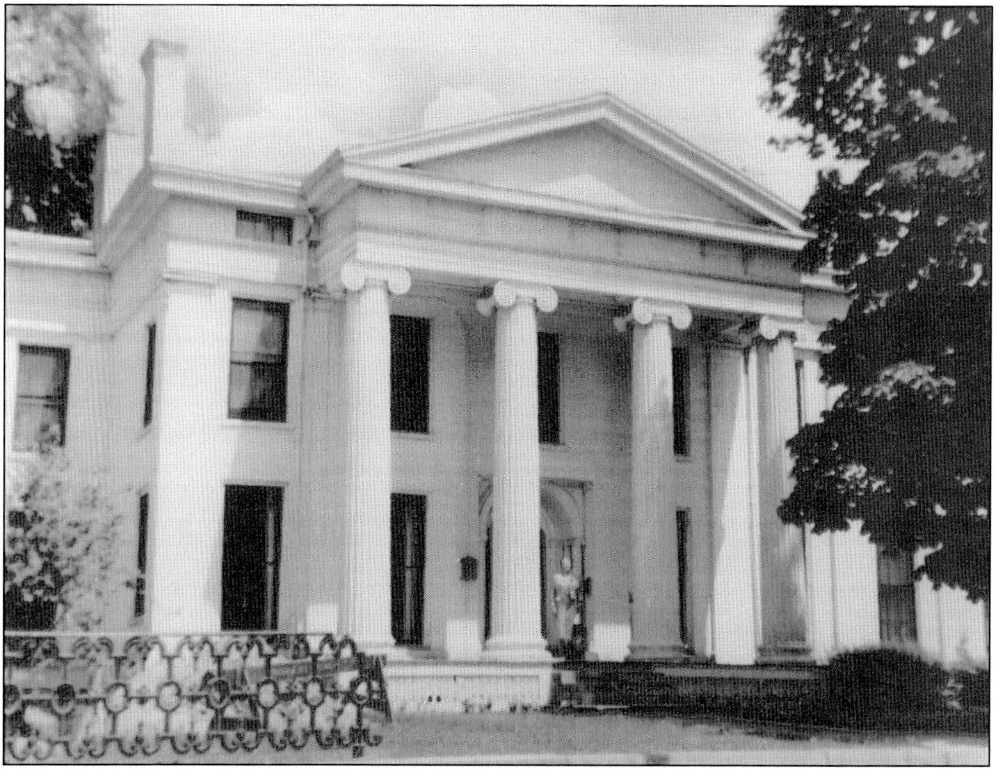

This photograph shows the Richmond Mansion, with Mary Richmond standing on the porch. Dean Richmond, president of the New York Central Railroad, built this home; he and his family then moved to Batavia.

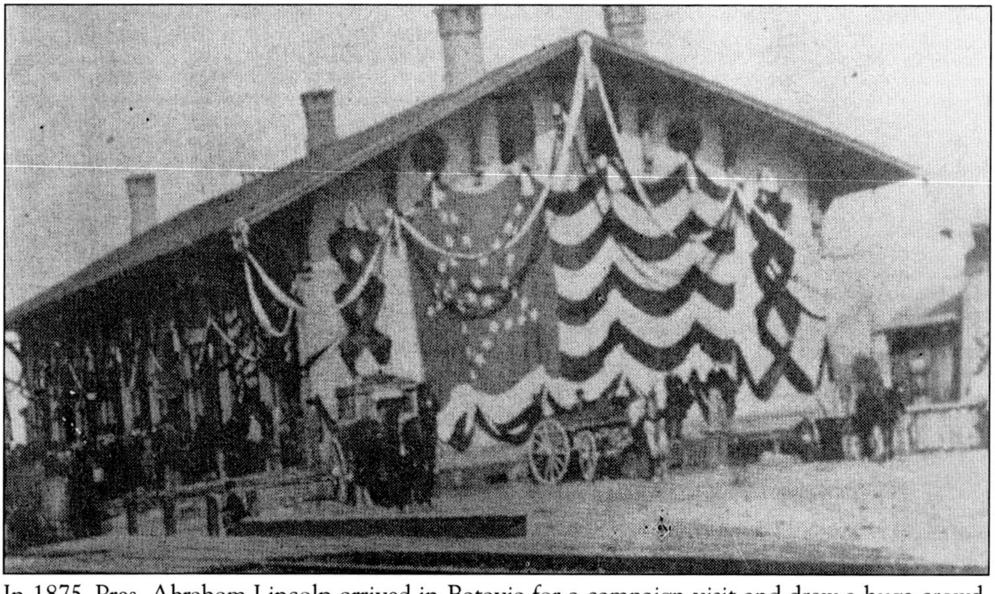

In 1875, Pres. Abraham Lincoln arrived in Batavia for a campaign visit and drew a huge crowd. After his assassination, his remains passed through Batavia on the way to his final resting place.

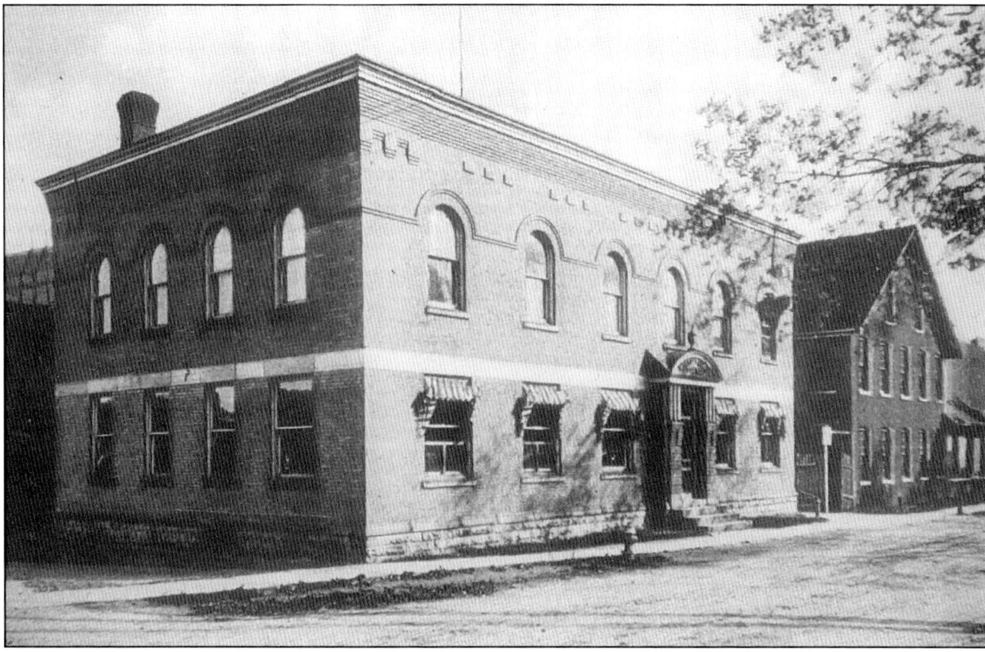

The Wiard Plow Company came to Batavia in 1876 to take advantage of the city's excellent railroad connections. It operated successfully at its Swan Street location until 1954. At that time, the company claimed to be the oldest plow manufacturer in the United States.

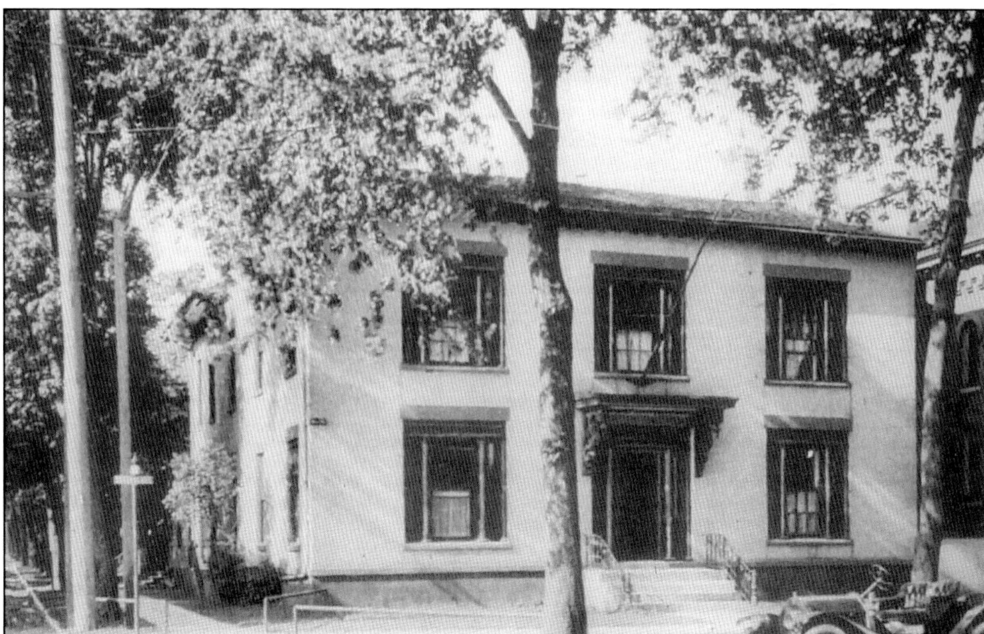

The Batavia Club was formed by a group of men who had been meeting informally for a year or two at the Cary house. The Bank of Genesee offered the men its old building at 109–111 Main Street. The club leased the building for two months and then initiated proceedings to purchase the structure.

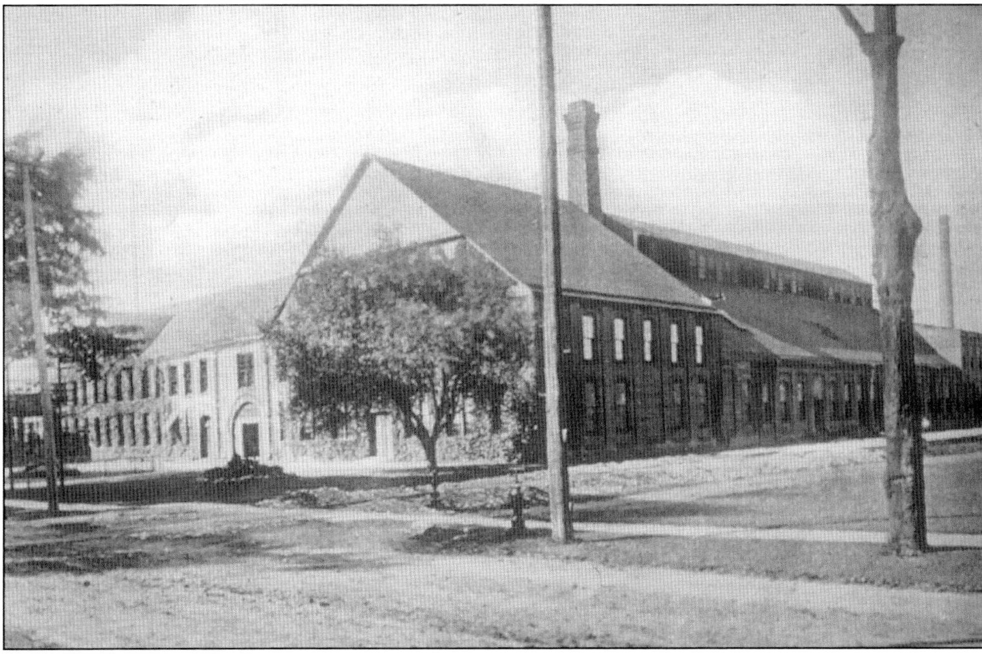

The Johnston-Harvester Company, shown *c.* 1882, manufactured farm equipment. It later became the Massey-Harris Harvester Company.

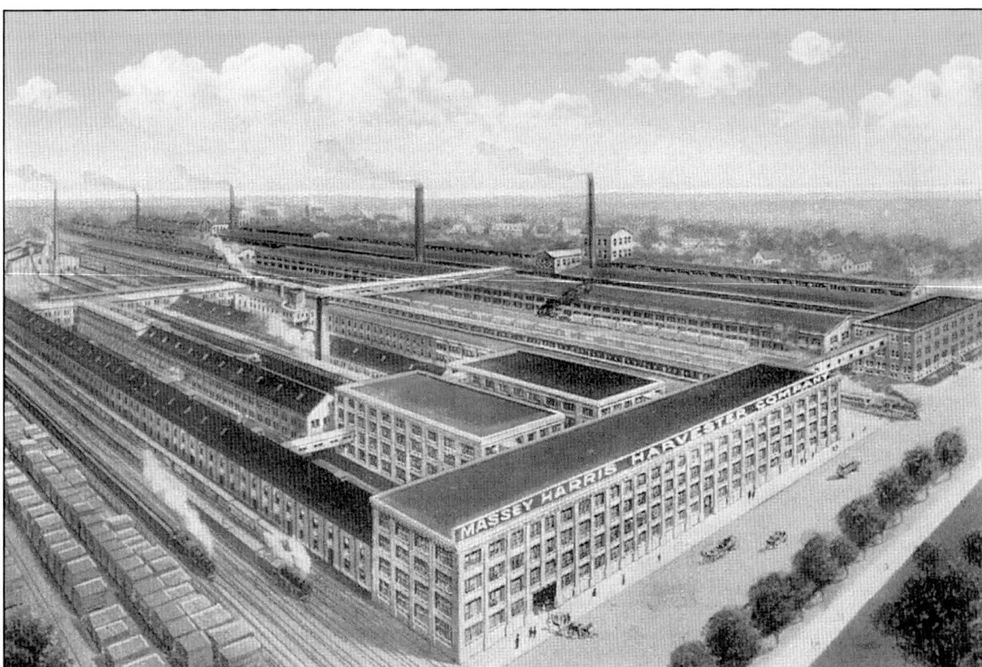

The Massey-Harris Harvester Company, formerly the Johnston-Harvester Company, continued to make agricultural equipment

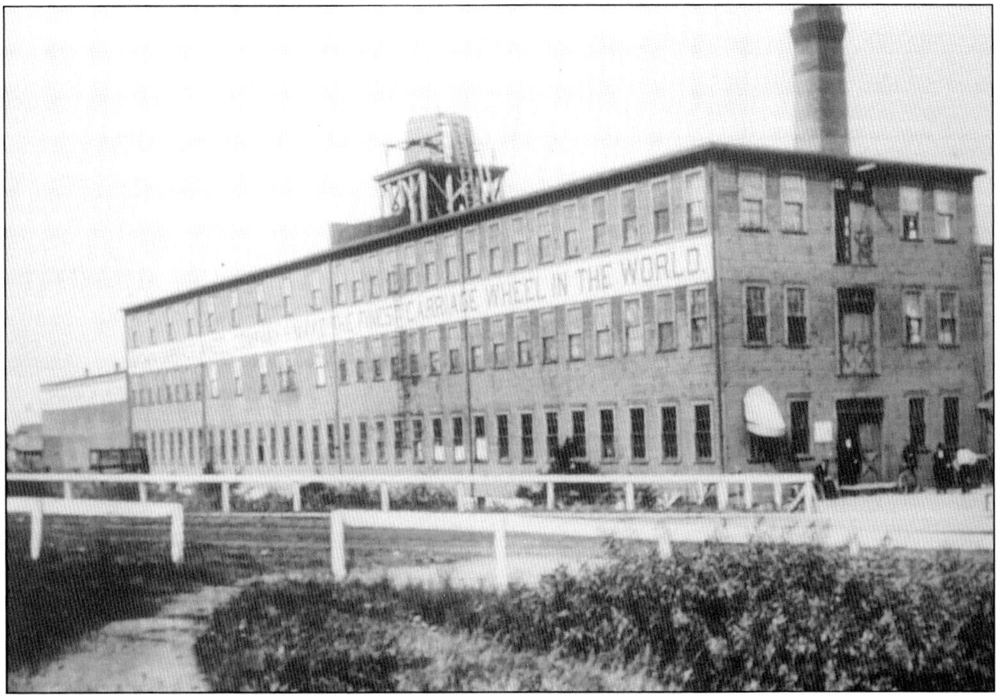

The Batavia Carriage Wheel Company, which advertised itself as making "the finest carriage wheel in the world," was the outgrowth of an industry founded on a modest scale by the A.M. Colt Company. Located on Exchange Place, the factory was destroyed by fire in 1887. The company had an office building on Walnut Street.

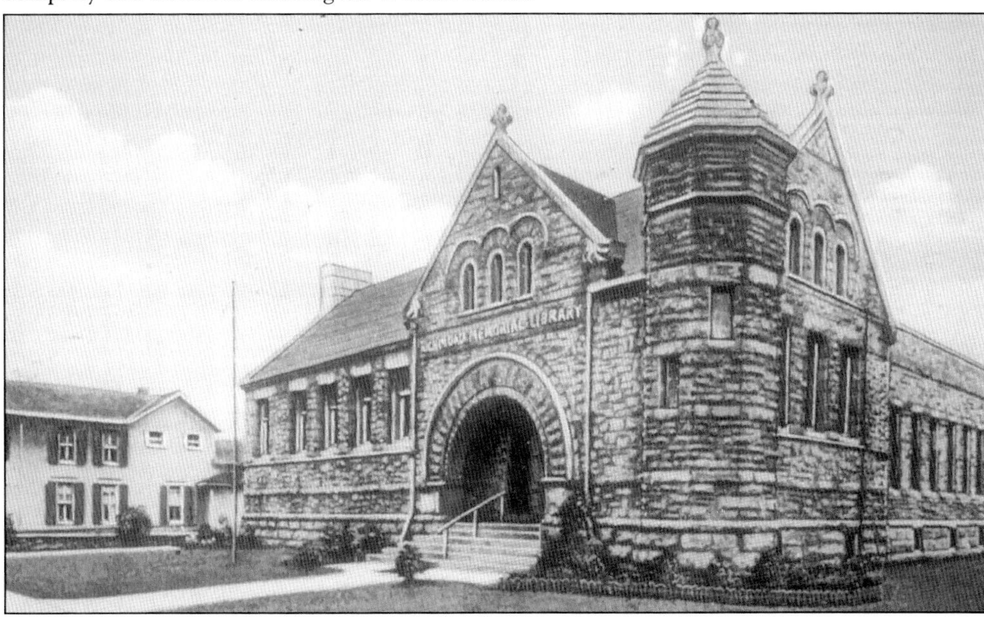

The Richmond Memorial Library was built at the behest of Mary Richmond, the widow of Dean Richmond, as a memorial to their son who died in 1885. The building's style is Romanesque, and its structure is fireproof. Its front is light gray Fredonia sandstone and red Albion stone. It was completed and presented to the village of Batavia on March 12, 1889.

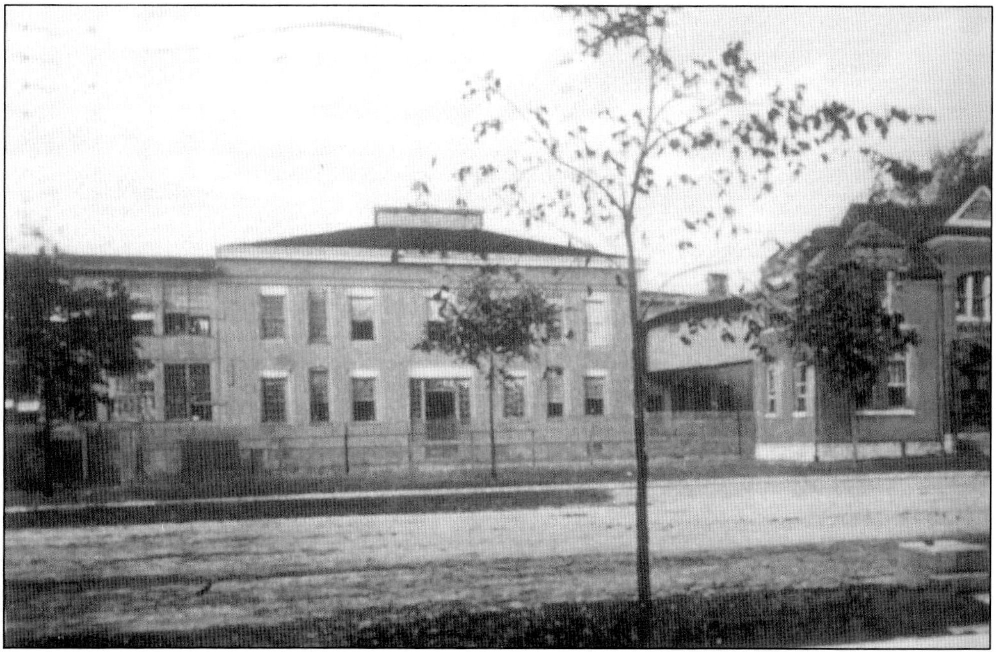

The Baker Gun Works opened in Batavia *c.* 1889. The company was known for its Baker hammerless shotguns. It moved here from Syracuse and was reorganized and renamed.

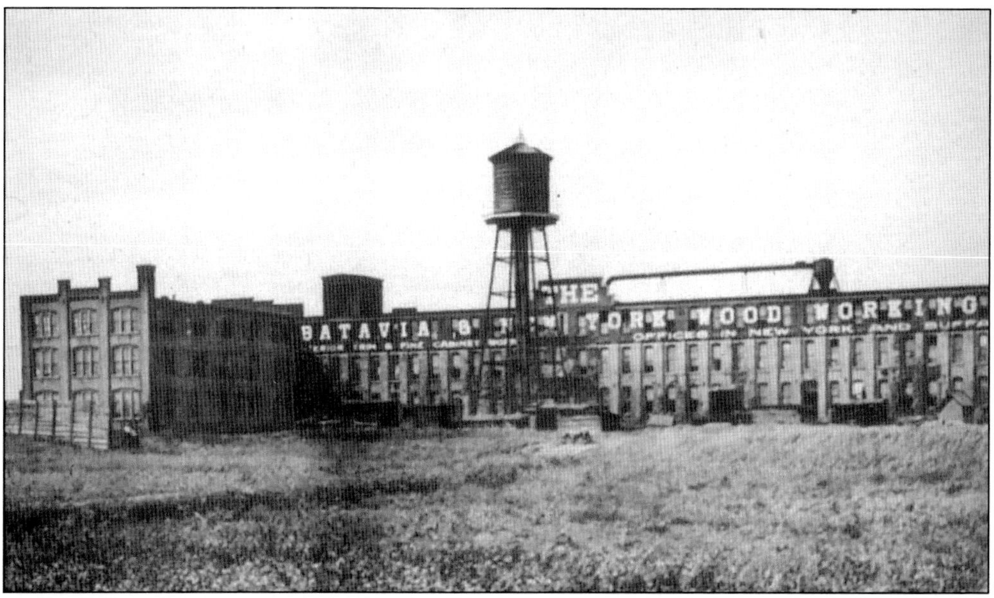

One of Batavia's finest industries in the early 1900s was the Batavia and New York Wood Working Company, which produced the interior wood used in banks, hotels, and offices. Its products included doors for Harvard University. The company flourished for many years before closing as a result of the Great Depression in 1939.

Three

BUSINESSES, SCHOOLS, AND TRANSPORTATION

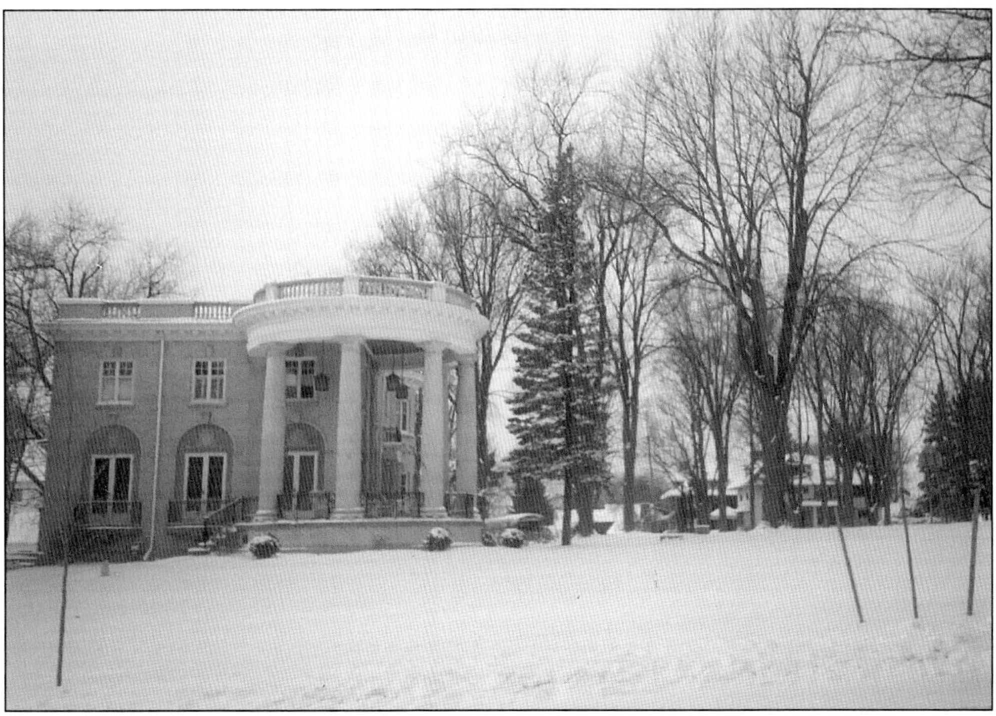

The E.N. Rowell Mansion is located at the corner of Ellicott and Richmond Avenues. Edwin Newton Rowell came to Batavia in 1888 and operated a successful box factory until he died in 1929. Today, Terry Platt and his wife own the E.N. Rowell Mansion.

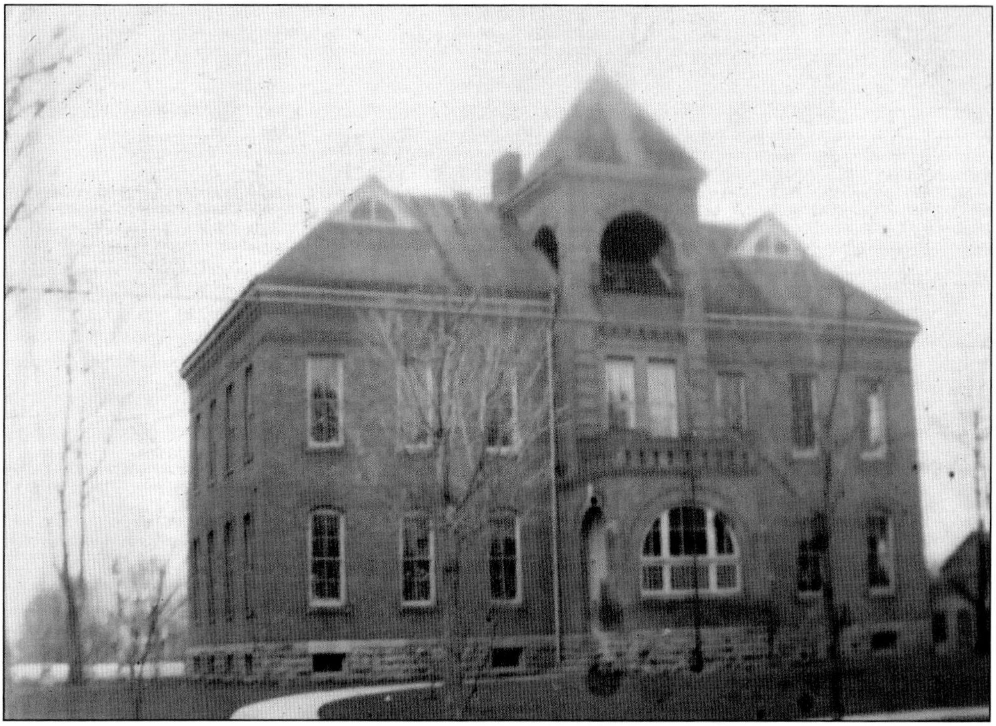

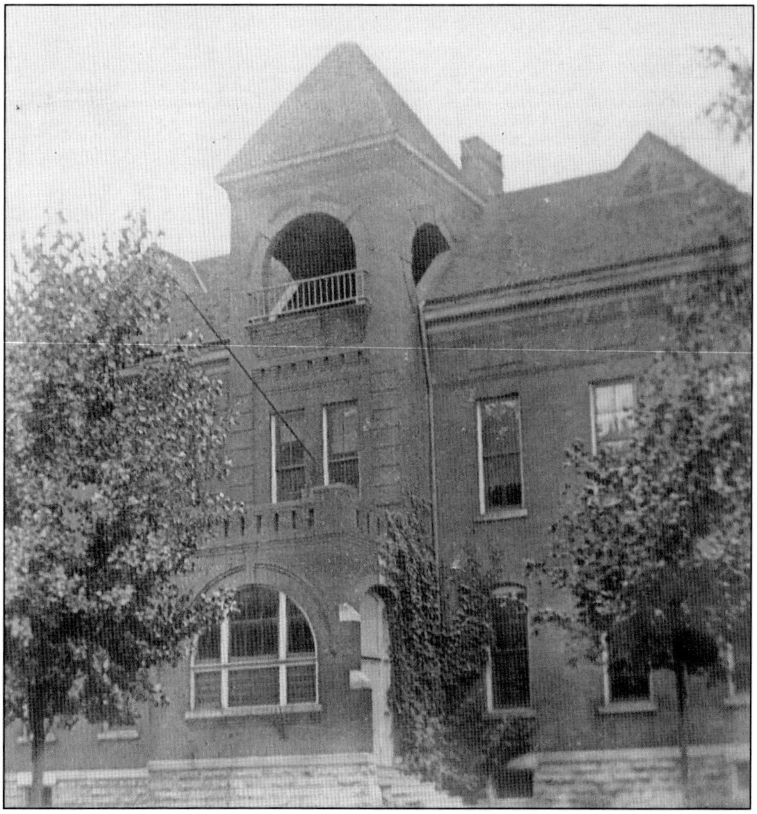

Both the West Main Street School, above, and the East Main Street School, at the left, were constructed *c.* 1892. The West Main Street School remained at 253–259 West Main Street until 1963, when it was razed and the property was sold by the board of education. On the site today is the restaurant Katie's Place, which is operated by the Feldman family.

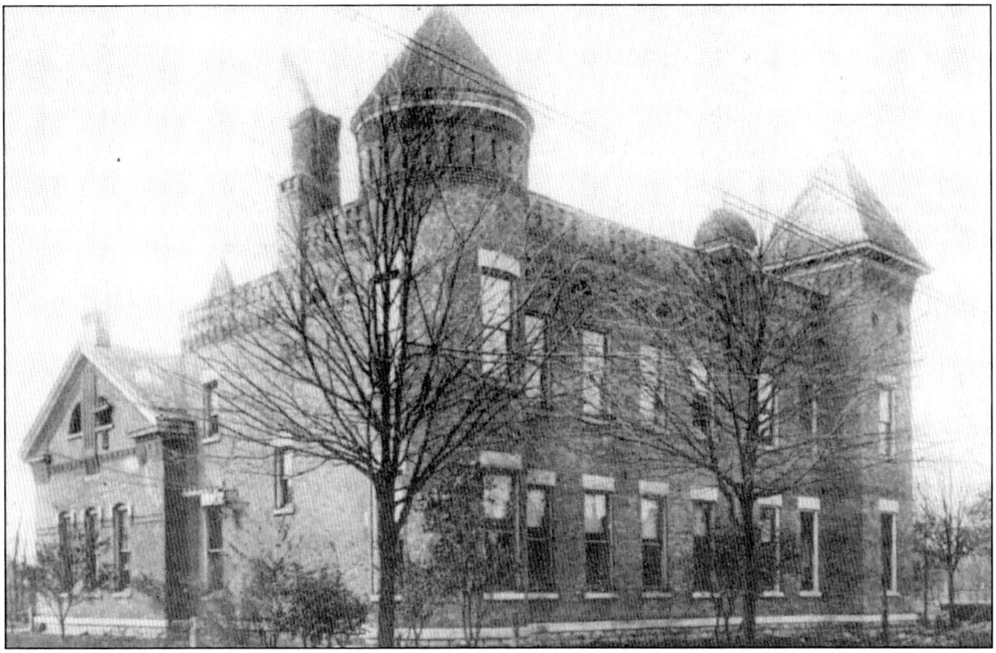

The Waterworks was built *c.* 1894 on the former site of the Genesee County Mills, a gristmill used for grinding grain into flour. In 1912, a new sewage collection station was added to the Waterworks, which later was renamed the Batavia Municipal Building.

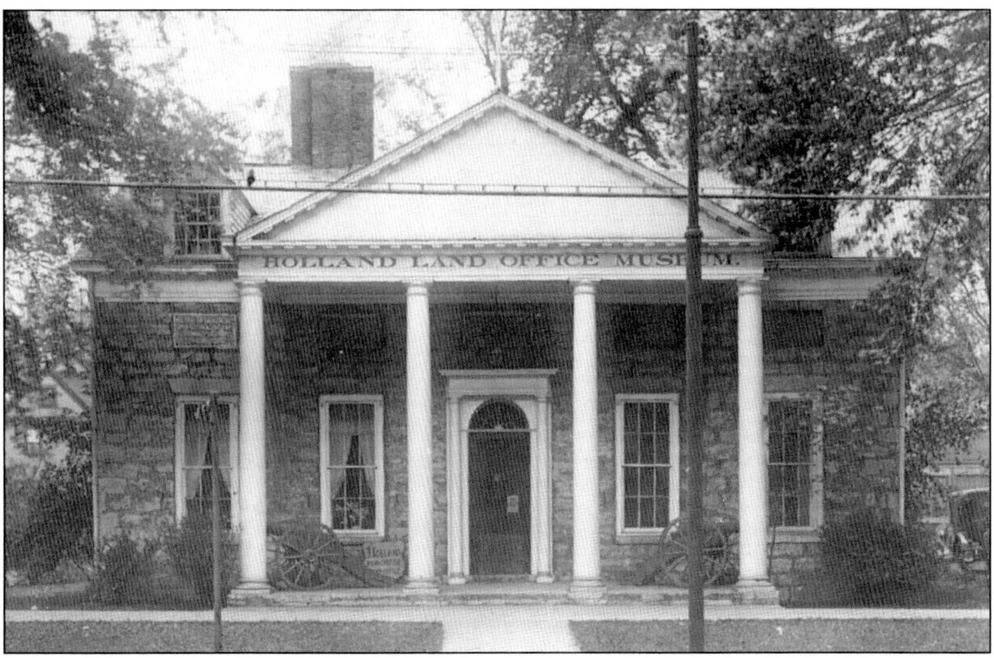

On Saturday, October 13, 1894, the Old Holland Land Company on West Main Street was dedicated to the memory of Robert Morris, the man who secured the Holland Land Purchase and established its office in the old stone building in Batavia.

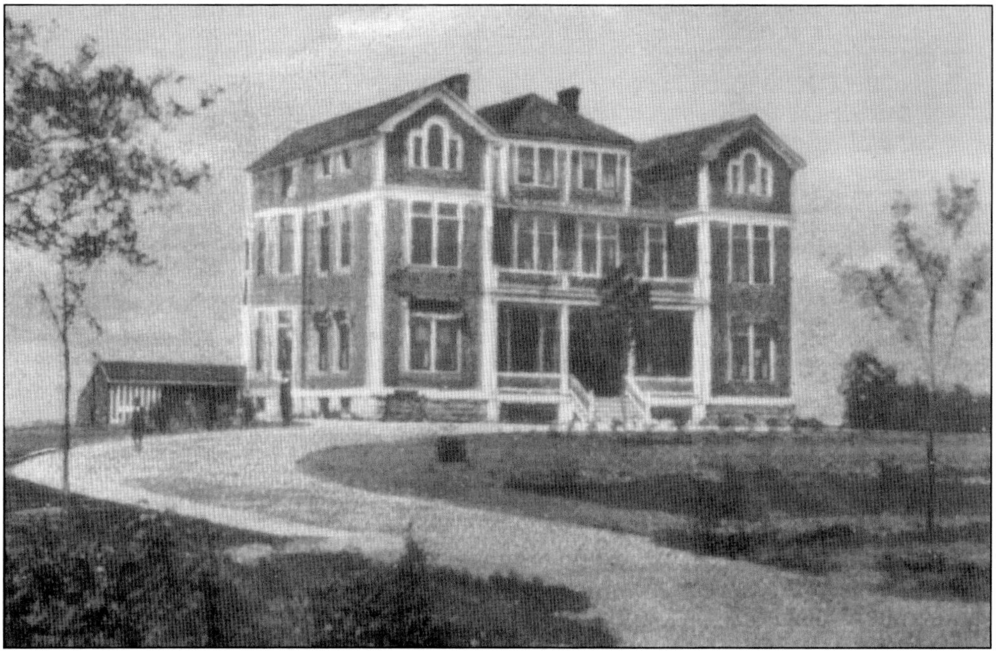

The Batavia Hospital opened on North Street *c*. 1902.

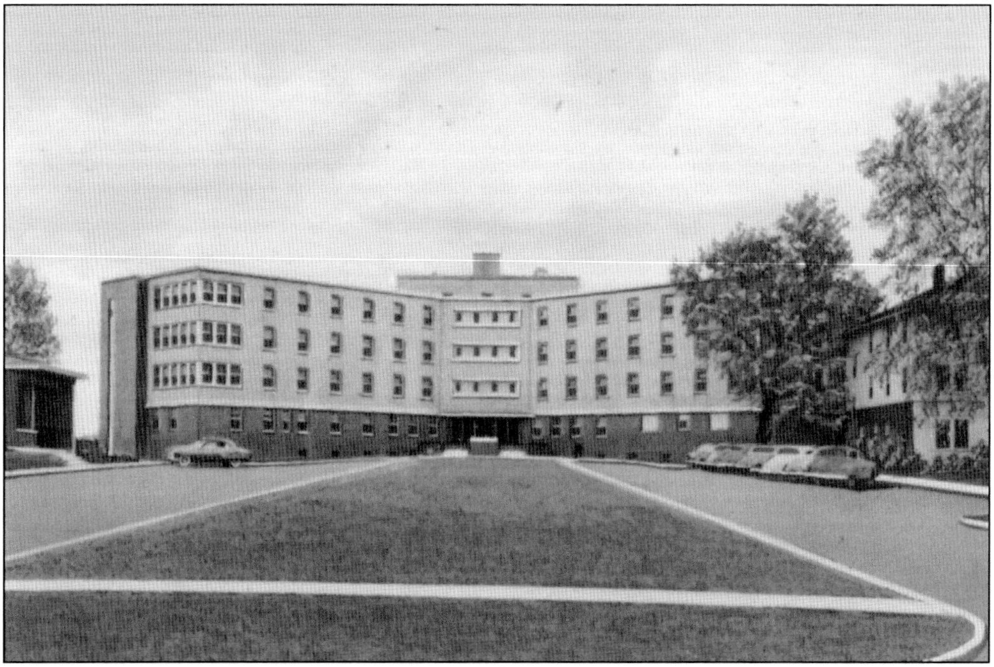

In 1967, a new hospital was built on the North Street site. It was named the Genesee Memorial Hospital, and it still stands today.

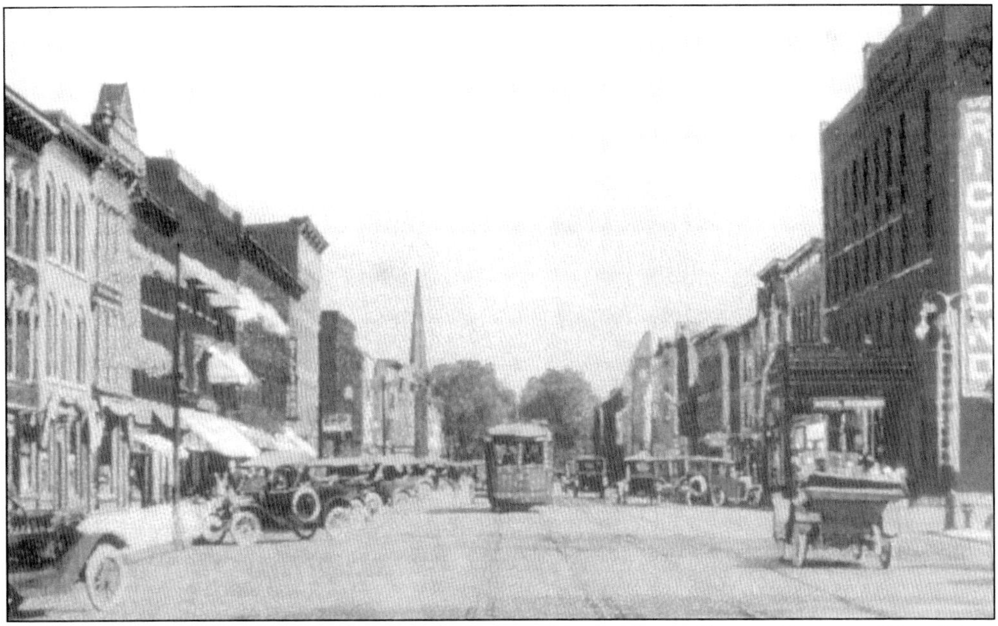

Trolley cars came to Batavia *c.* 1903 and ran for 1.5 miles from Clinton Street to West Main Street. The cost of a round-trip ride was 5¢.

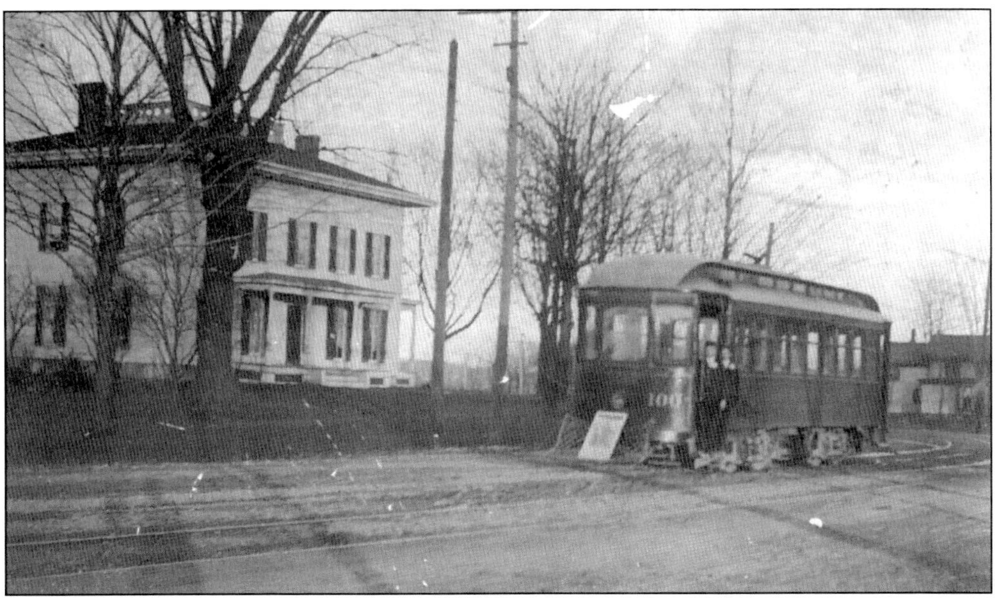

This is a close-up view of one of the trolley cars used in Batavia in 1903.

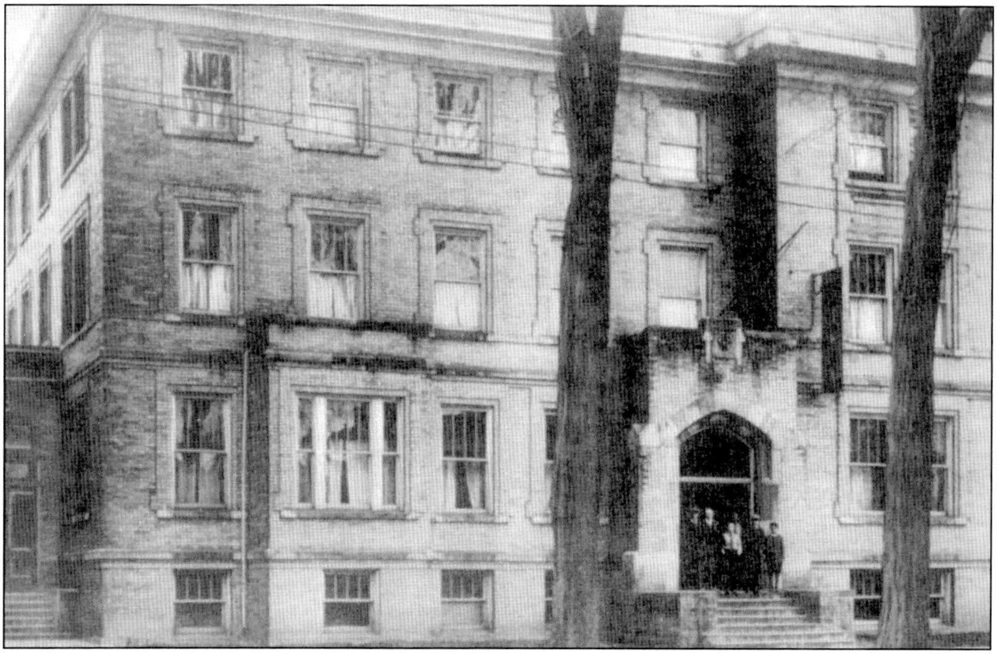

The Batavia YWCA received its association charter in 1903. A group of women headed by Frances B. Fisher met and organized the local branch.

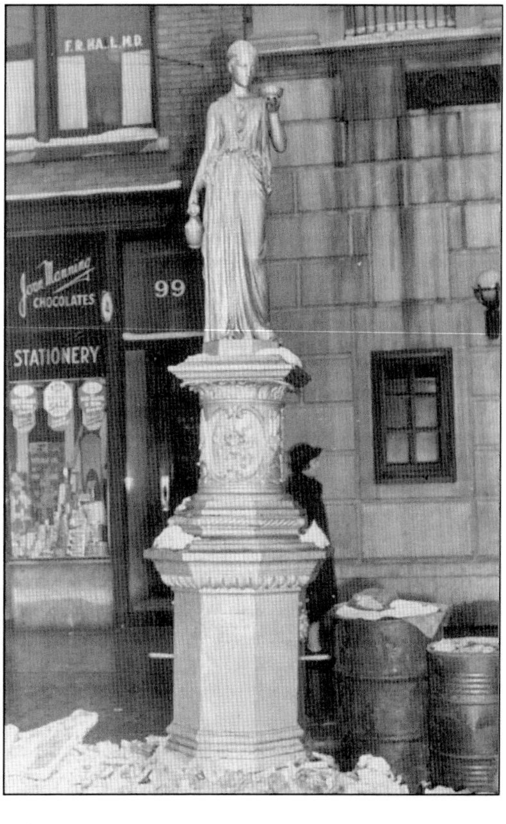

The Women's Christian Temperance Union fountain stood on the corner of Jackson and Main Streets. Made of white marble, it had three fountains with running water: one for horses, one for humans, and one for dogs. The fountain was removed *c.* 1904.

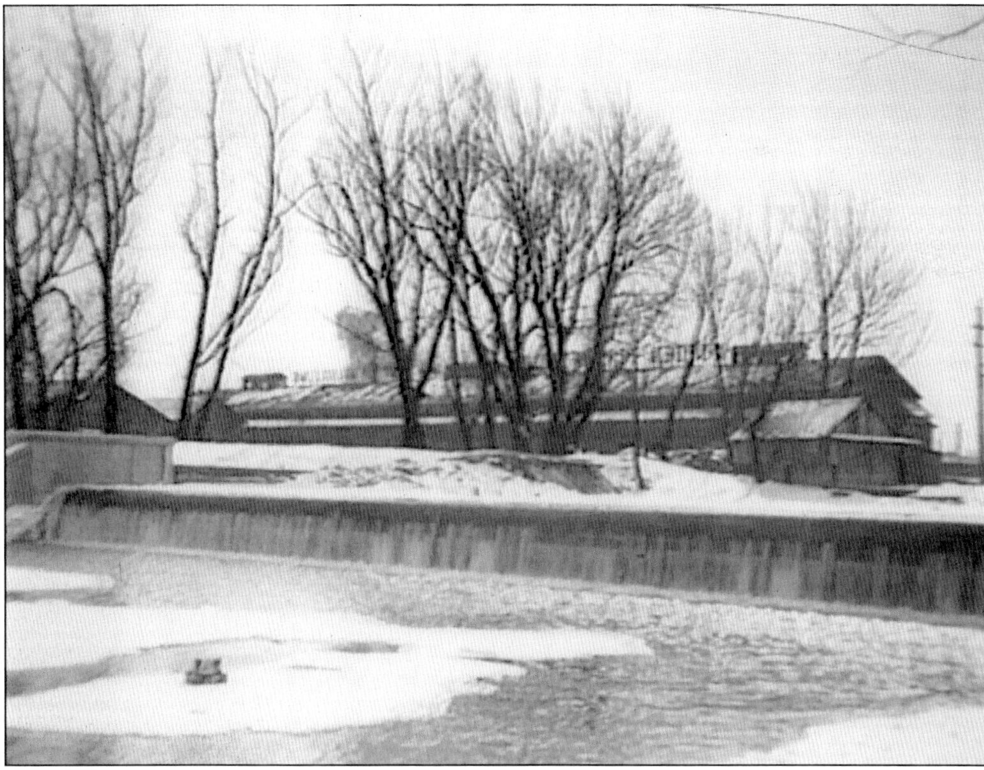

The Worden Monument Company began operations *c.* 1904 near the bend in the Tonawanda Creek. The company cut and designed monuments, among them those that still stand today in Batavia, several other New York locations, and Gettysburg, Pennsylvania.

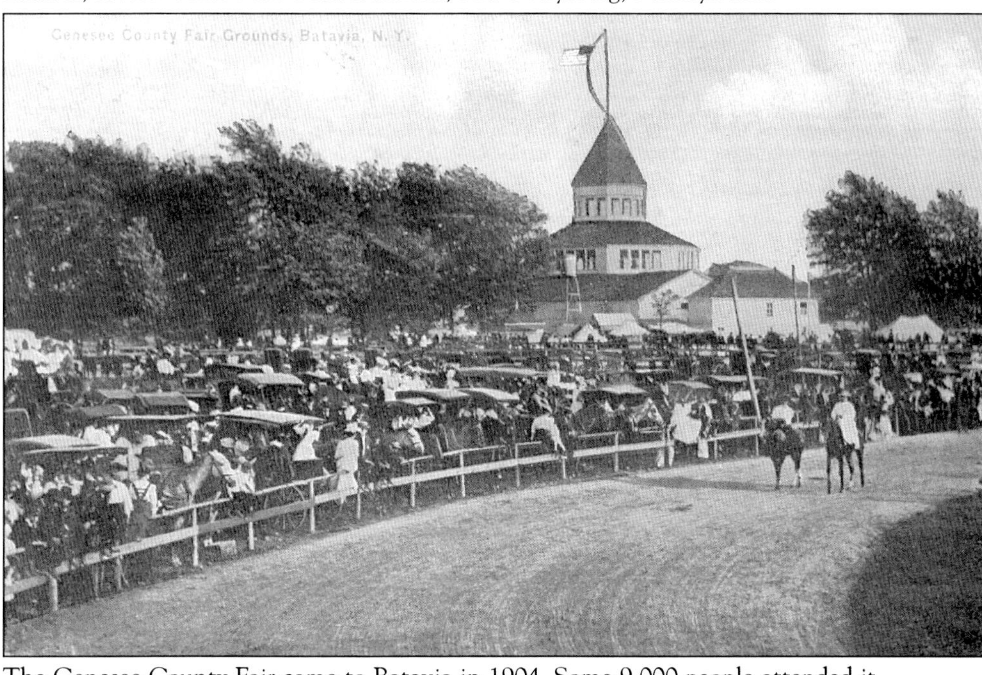

The Genesee County Fair came to Batavia in 1904. Some 9,000 people attended it.

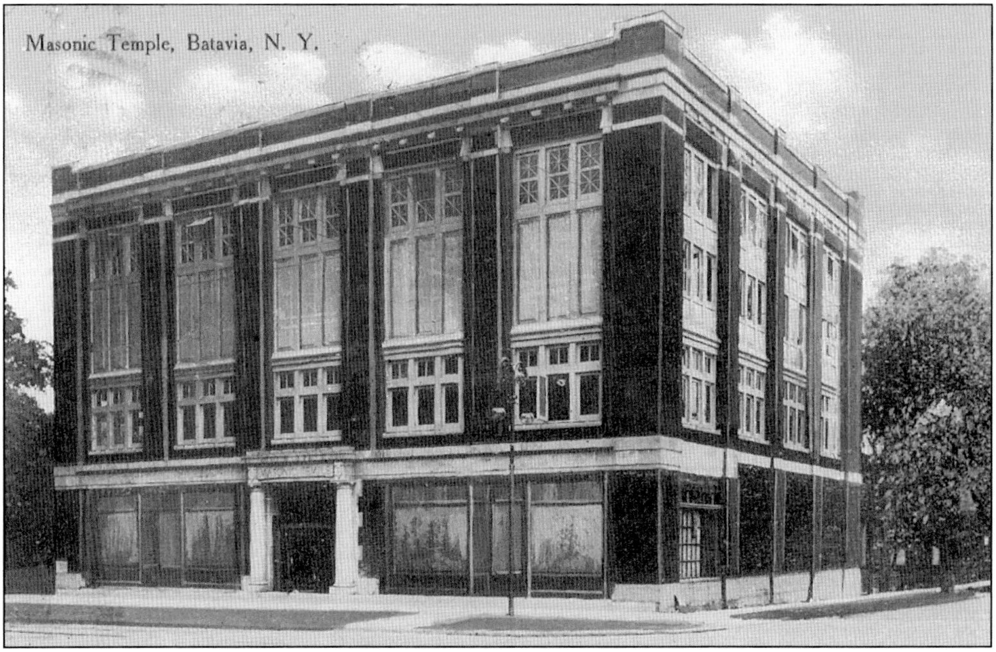

The cornerstone for the three-story brick Masonic Temple was placed on November 11, 1908. The is a postcard view of that building. The present Masonic lodge dates from 1859.

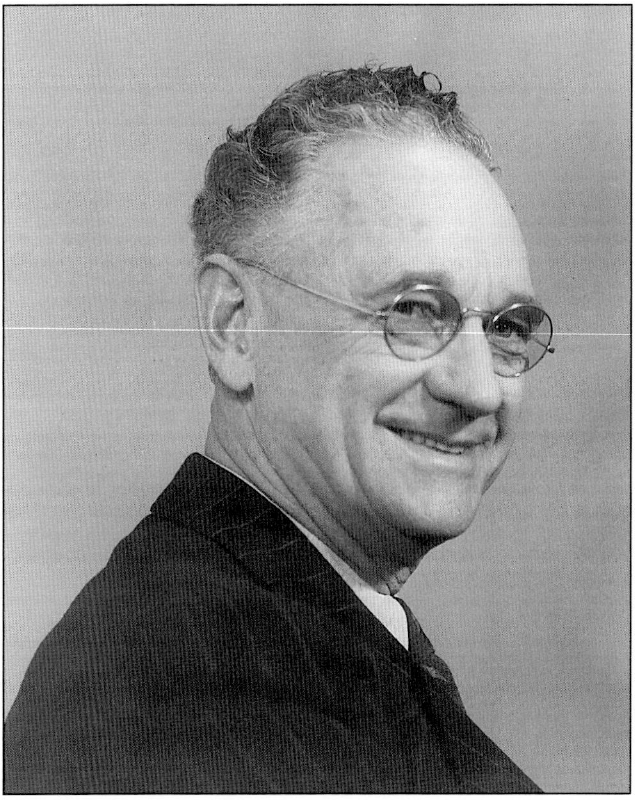

Local artist Roy Mason learned the essentials of painting and design from his father, Frank E. Mason. Roy Mason and his sister Nina opened a commercial art studio together. Their father came to Batavia as an artist, worked at the Baker Gun Company, and set up a small embossed seal and label-manufacturing business at 24 Main Street c. 1907.

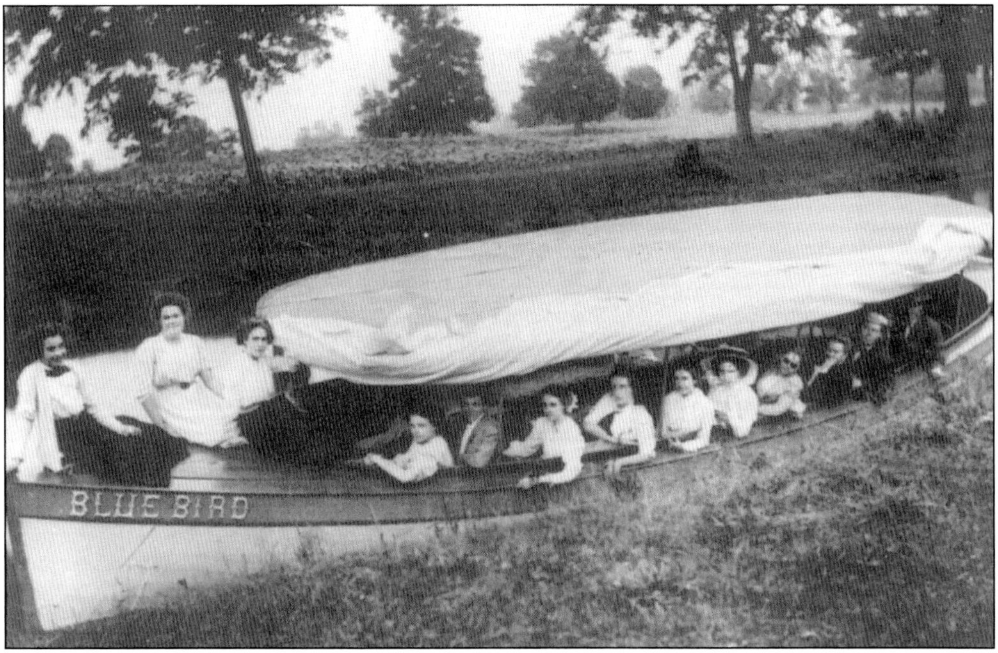

The Tonawanda Creek was used for recreation and pleasure. Ed Follett and his brother built the boats named *Bluebird*, *Irene*, and *Cynthia* c. 1910.

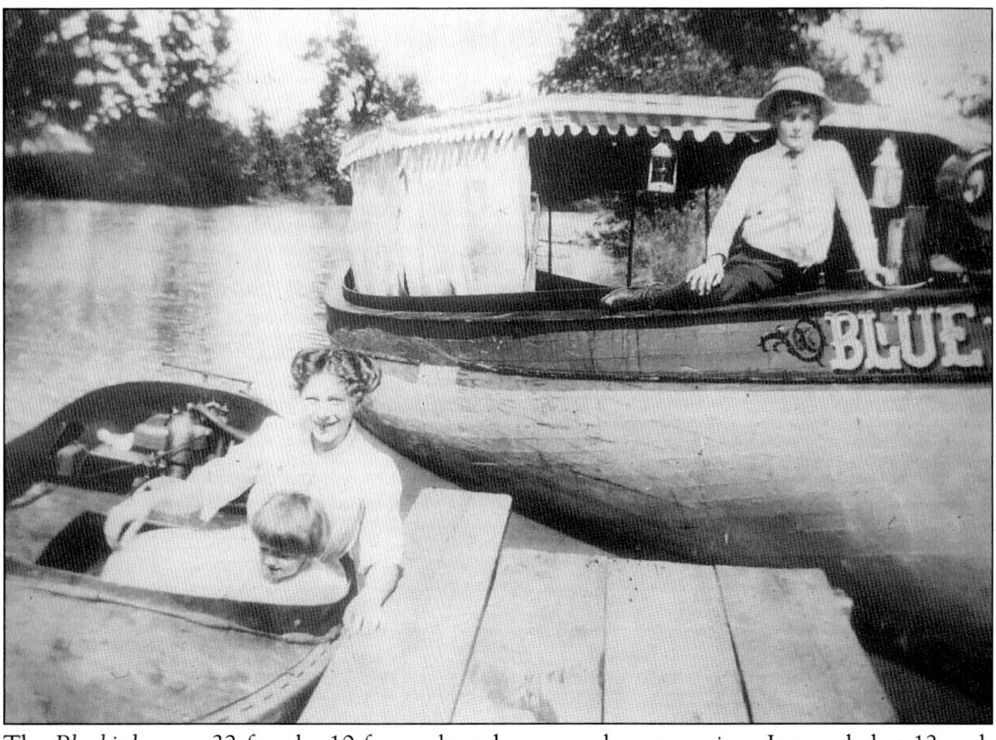

The *Bluebird* was a 32-foot by 10-foot oak and cypress pleasure cruiser. It traveled at 12 mph and was used until it was lost in the flood of 1922.

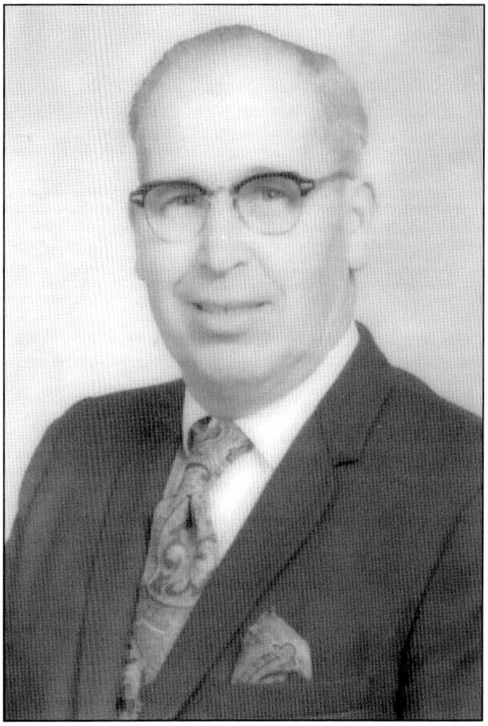

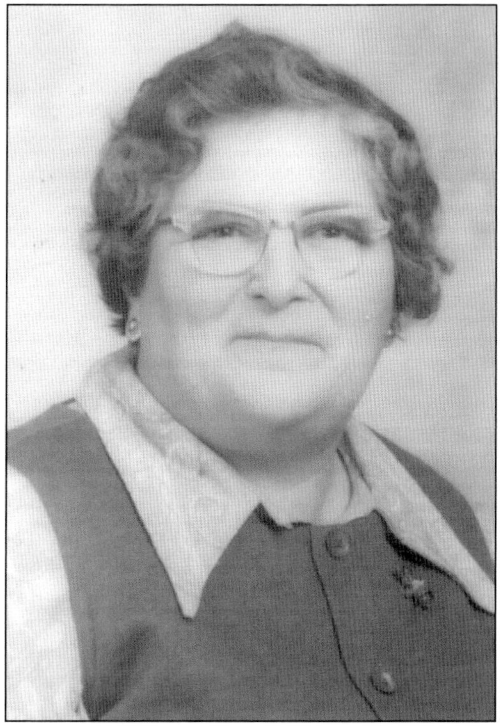

Dwight S. Toal, left, was a master plumber. He owned and operated a plumbing, heating, and electrical company. He has been given credit for establishing the first public rest rooms in Batavia's downtown area. His wife, Ruth Elizabeth, handled the accounting end of Toal's plumbing business. The couple were active members of the East Pembroke Federated Church.

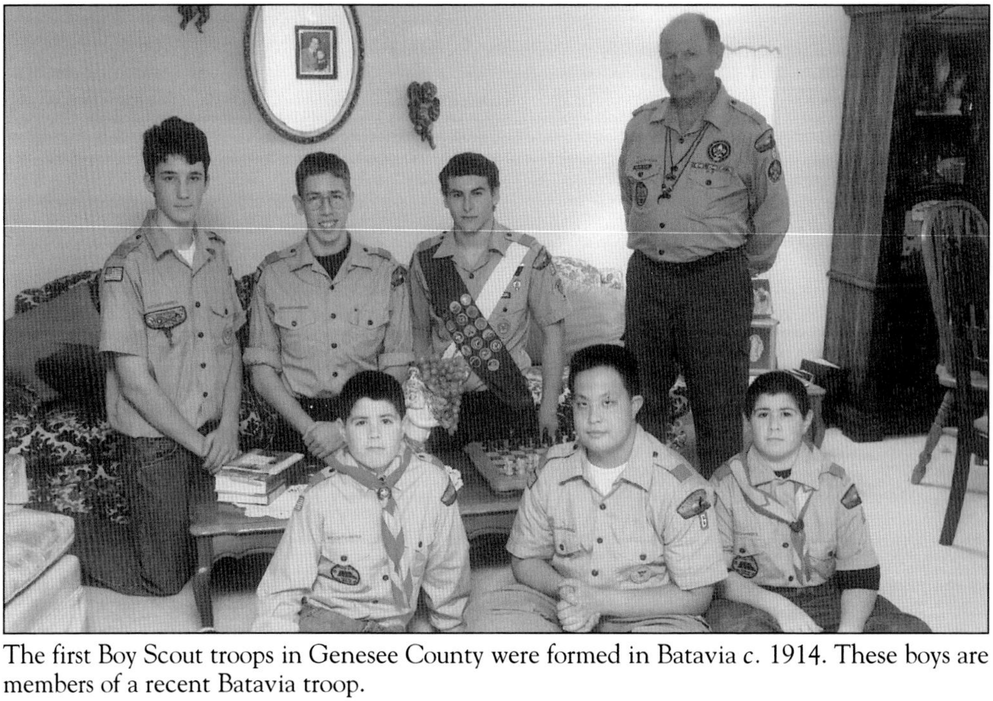

The first Boy Scout troops in Genesee County were formed in Batavia c. 1914. These boys are members of a recent Batavia troop.

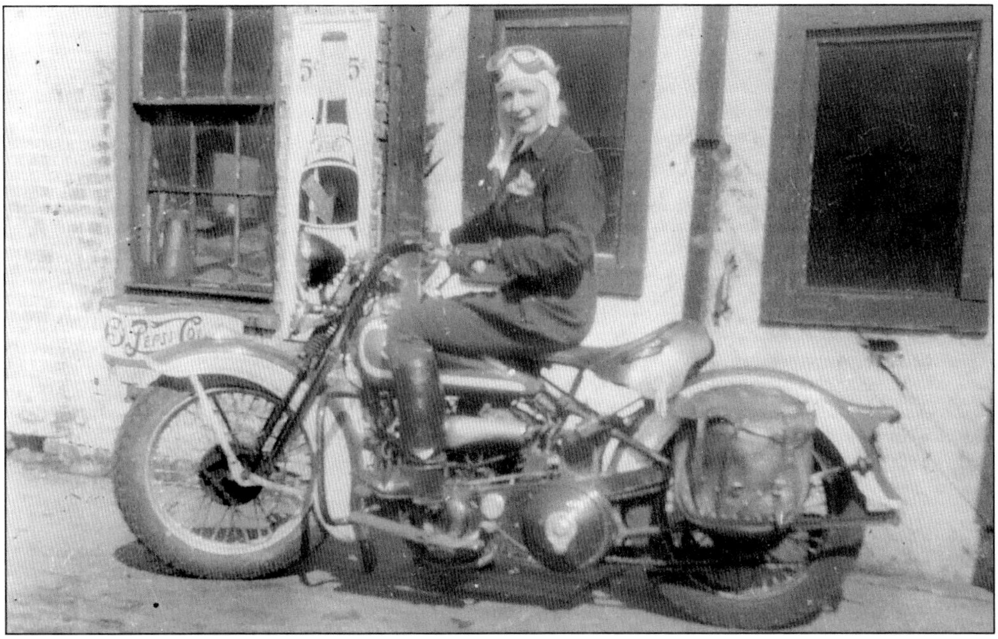

The automobile arrived in Batavia and with it, *c.* 1915, came a baby blue Harley-Davidson motorcycle. The owner was Louise "Blondie" Bailey, who is best remembered for her superb handling of the vehicle: she once rode the motorcycle down Main Street standing on the seat— with no hands.

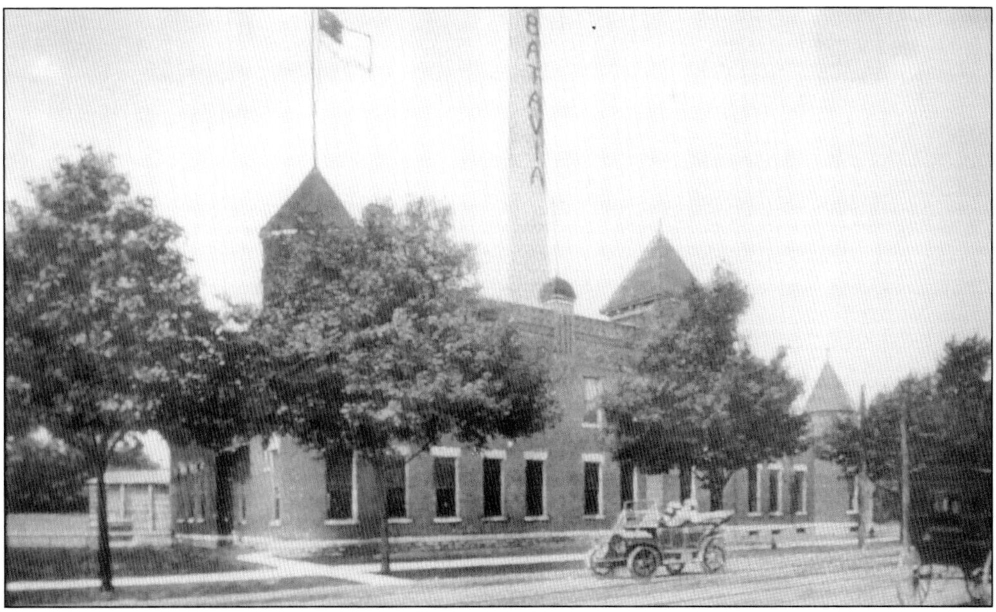

The city inherited the municipal building from the village of Batavia *c.* 1915. Raw sewage was pumped to a facility at Hillcrest Avenue, where it was treated and sent on to the creek by a gravity flow system at 3 West Main Street. The structure was rebuilt *c.* 1948, after being heavily damaged by an explosion caused by a sewer gas leak. Later, the building served as a firehouse and then as a restaurant. In 1996, it was bought by Genesee County. The building was restored, and a portion of it was converted into the Genesee County History Department.

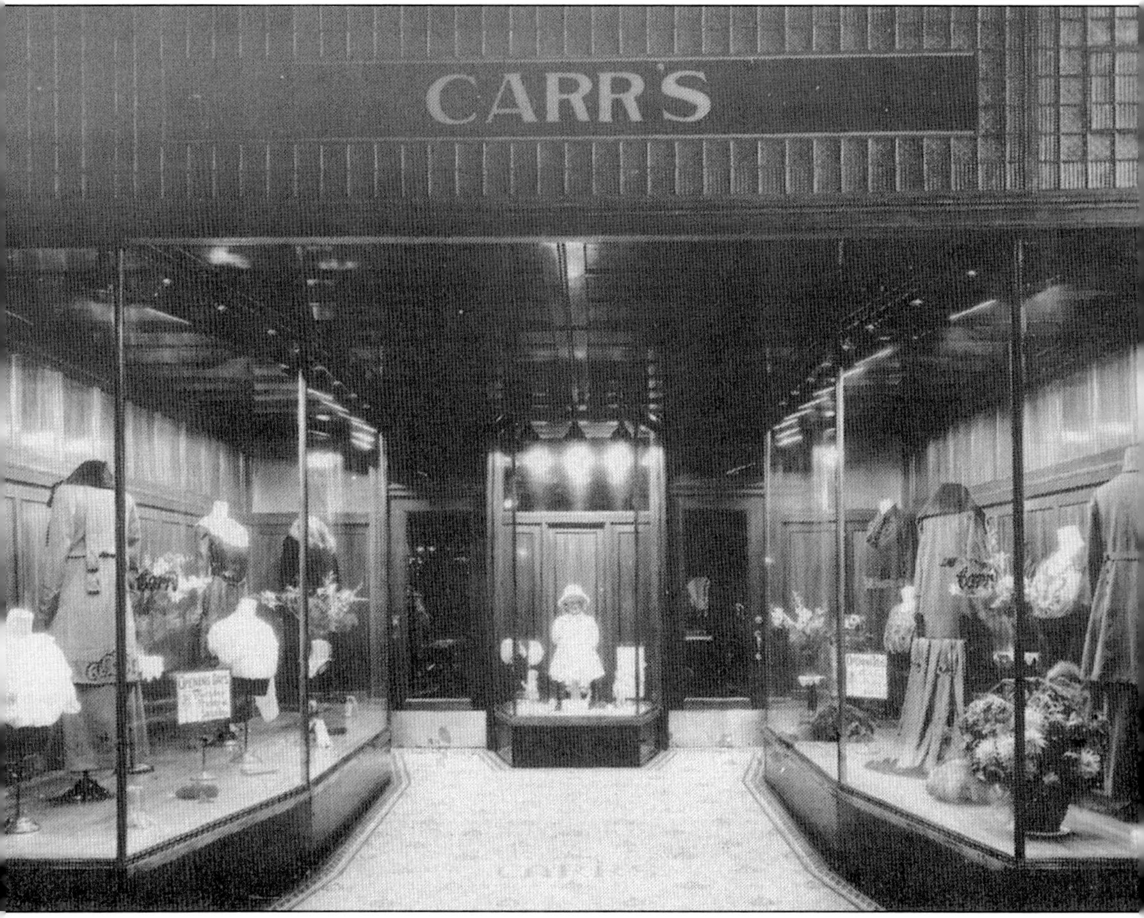

C.L. Carr's Department Store was founded *c.* 1915 on Main Street in the heart of downtown Batavia. It is the oldest family-owned and operated department store in Batavia.

This was one of Batavia's earliest police officers, hired to stop speeders. When Batavia became a city, the speed limit was 15 mph.

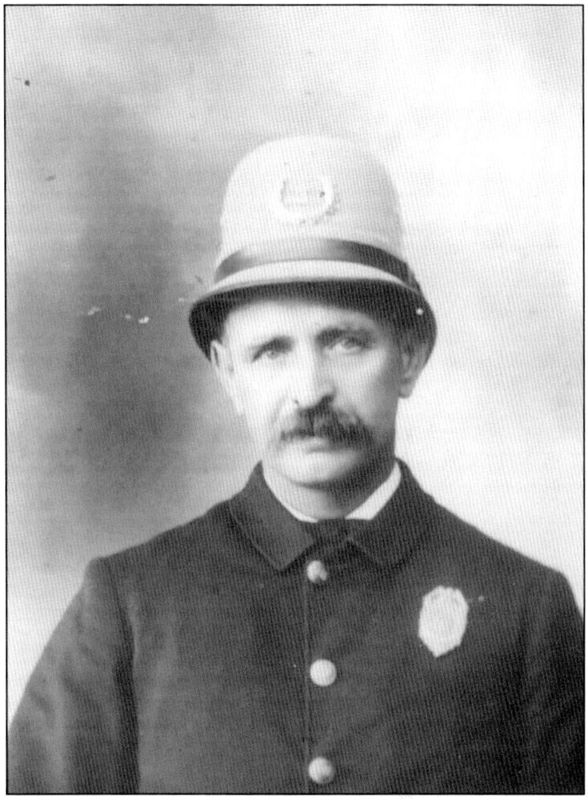

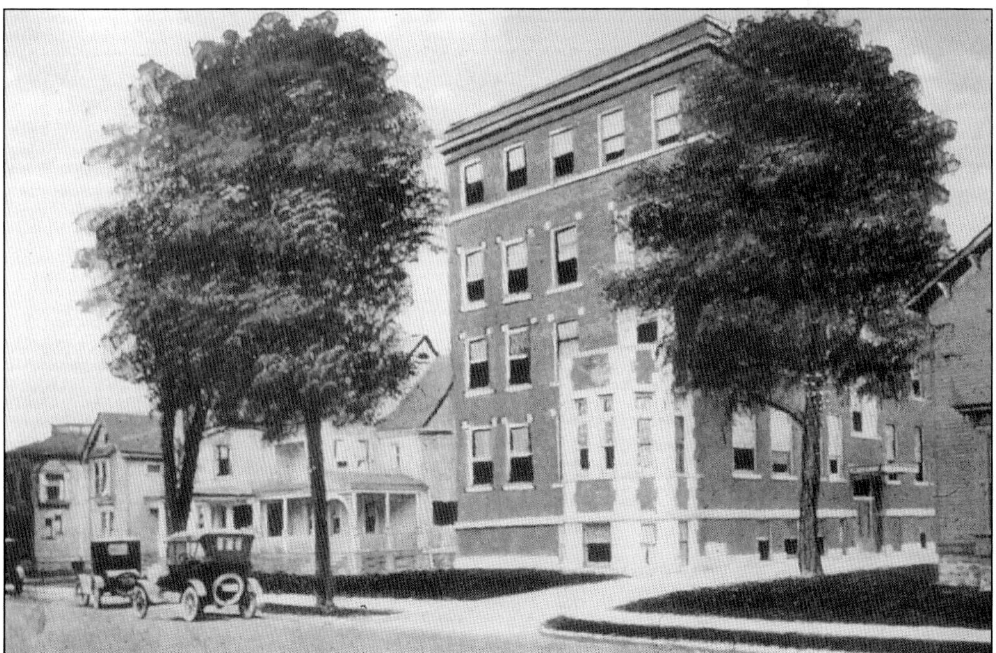

In 1916, Rose A. Jerome bequeathed her double home at 16 Bank Street as a home for girls to be maintained and conducted by the Sisters of Mercy of the Buffalo Diocese.

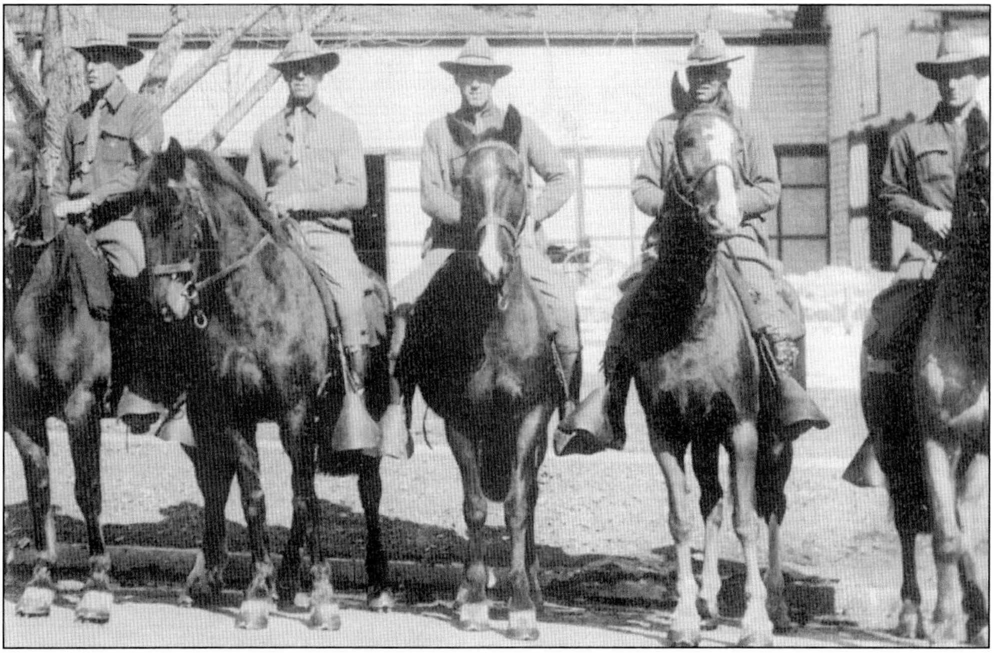

New York State Troopers arrived *c.* 1917. Troop A Headquarters was established in the Dyke Roller Rink, with the basement converted into stables for the horses. In October 1920, the troop moved to a new location farther east on East Main Street and, in 1976, it moved to a new building on Saile Drive.

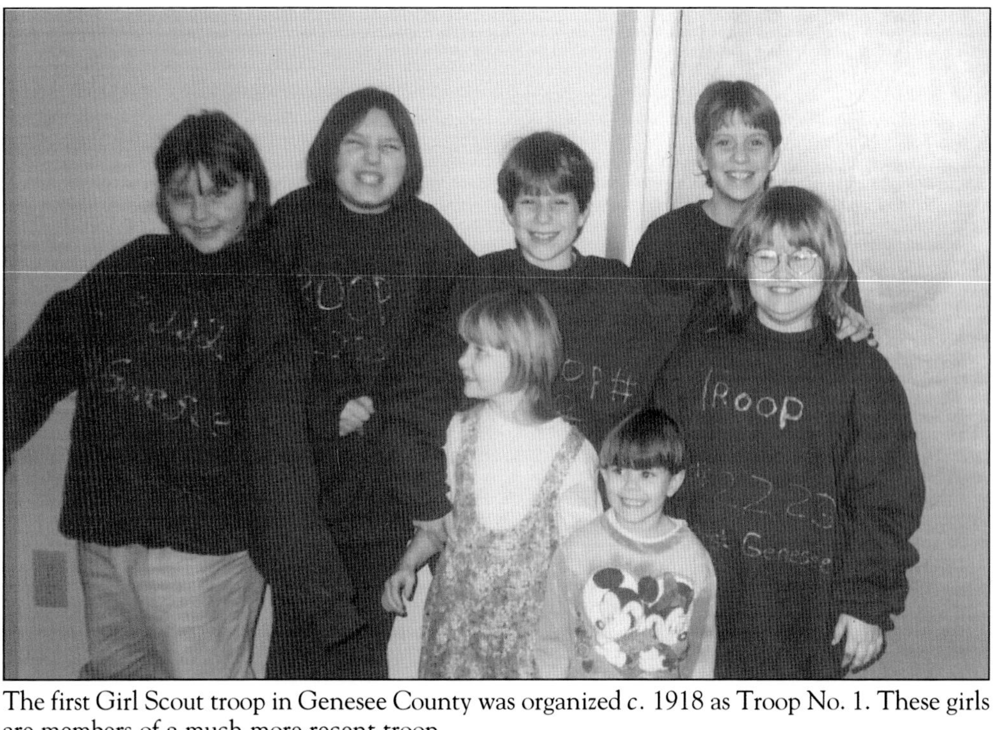

The first Girl Scout troop in Genesee County was organized *c.* 1918 as Troop No. 1. These girls are members of a much more recent troop.

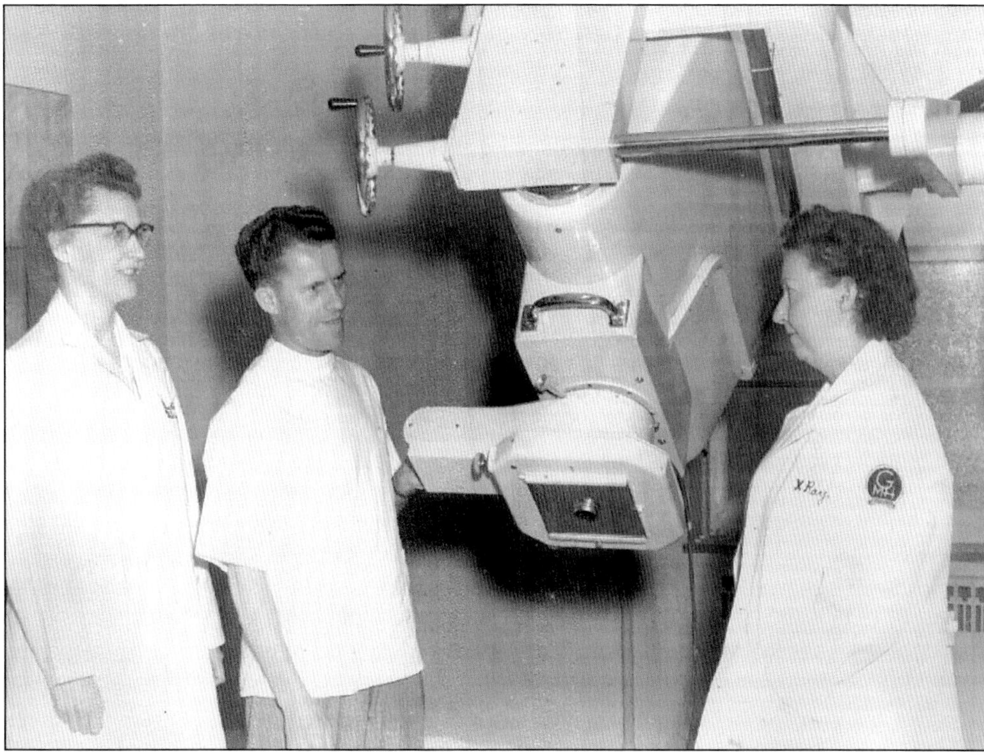

Batavia Hospital acquired its first X-ray machine *c.* 1918. Around the same time, a group of 50 women established the Batavia branch of the Red Cross.

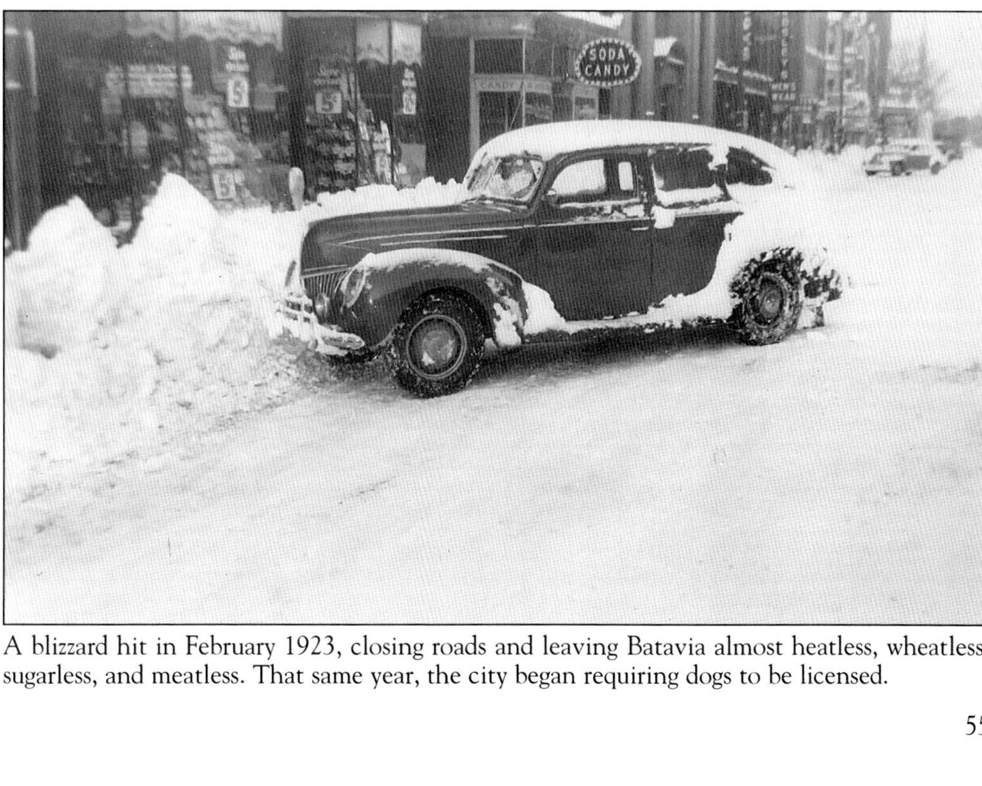

A blizzard hit in February 1923, closing roads and leaving Batavia almost heatless, wheatless, sugarless, and meatless. That same year, the city began requiring dogs to be licensed.

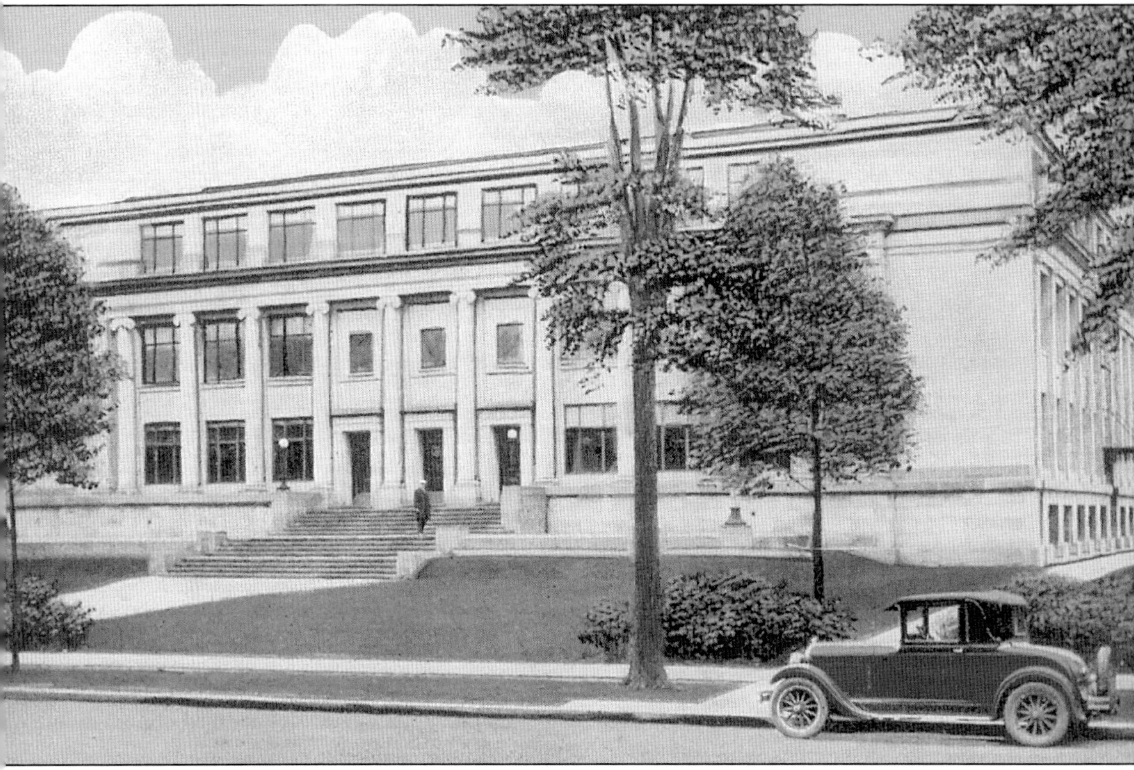

The Batavia Middle School was constructed *c.* 1924 on Ross Street at the end of Washington Avenue. A gymnasium was added in 1964.

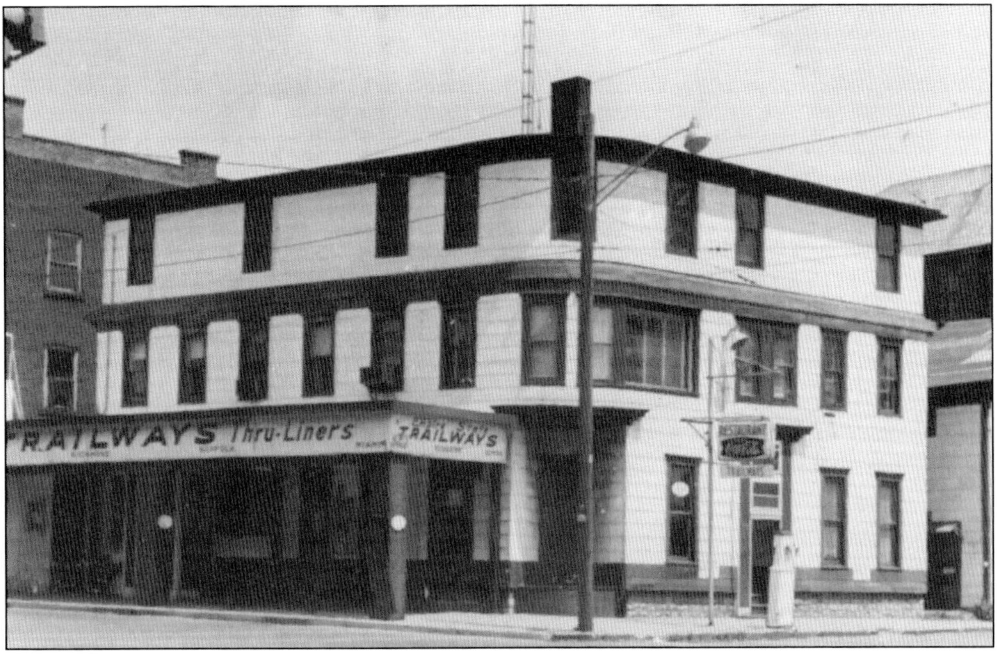

The Empire State Trailways bus station was on the corner of Court and Ellicott Streets. The sign in this 1958 view offers buses to—among other places—Rochester and Elmira, and advertises Thru-Liners to Richmond, Norfolk, Miami, and so forth.

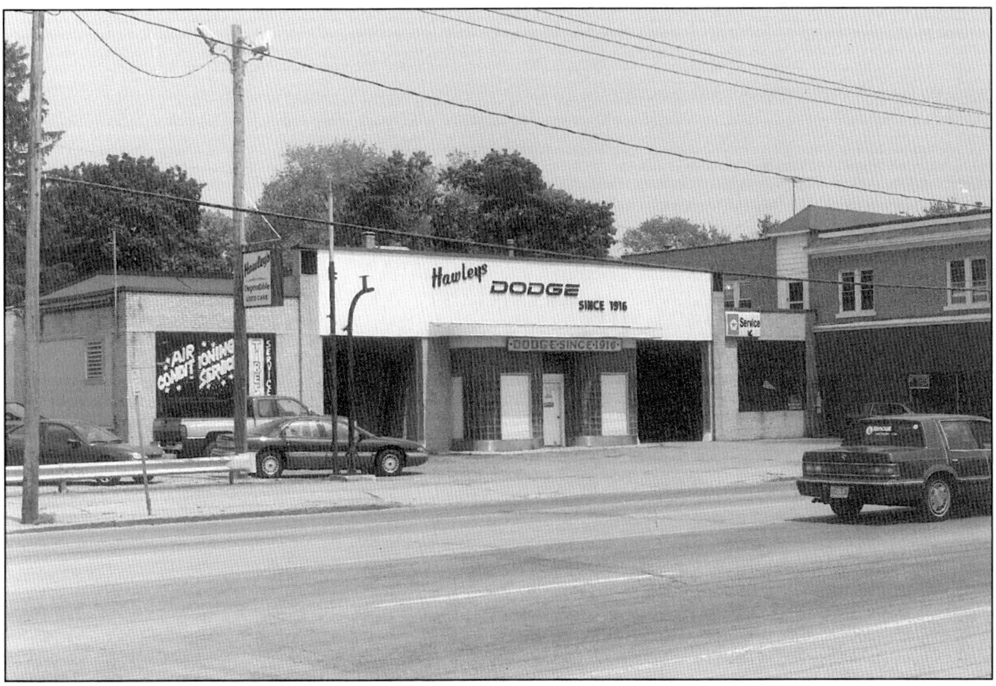

Hawley Motors began in 1923. This is the oldest family-owned and operated Dodge dealer in western New York.

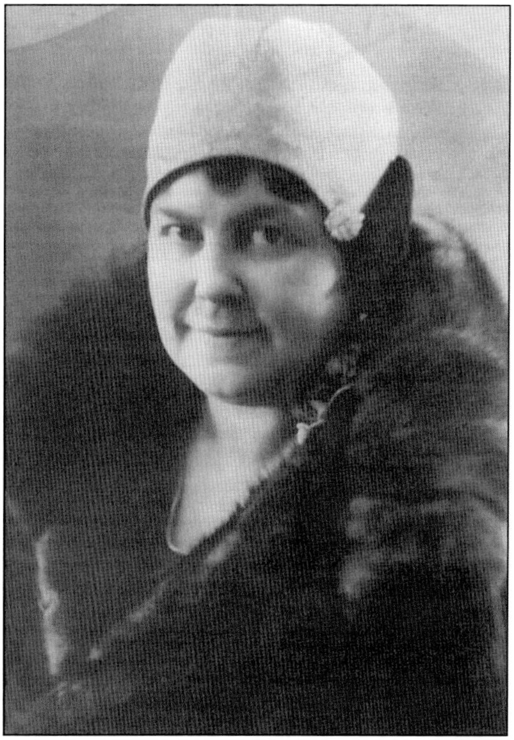

Edna Gruber moved from East Pembroke and purchased a large house on Jackson Street *c.* 1926. She was Batavia's famous madam.

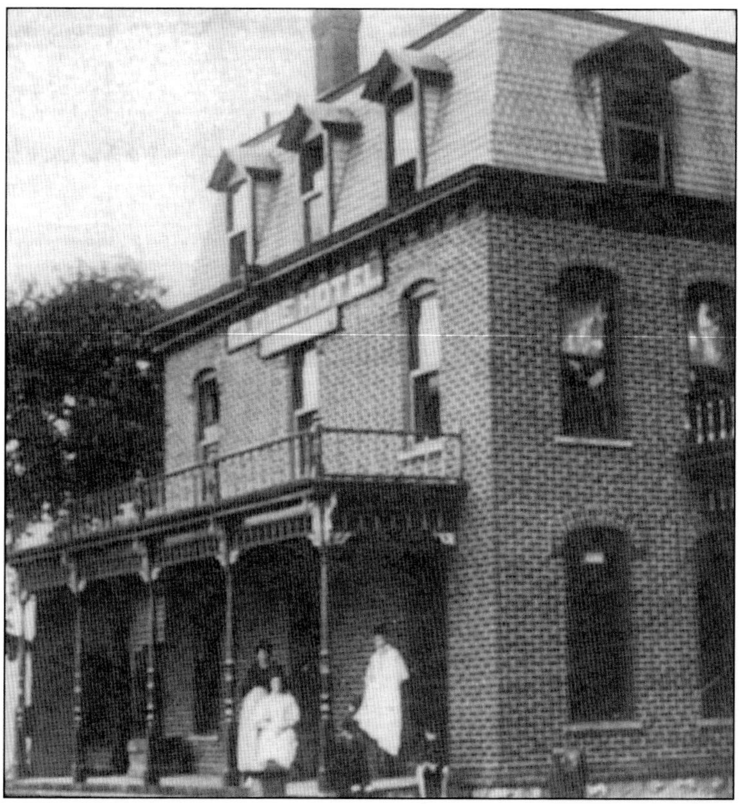

Edna Gruber was married and had a son, a daughter, and a granddaughter. Her house at 103 Jackson Street was generally known as the Central Hotel. Gruber renamed it the Palace Hotel, and today it is known as the Globe. The house was recently remodeled into multiple units.

Four

Sports and Other Events

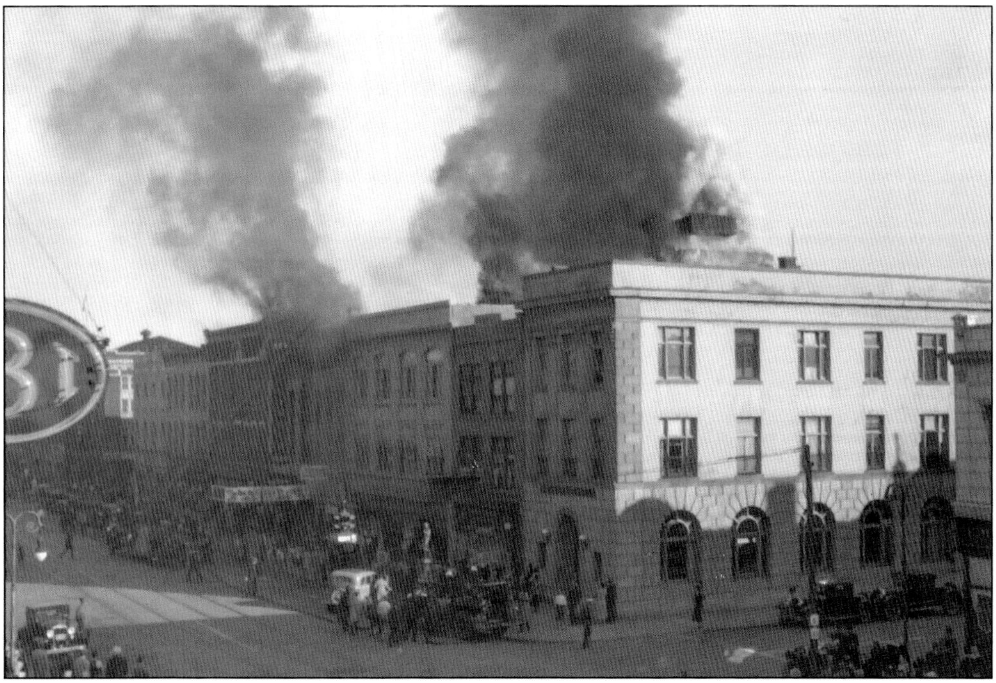

The Dellinger Theater was destroyed by fire in the mid-1930s. This photograph shows the building in flames. Some 75 firemen battled the blaze for four hours. However, the theater was lost. Fire walls, 16 inches thick, were credited with keeping the adjacent C.L. Carr Company from also being destroyed.

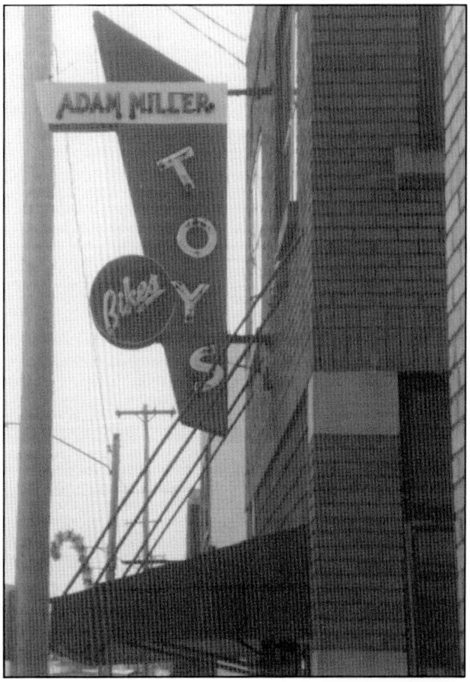

Walter J. Davis, a bicycle dealer, constructed a building at 6 Center Street *c.* 1929. He sold and repaired bicycles there until 1946. Adam Miller bought the bicycle business in February 1946. Today, the shop is still owned and operated by members of the Miller family.

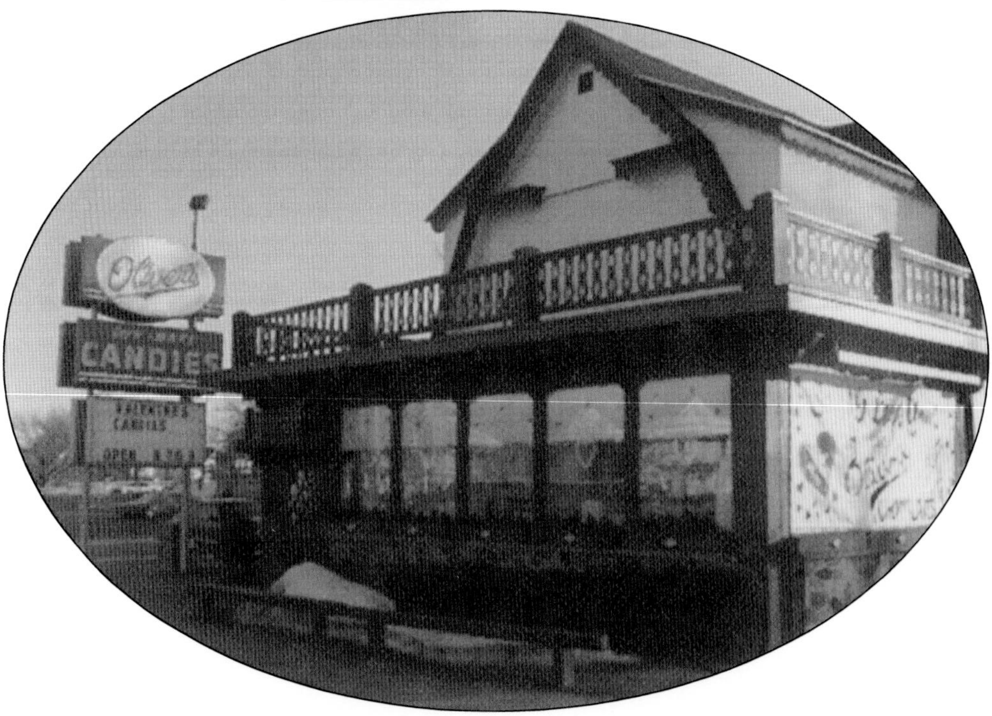

Oliver's, located at 211 West Main Street, was established by Joseph Boyd Oliver *c.* 1932. Famous for its award-winning chocolates, Oliver's continues to maintain highest quality and customer service by using original family-proven recipes and the best ingredients, including real butter, cream, honey, and other natural products. It is currently owned by the Quincey family.

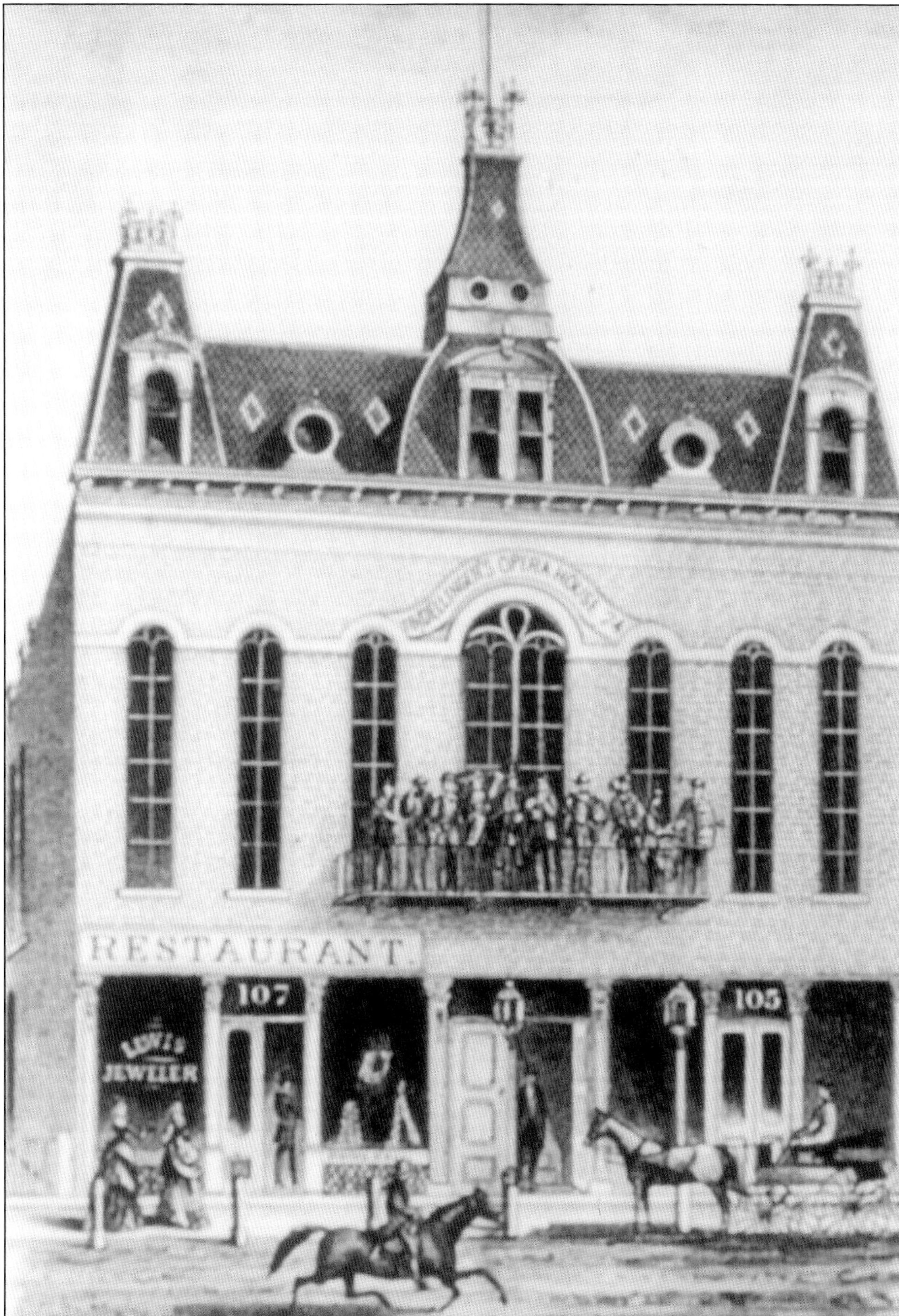

The Dellinger Opera House opened on Main Street c. 1874. Also called the Dellinger Theater, the business thrived until the building burned in a Columbus Day fire in the mid-1930s. This picture shows the building with a restaurant and a jeweler on the street level.

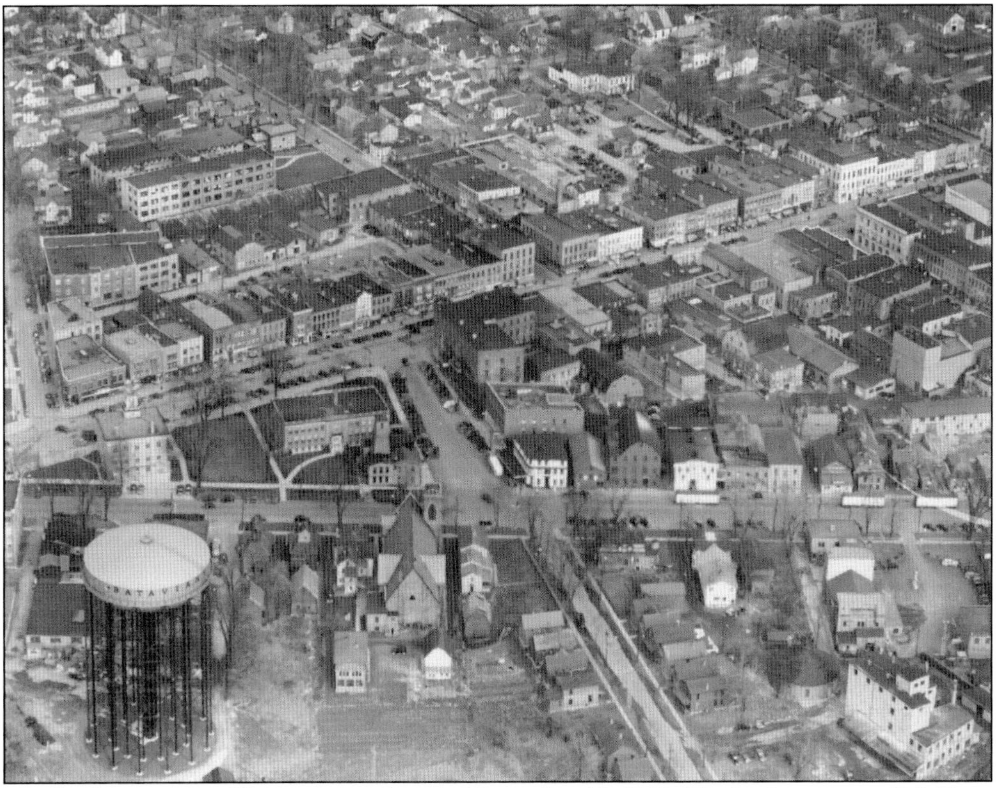

This bird's-eye view of Batavia was taken on November 15, 1939. The back is stamped H. Gene Lyon & H. DeWolf, Aerial Photographers, Rochester. The city's water storage tank appears at the left in the photograph.

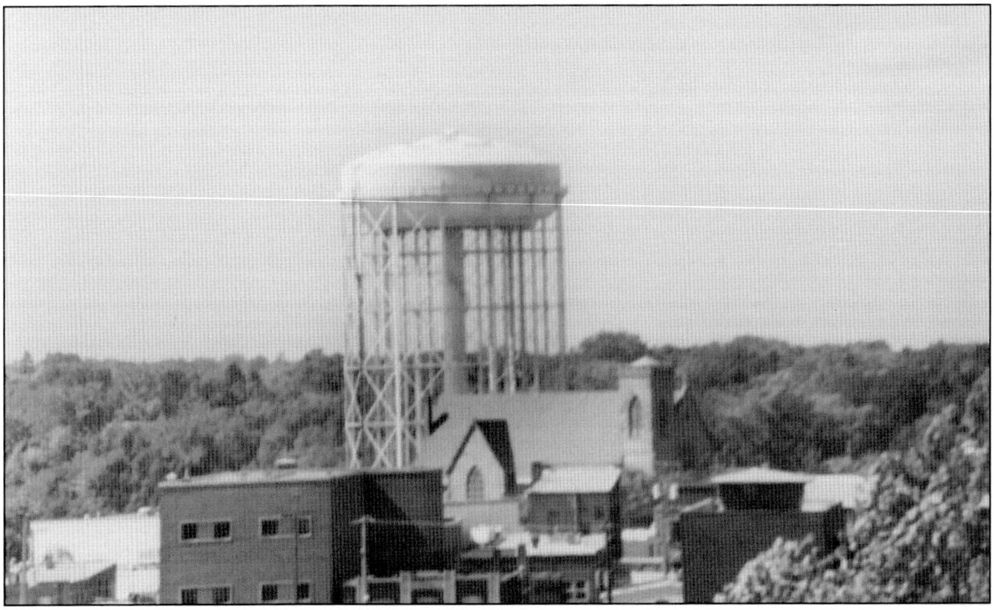

The Ellicott Street water storage tank was completed at a cost of $175,000 *c.* 1938. At the time, it was the highest elevated tank of its capacity: 1.5 million gallons.

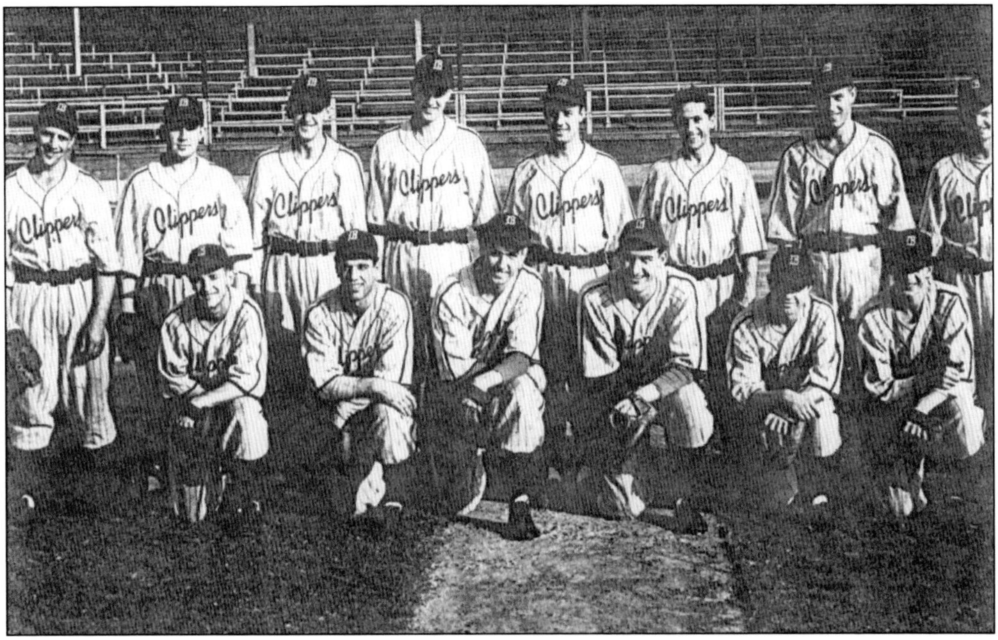

Members of the Batavia Clippers baseball team played their first game *c.* 1939.

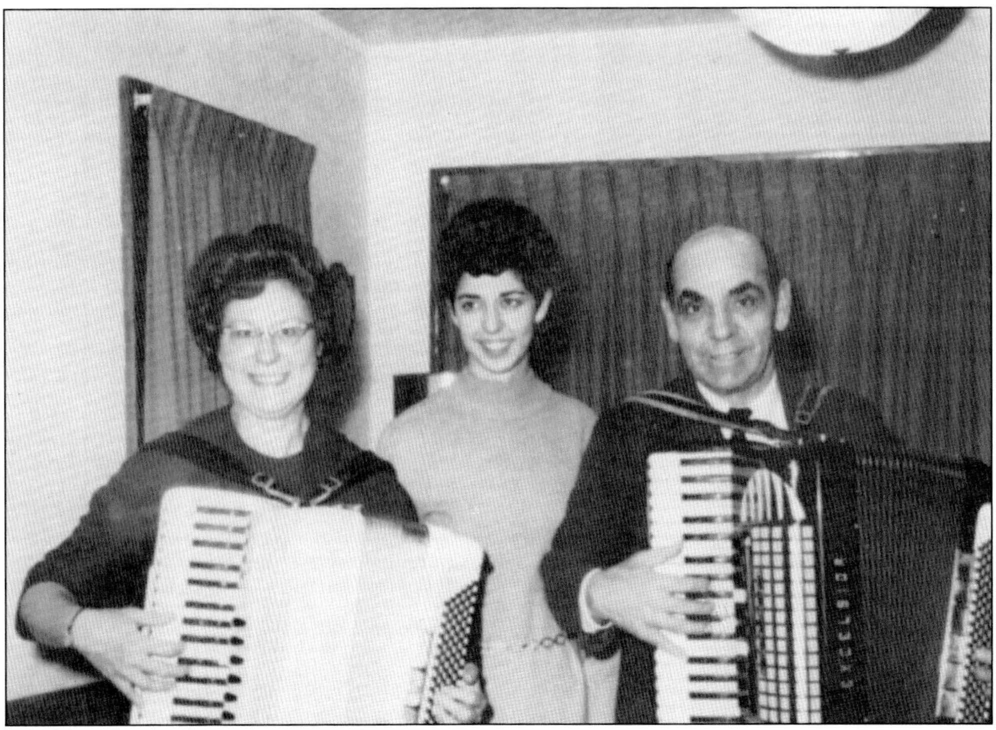

Roxy and Nellie Caccamise opened a music studio at 331 West Main Street *c.* 1939. Roxy Caccamise was known far beyond Batavia and performed with many well-known musicians. Daughter Rose Caccamise took over the store in the 1960s and later moved the business to the Genesee Country Mall.

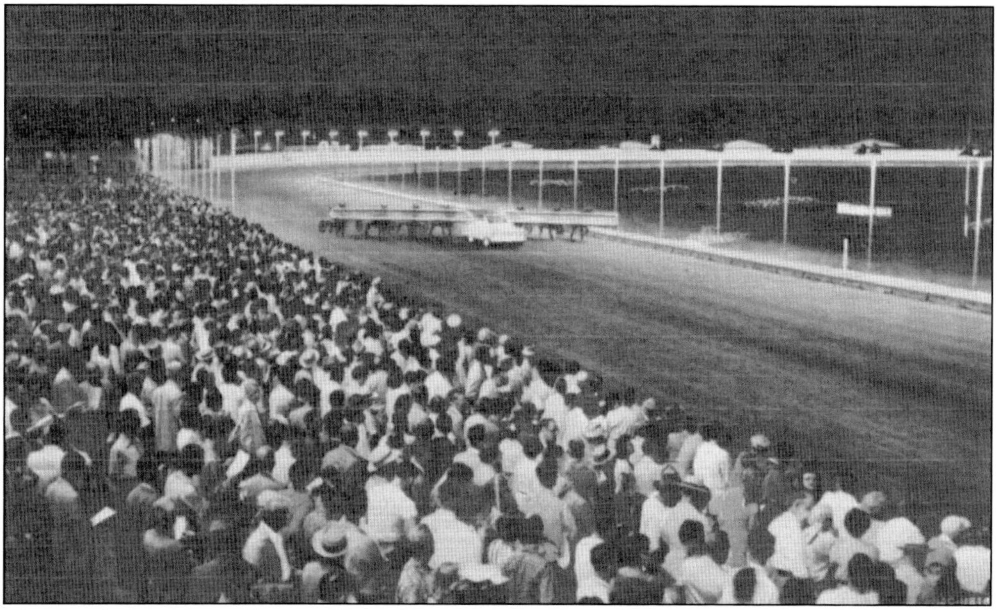

The first horse race at Batavia Downs was run c. 1940. The harness racing track drew many fine horses and drivers throughout the years. At the time this picture was taken, the track held races nightly at 8:30 from August through October. Recently, Batavia Downs was sold to Off-Track Betting.

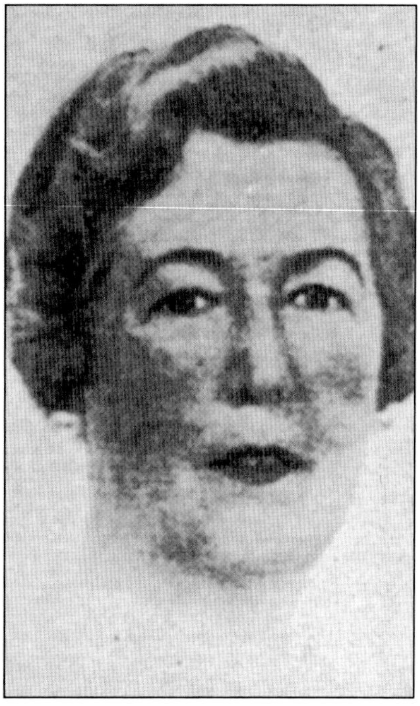

Maud Homelius was appointed as Batavia's first female mayor c. 1941. To date, she is the only woman to serve as the city's mayor.

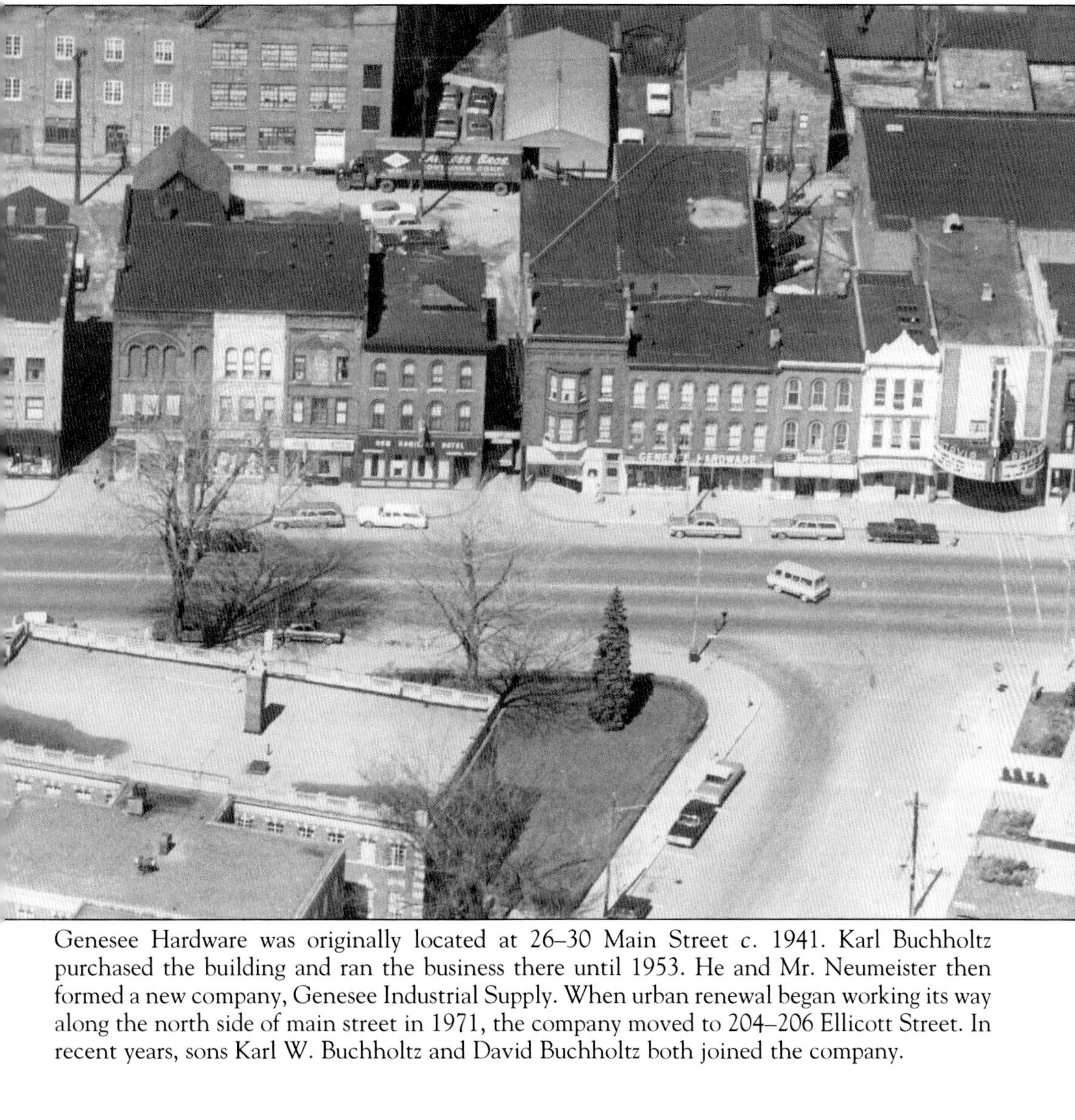

Genesee Hardware was originally located at 26–30 Main Street *c.* 1941. Karl Buchholtz purchased the building and ran the business there until 1953. He and Mr. Neumeister then formed a new company, Genesee Industrial Supply. When urban renewal began working its way along the north side of main street in 1971, the company moved to 204–206 Ellicott Street. In recent years, sons Karl W. Buchholtz and David Buchholtz both joined the company.

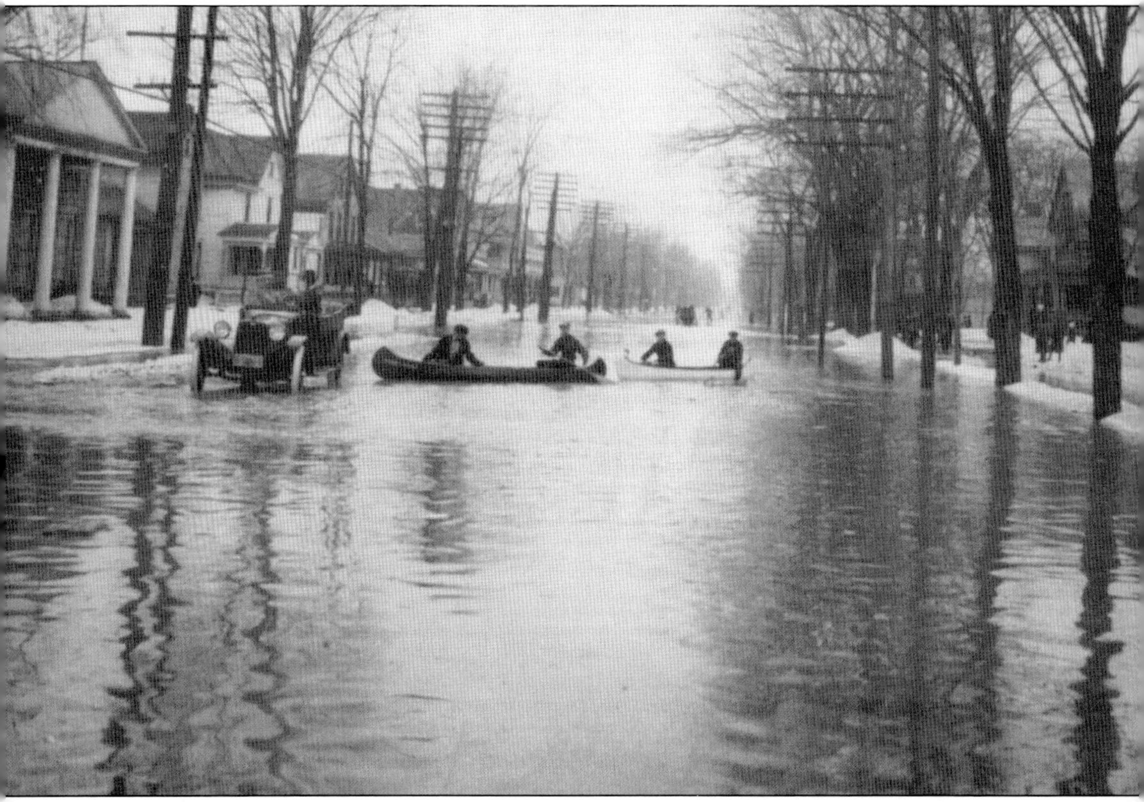

The greatest flood in the history of Batavia hit the area on St. Patrick's Day in 1942. The flood marooned hundreds of south side residents and caused at least $500,000 worth of damage.

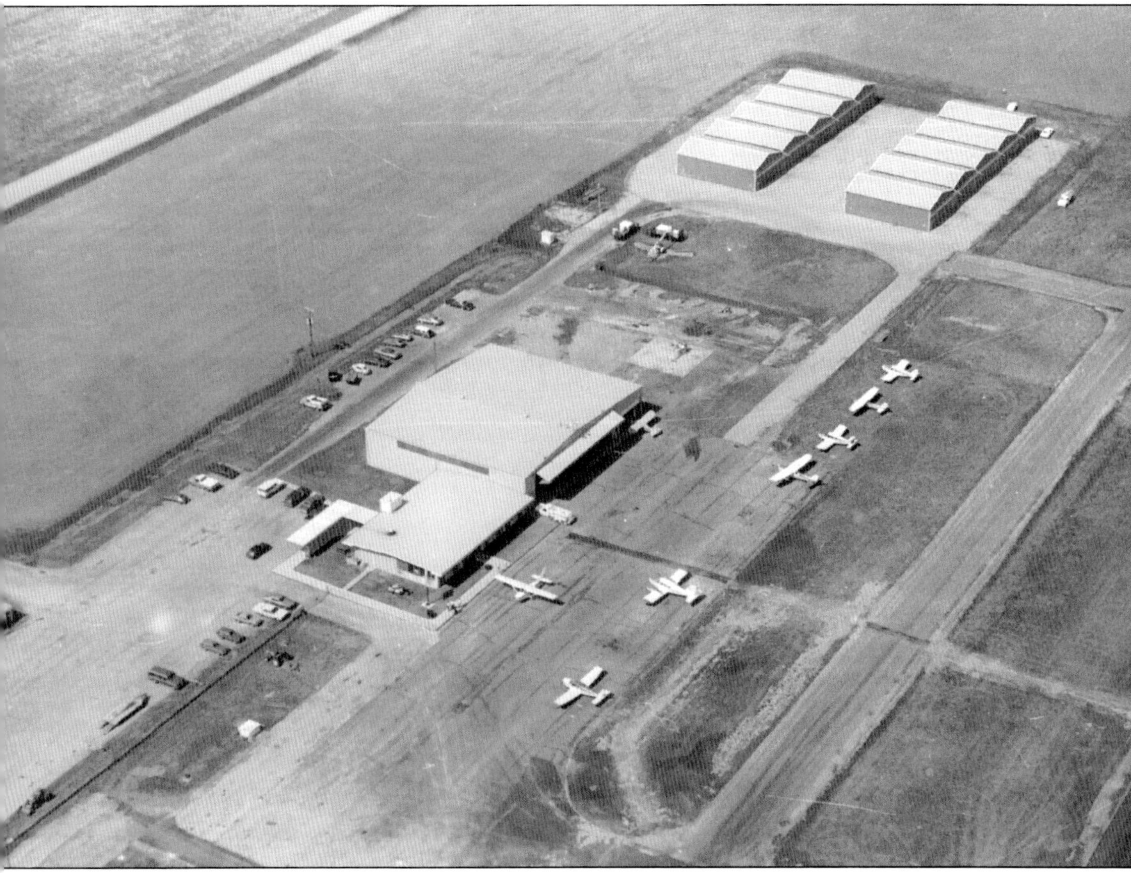

The Batavia Airport first opened *c.* 1943. It was owned by Gilbert Chapel until being taken over by the county of Genesee in 1963. In 1965, it was expanded to 20 hangars.

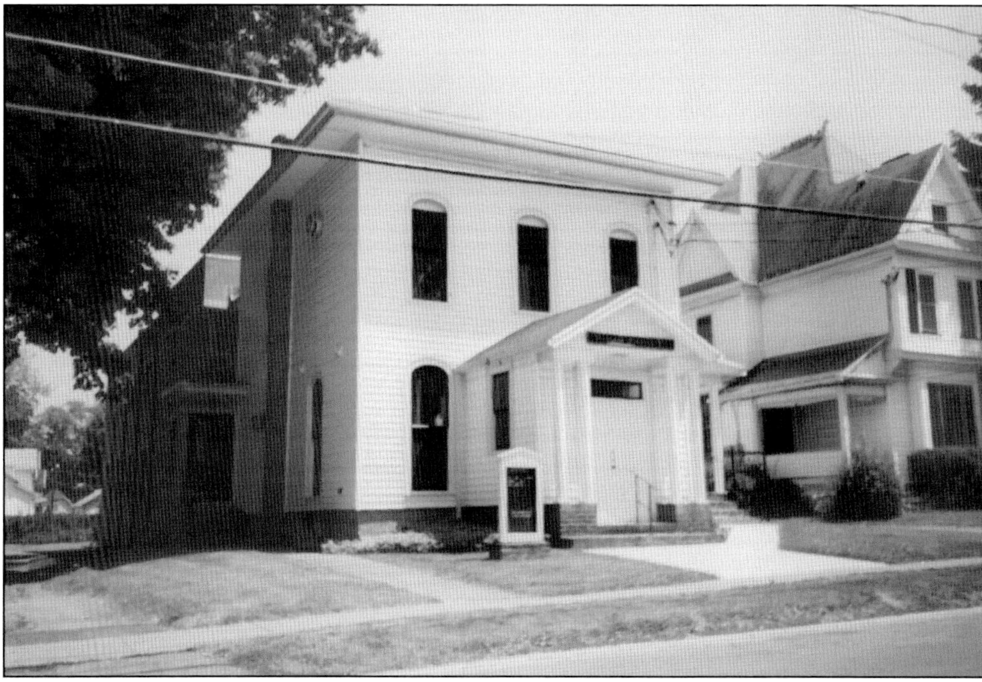

The growing Jewish community of Batavia purchased a home at 124 Bank Street and converted it into a temple on September 12, 1945. Temple Emanu-El was established and, following its merger with Shomrei Emunah Synagogue, jewelry store owner Herbert Brenner became its first president.

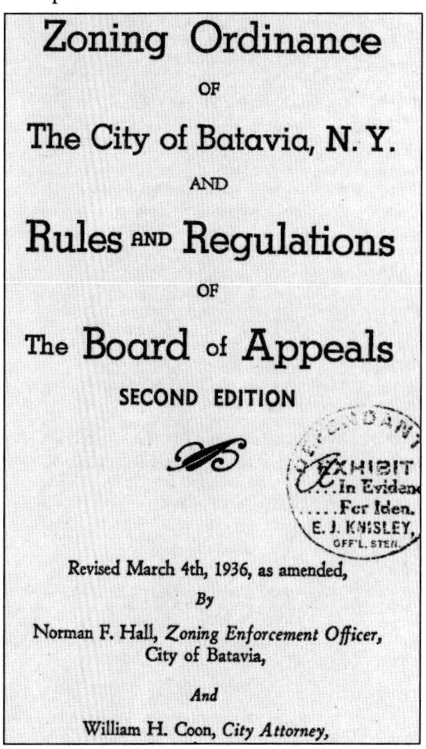

Zoning Ordinance

OF

The City of Batavia, N. Y.

AND

Rules AND Regulations

OF

The Board of Appeals

SECOND EDITION

EXHIBIT
In Eviden
For Iden.
E. J. KNISLEY,
OFF'L. STEN.

Revised March 4th, 1936, as amended,

By

Norman F. Hall, *Zoning Enforcement Officer,*
City of Batavia,

And

William H. Coon, *City Attorney,*

Batavia established its zoning ordinance *c.* 1925 to regulate future homes, industries, and businesses. This depicts the second edition of the ordinance, as revised on March 4, 1936.

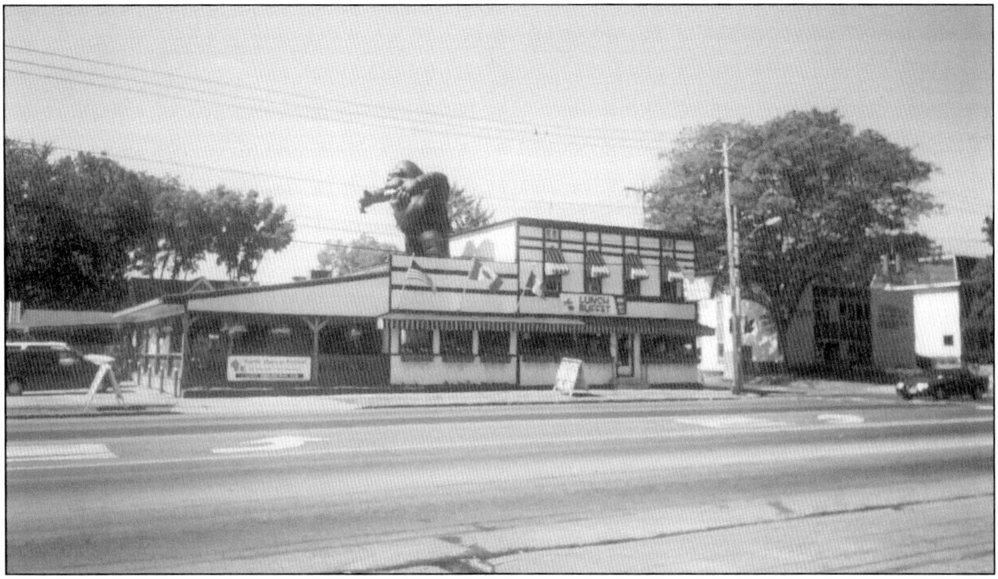

Pontillo's Pizzeria opened on Ellicott Street *c.* 1947, becoming Batavia's first pizza shop. The cost of a pizza pie was 85¢.

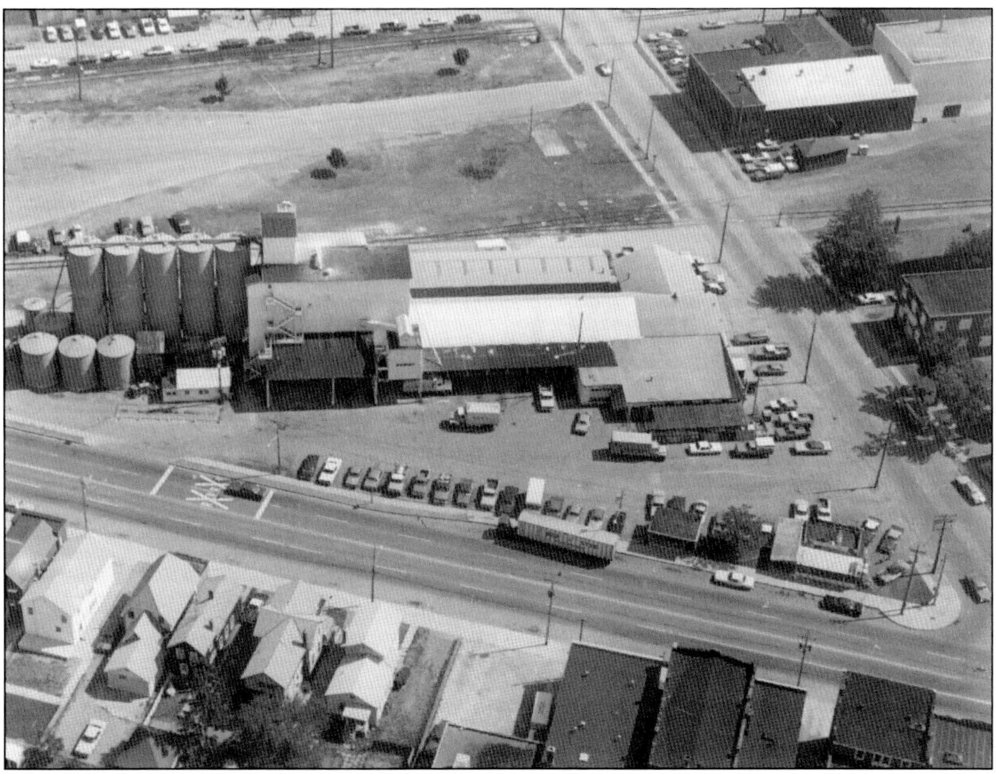

The GLF (Agway) plant, which supplied the agricultural needs of Genesee County, burned in a fire *c.* 1948. The two streets in this aerial view are Ellicott Street in the foreground and Liberty Street on the right.

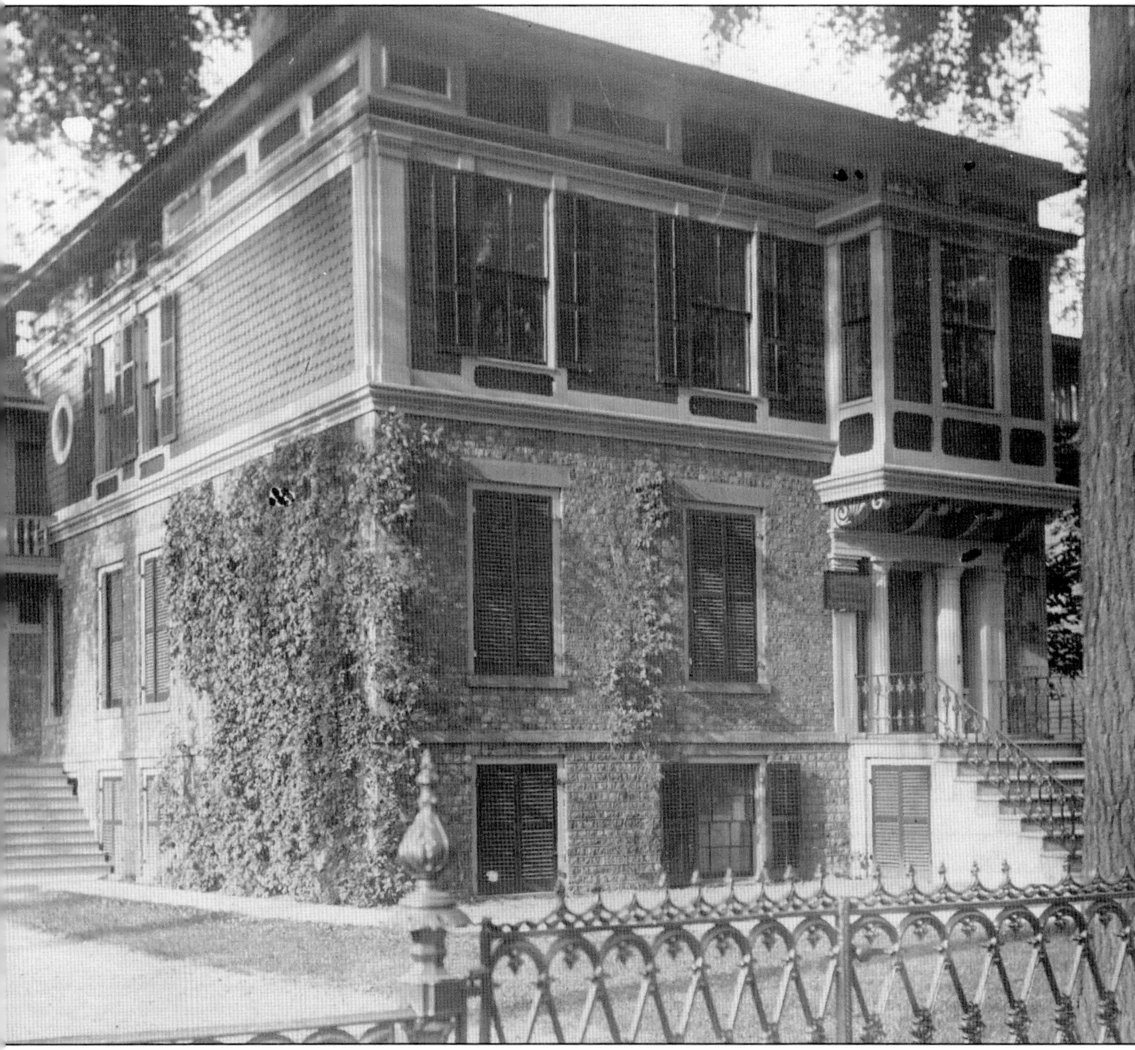

The Christian Science congregation built this church at 427 East Main Street after outgrowing the private home that was being used for services. The new church opened *c.* 1948.

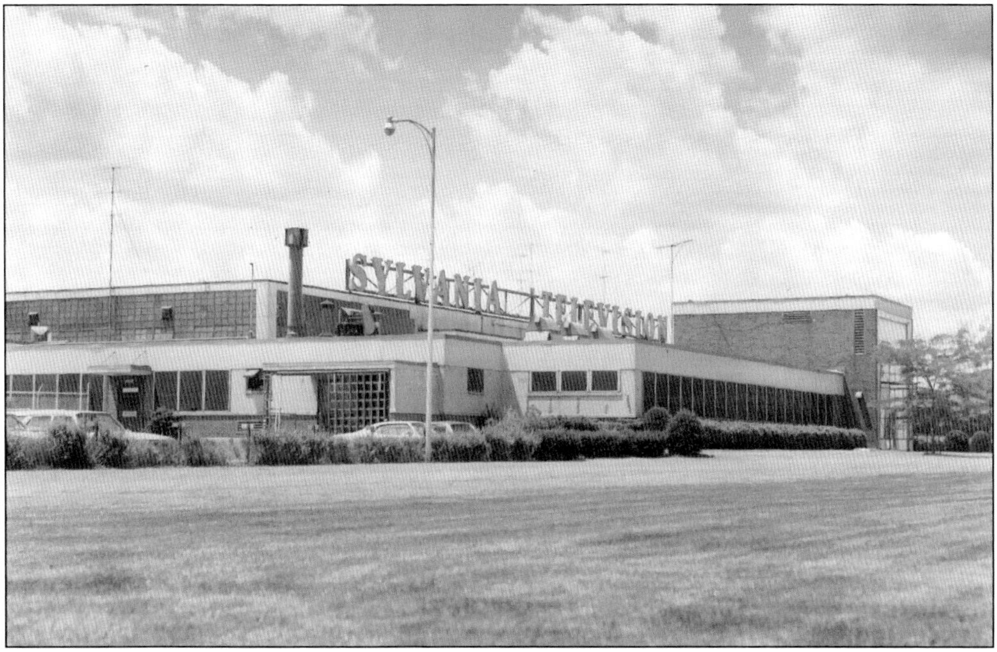

GTE Sylvania Products announced in 1953 that Batavia was the site chosen for a new television assembly plant, the world's largest such factory under one roof.

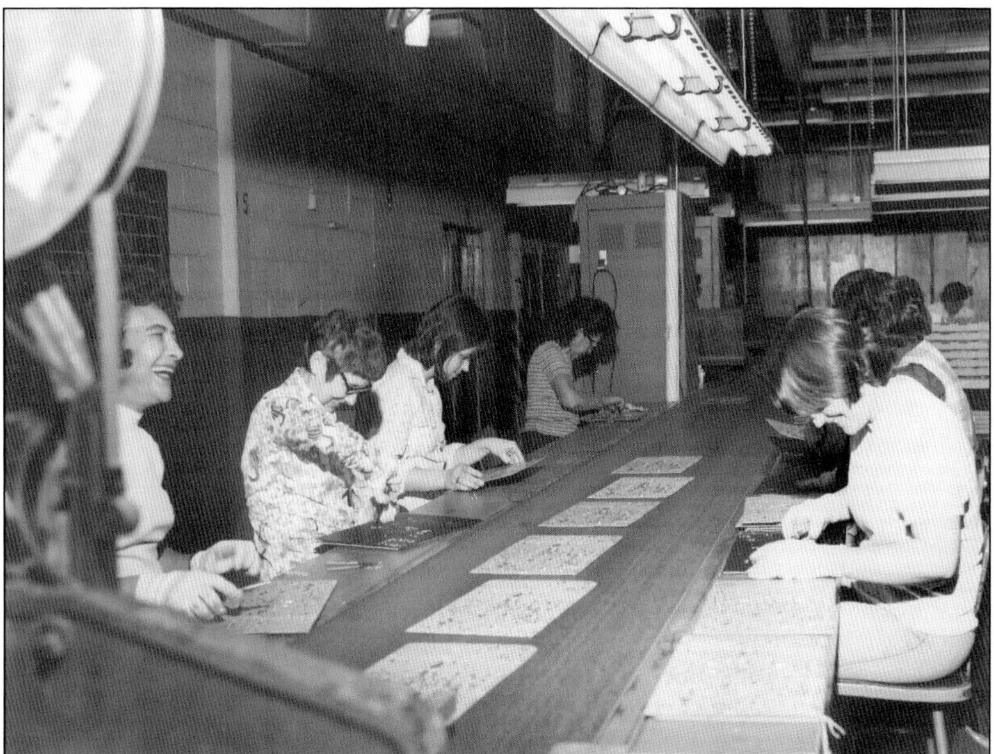
In 1954, GTE Sylvania opened its third assembly line but production was delayed by the shortage of women employees.

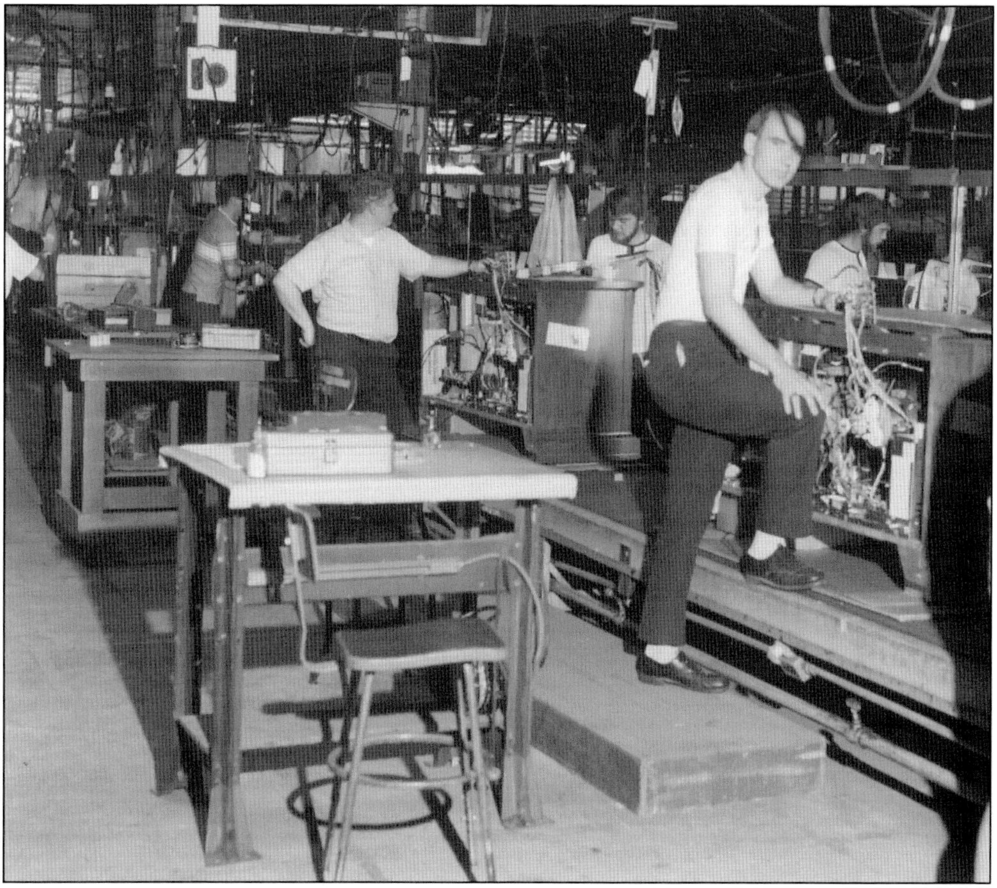

At one time, GTE Sylvania employed 2,000 people and output 750 color receivers and 900 monochrome receivers per day. The operation moved from Batavia to Smithfield, South Carolina, in 1981.

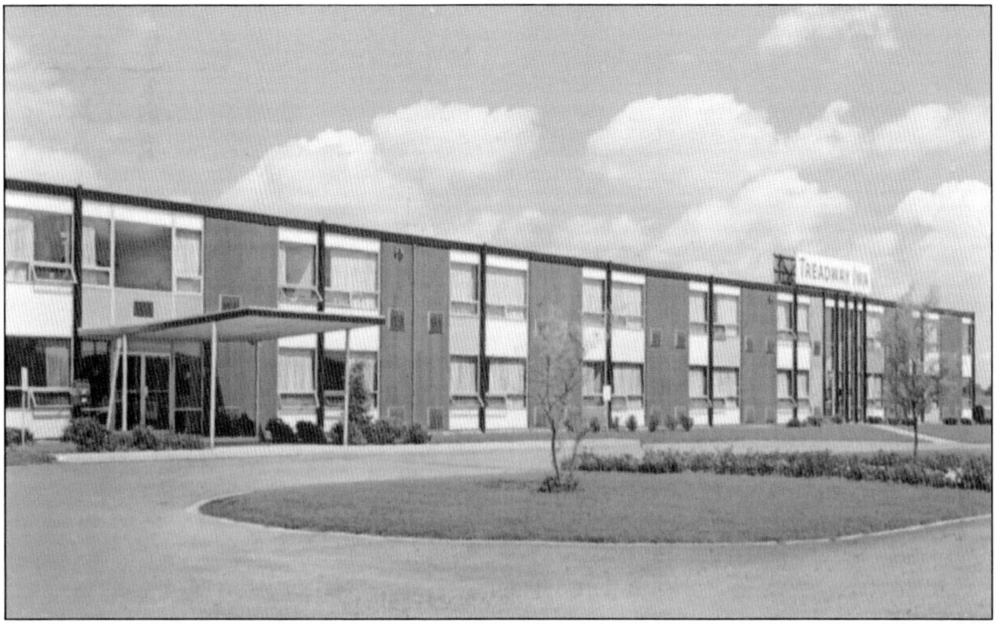

The New York State Thruway between Buffalo and Rochester, with the Batavia interchange, opened in August 1954. That same year, the Treadway Corporation came looking for a motel site near the interchange. In 1961, Treadway opened its Batavia motel, which had 152 bedroom units, a dining room, a bar, and several rooms for large gatherings. Later, it added a swimming pool. Today, Best Western owns and operates the motel.

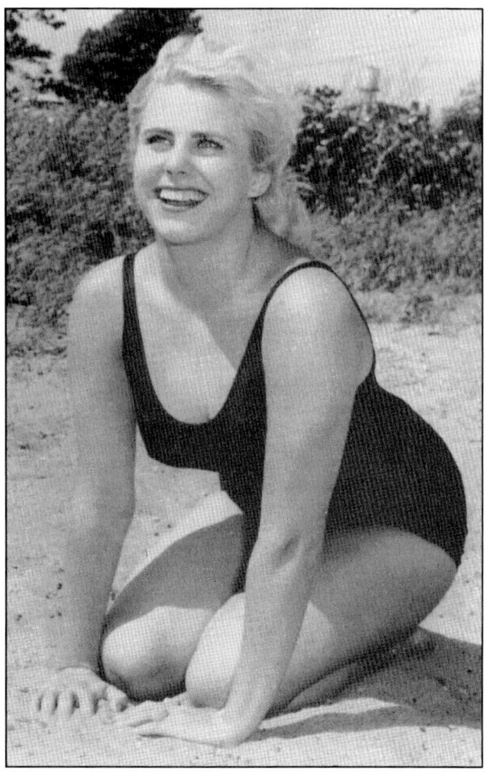

Greta Patterson, a native Batavian, swam 15 miles across Lake Erie in 1954, becoming the first person ever to do so.

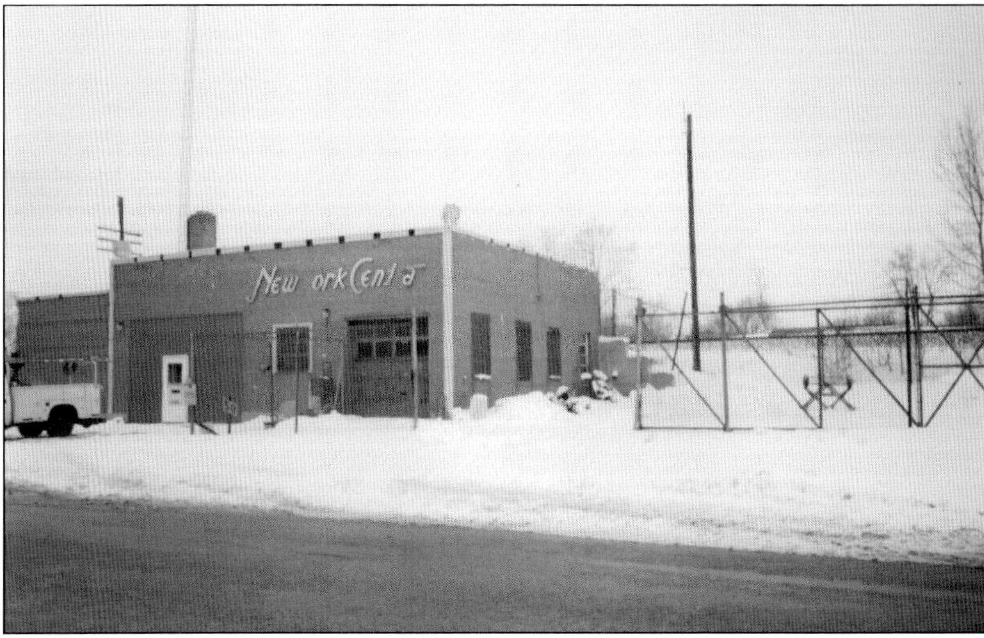

As early as 1951, fears of fatal accidents arose as the city grew and the central location of the railroad tracks increased difficulties for local traffic. In 1957, the tracks were moved southward and the New York Central Railroad Station was built on Lehigh Avenue.

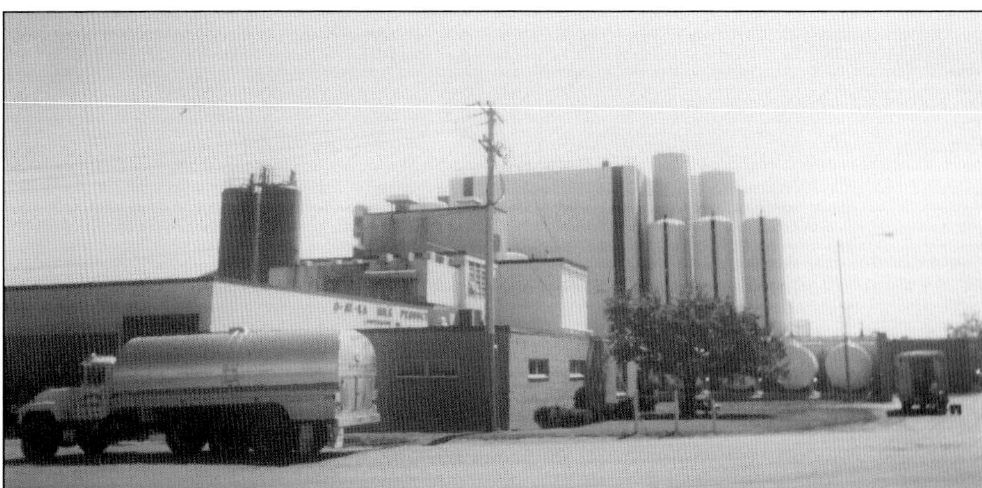

Oat-ka Milk Products Inc. opened on the corner of Ellicott and Cedar Streets and began production in 1959.

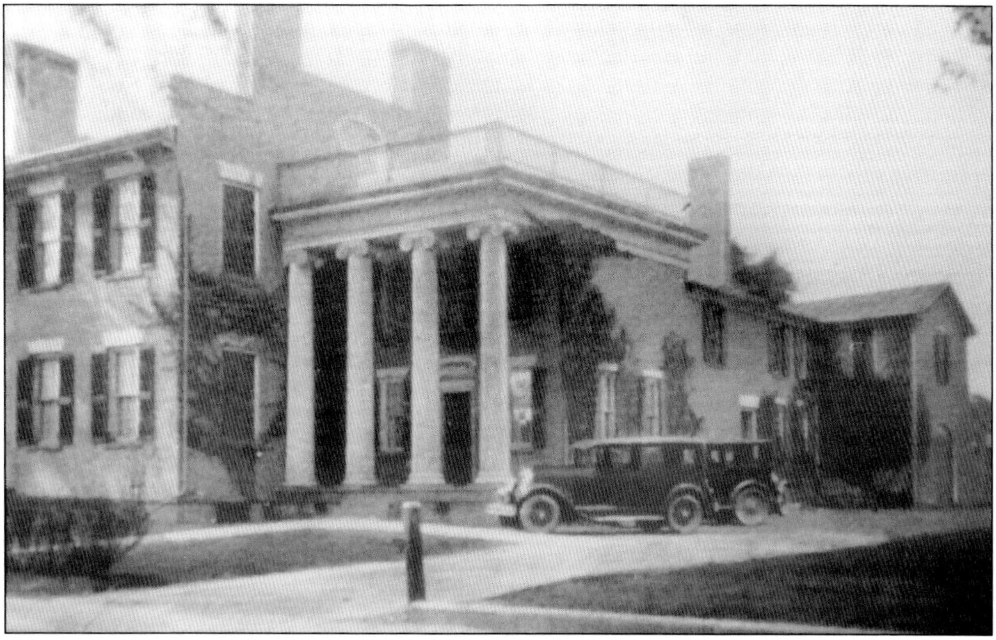

St. Jerome's Hospital purchased the Cary Mansion in 1959 and subsequently renovated it for the Catherine McAuley School of Practical Nursing.

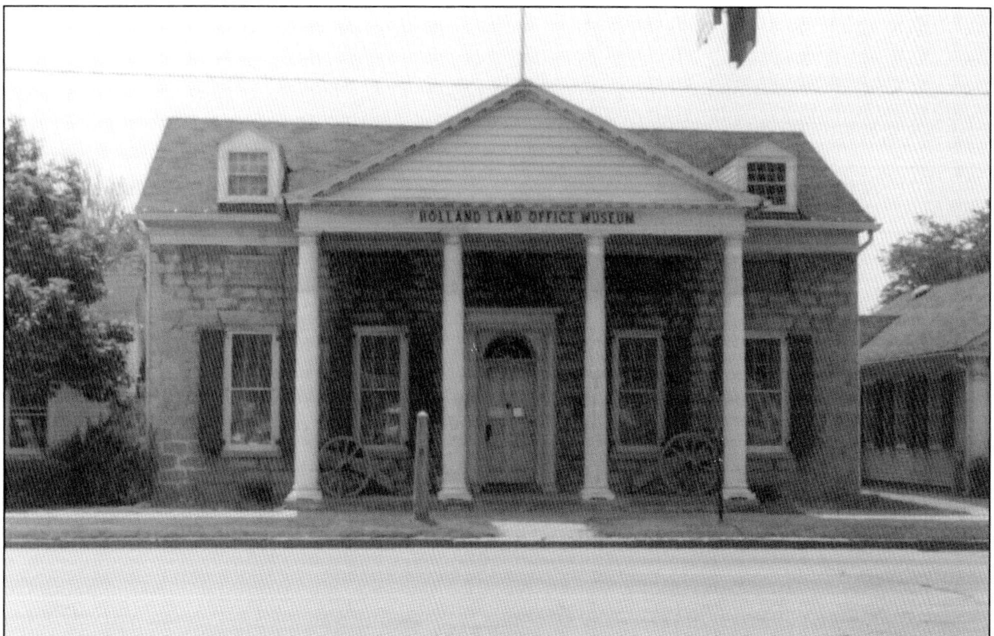

The Holland Land Office Museum was dedicated as a registered historical landmark in 1961.

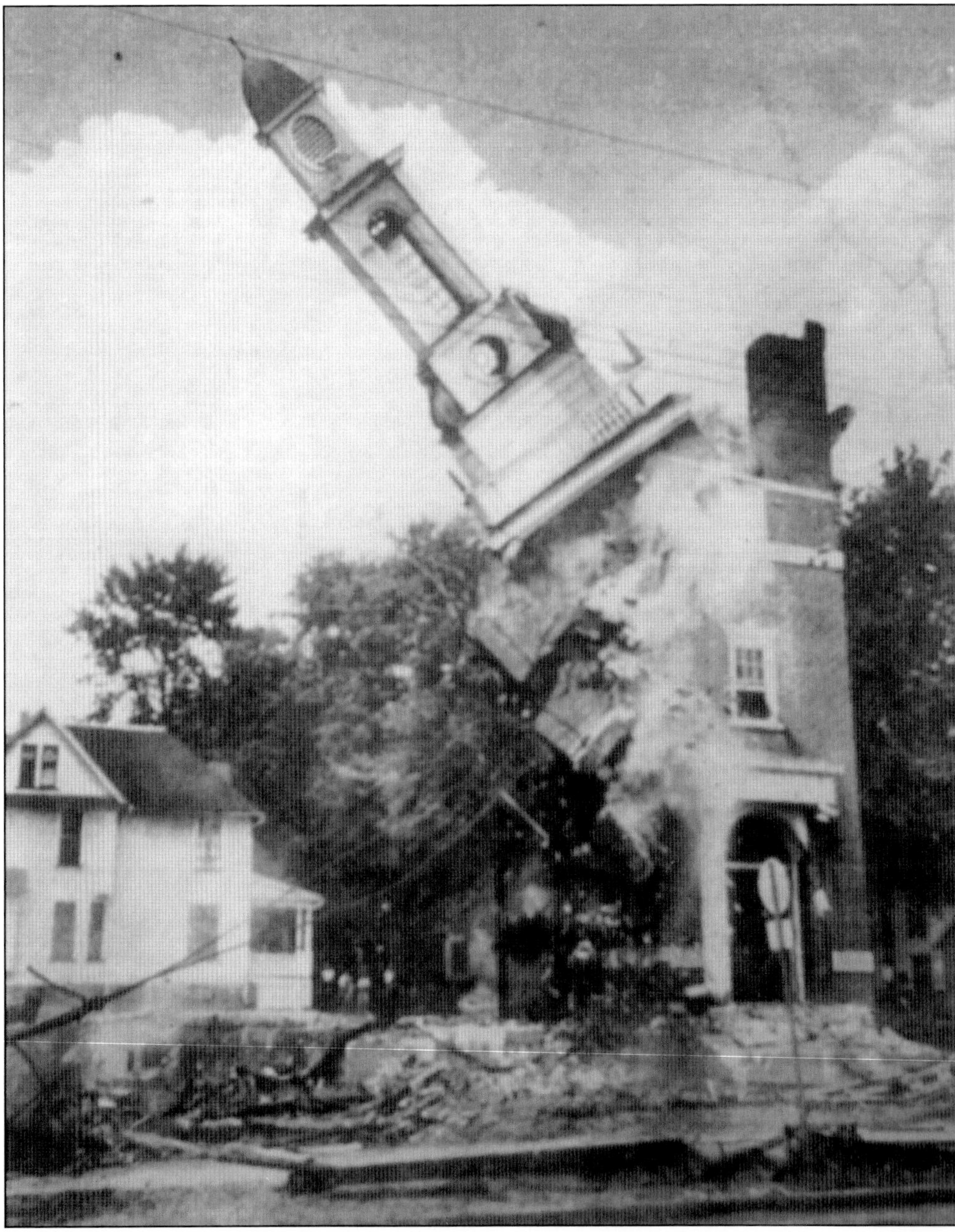

The Emmanuel Baptist Church, which stood at the corner of Main Street and Thomas Avenue, was destroyed by fire in 1961. This photograph shows the church steeple on its way down. The church was subsequently rebuilt on Oak Street.

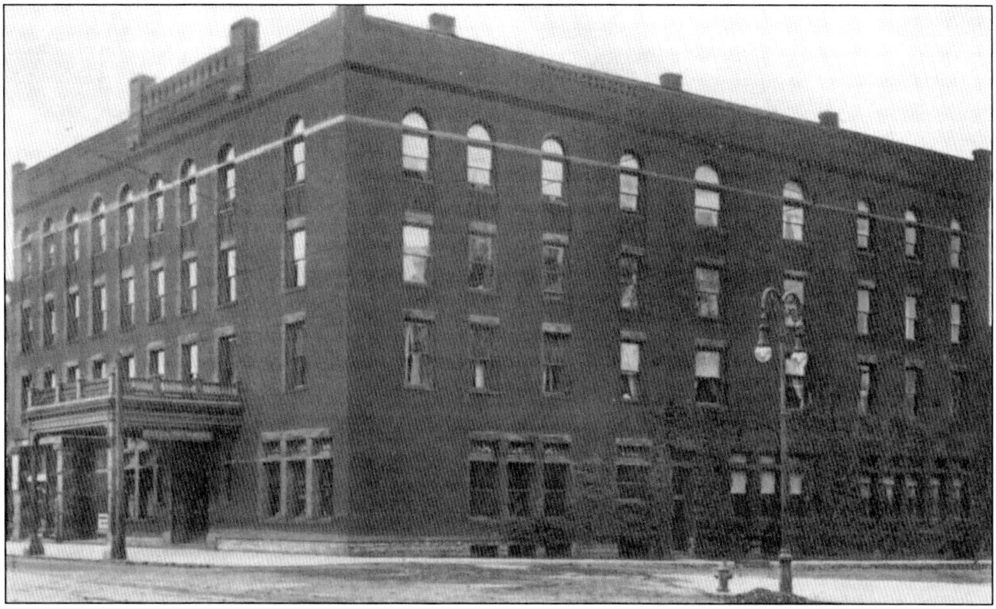

The Hotel Richmond was demolished in 1961 to make way for an office building at the corner of Main and Court Streets. The new building contains offices and a bank.

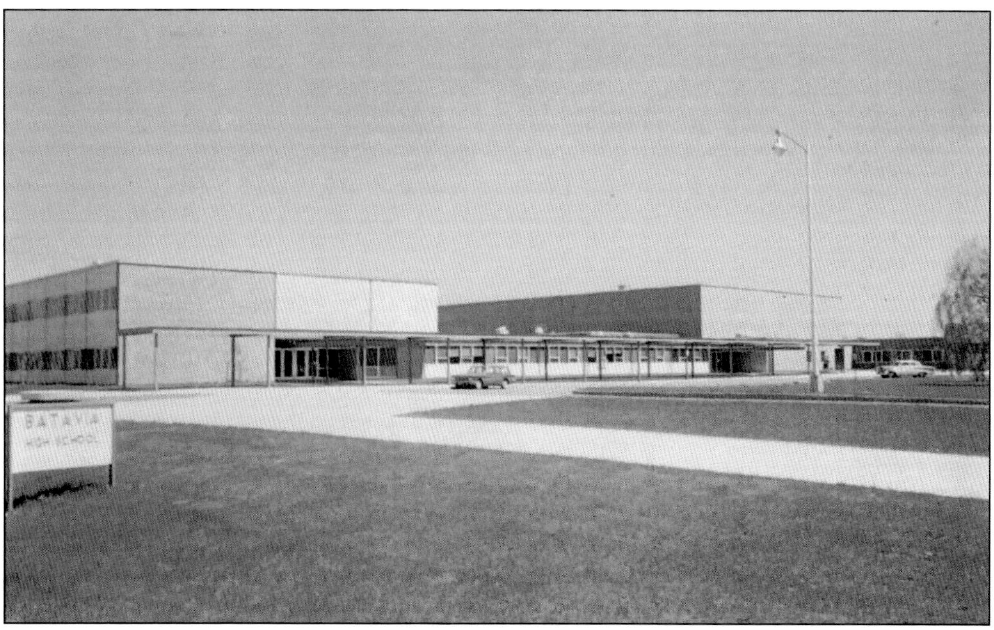

Batavia High School opened in 1961 on State Street. The school was built to handle an increase in student enrollment.

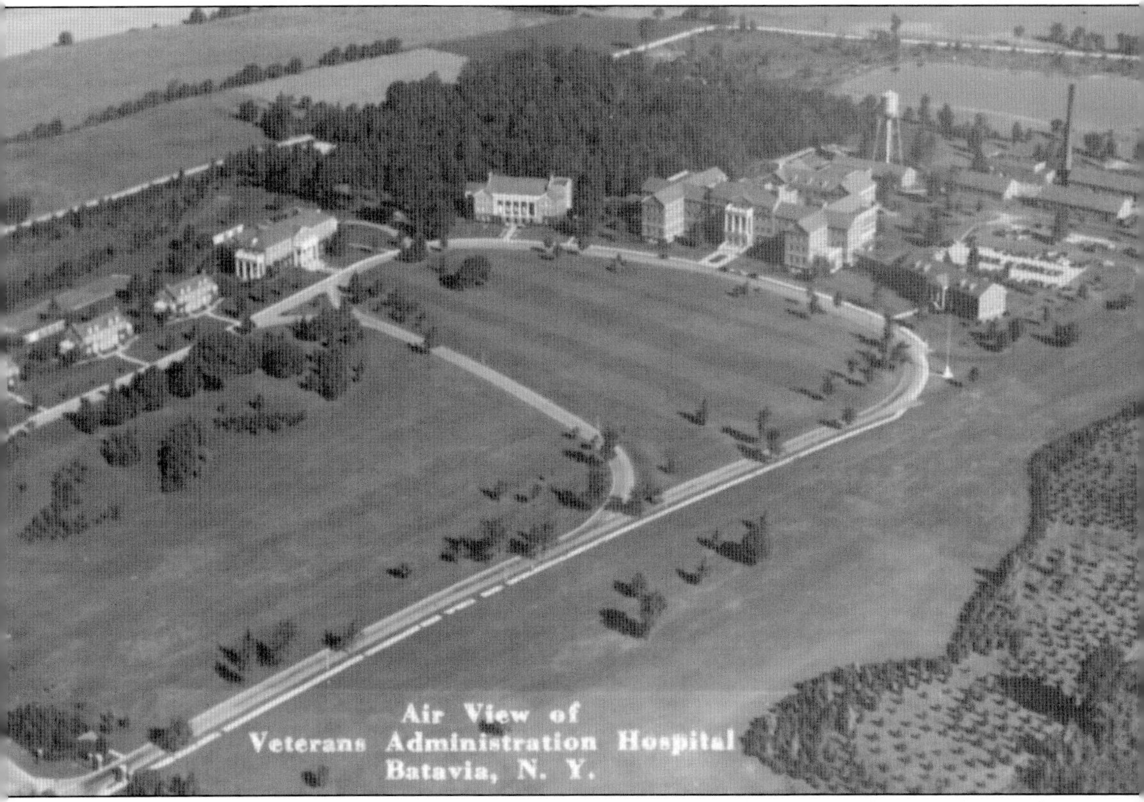

The Veterans Administration facility is located on Richmond Avenue. This aerial view shows the entire complex.

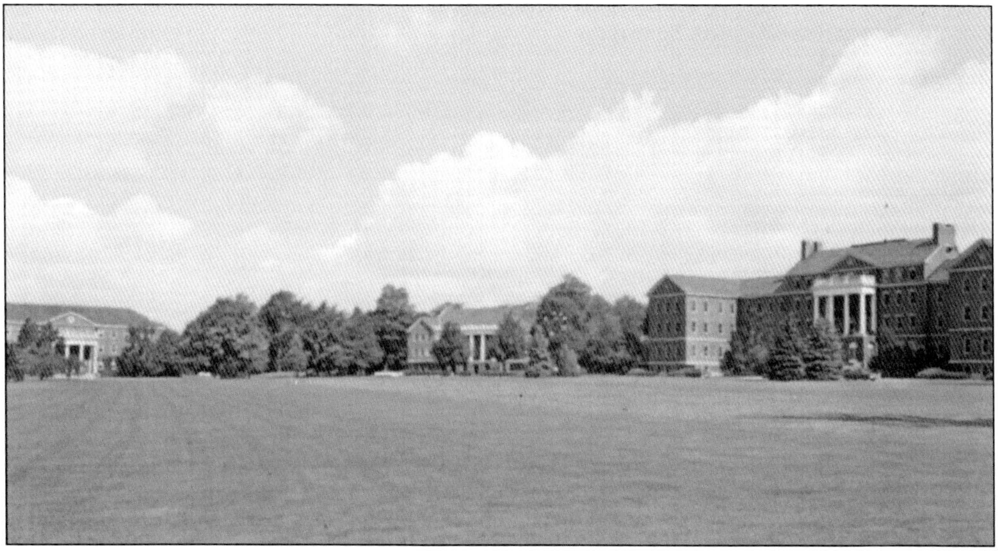

This view shows the hospital and the living quarters of the Veterans Administration facility on Richmond Avenue in Batavia.

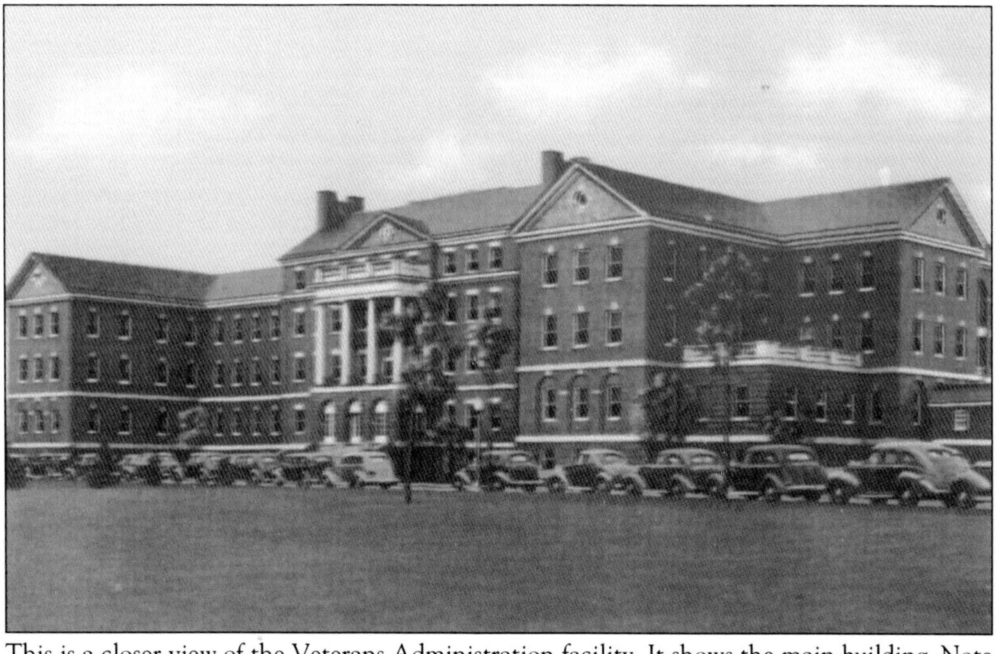

This is a closer view of the Veterans Administration facility. It shows the main building. Note the number of automobiles parked out front.

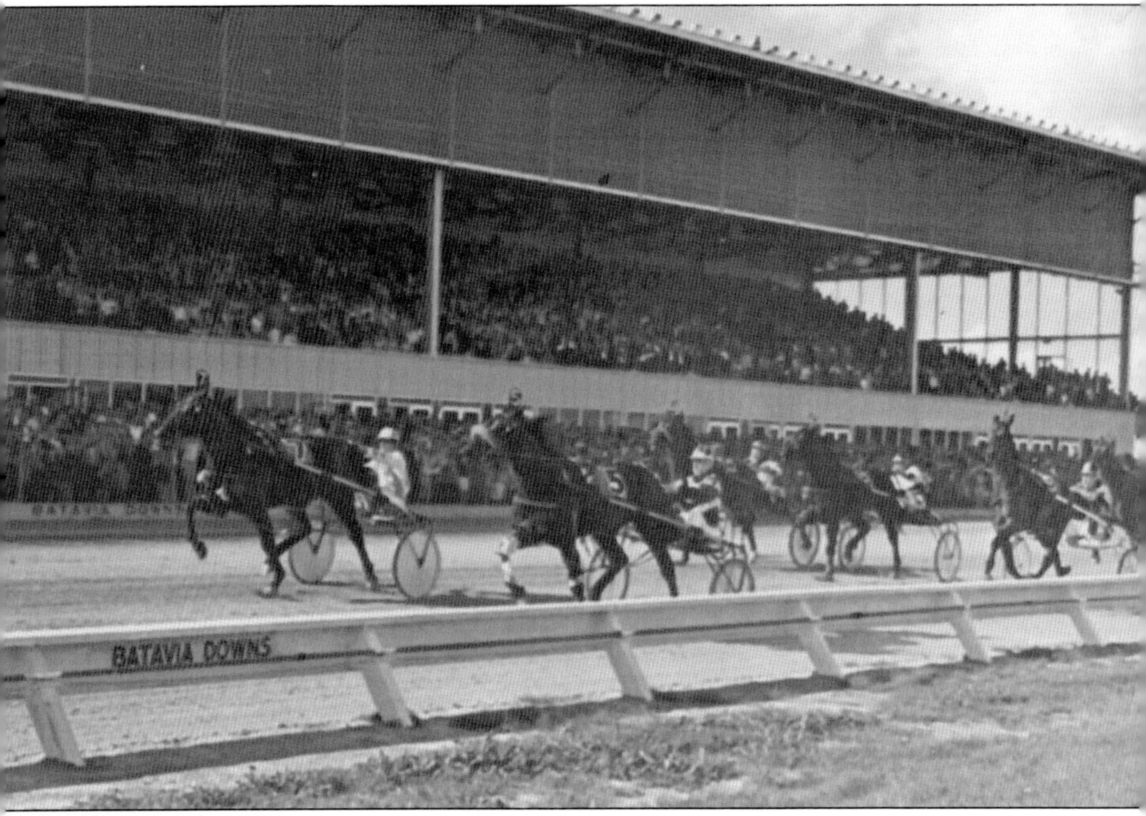

At Batavia Downs, the crowds are yelling and the horses are straining. The race is on.

Five

URBAN RENEWAL

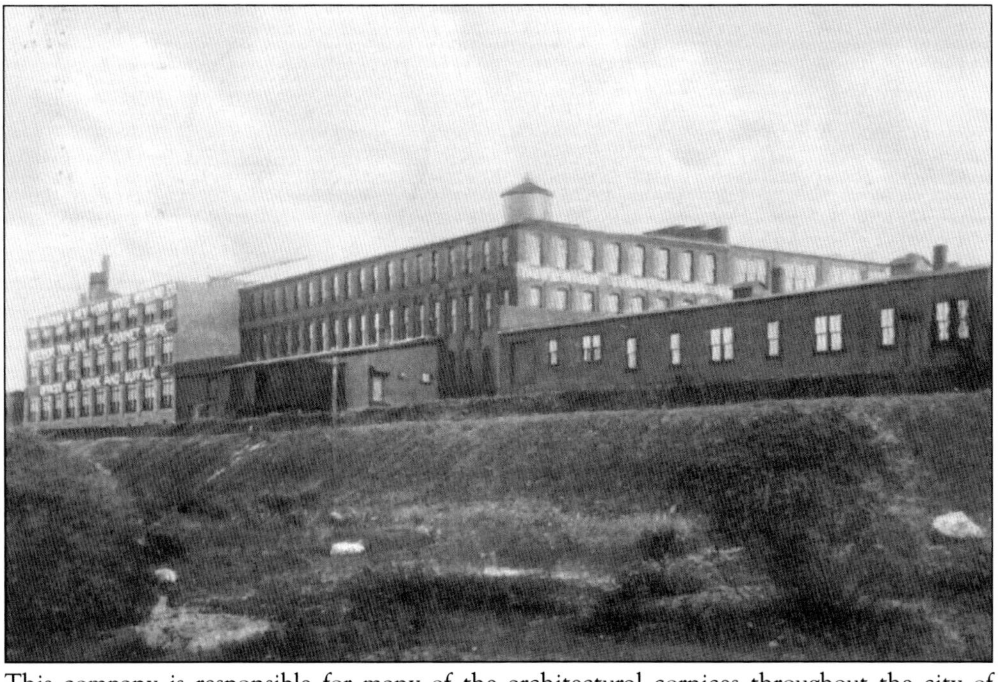

This company is responsible for many of the architectural cornices throughout the city of Batavia and for many of the finer interior woodworking designs as well. It is the Batavia and New York Wood Working Company.

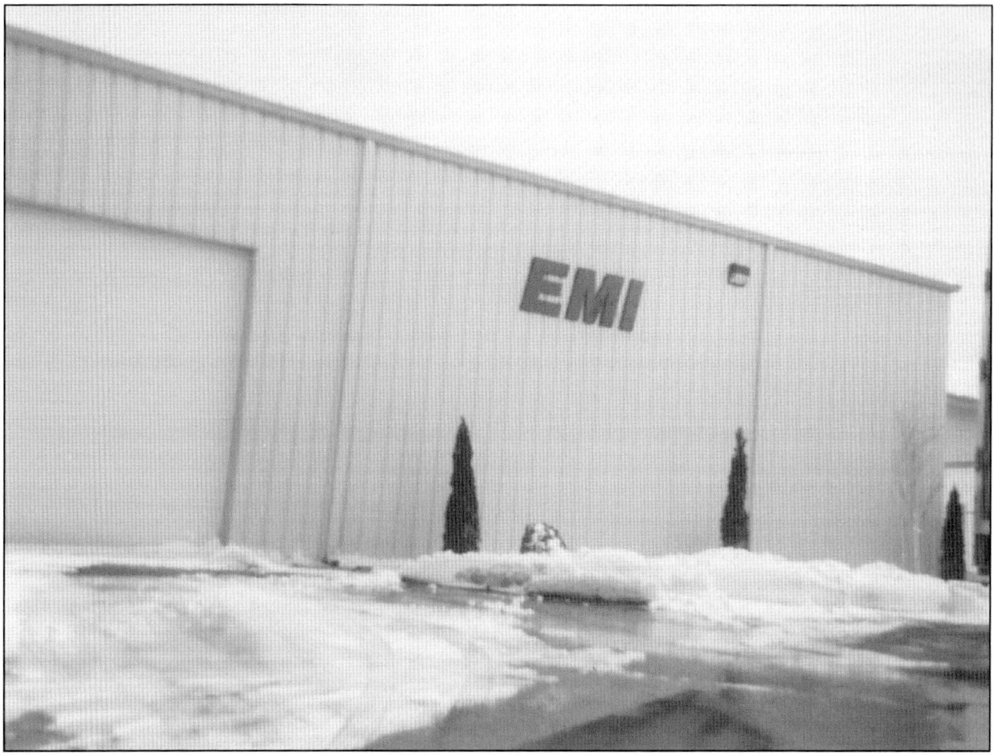

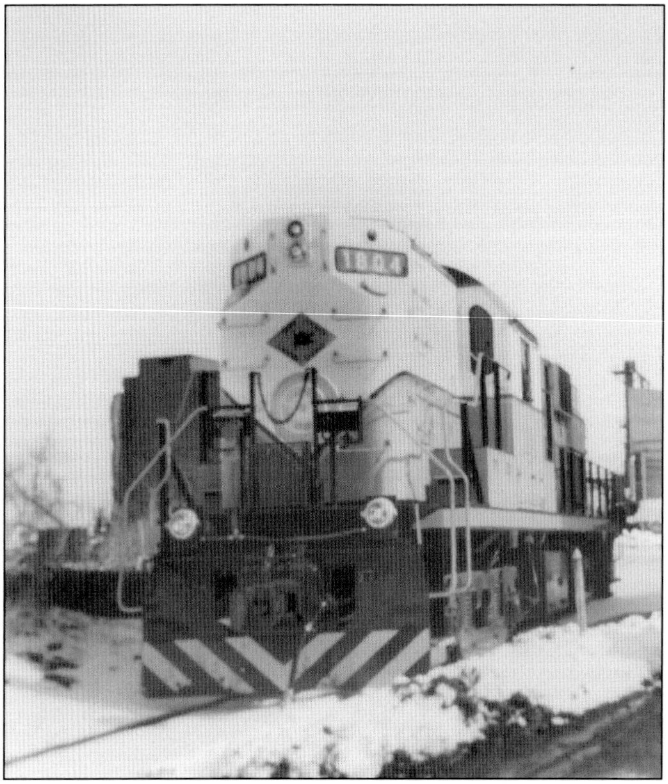

Fire destroyed the Wall and Grain Company plant in 1963, the former Batavia Wood Working Company. Later, Eastern Molding Industries (EMI) opened its headquarters on the site. That building burned in 1999, was rebuilt, and is in back operation today. Tracks run alongside the building, providing the company with direct access to the railroad, left.

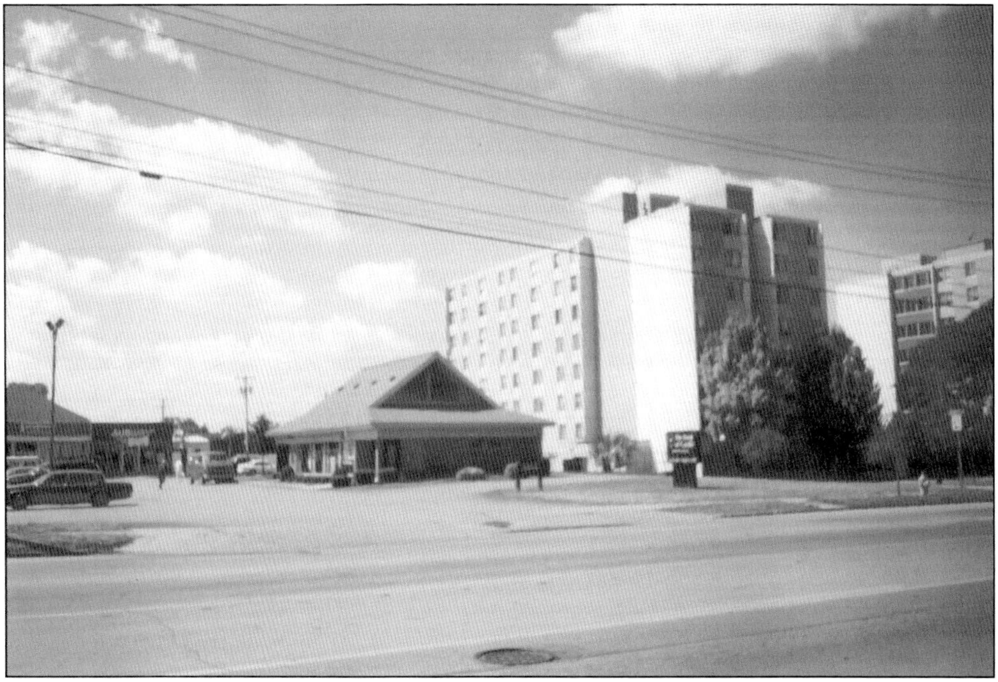

Four Hundred Towers, an eight-story two-tower apartment building for the elderly, was constructed in 1967 at 400 East Main Street. Owned and operated by the Batavia Housing Authority, the building was dedicated in 1971. It contains efficiency units, and one- and two-bedroom apartments. Its two towers are connected by a central lobby and a recreation area. The grounds includes lawns, walkways, and a parking area.

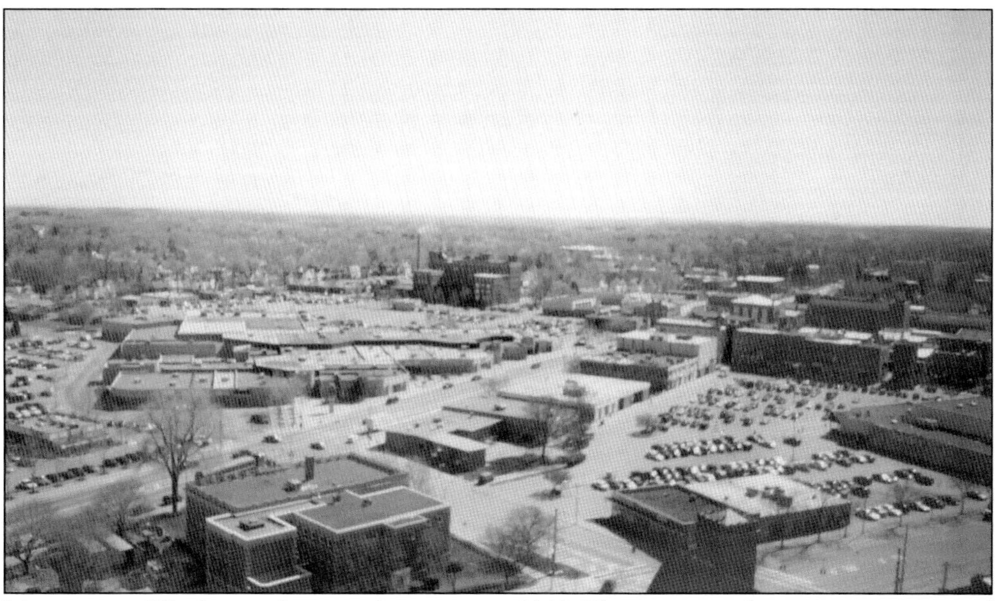

Montgomery Ward opened a store downtown in 1968. This was viewed as a major step toward rebuilding the downtown shopping area.

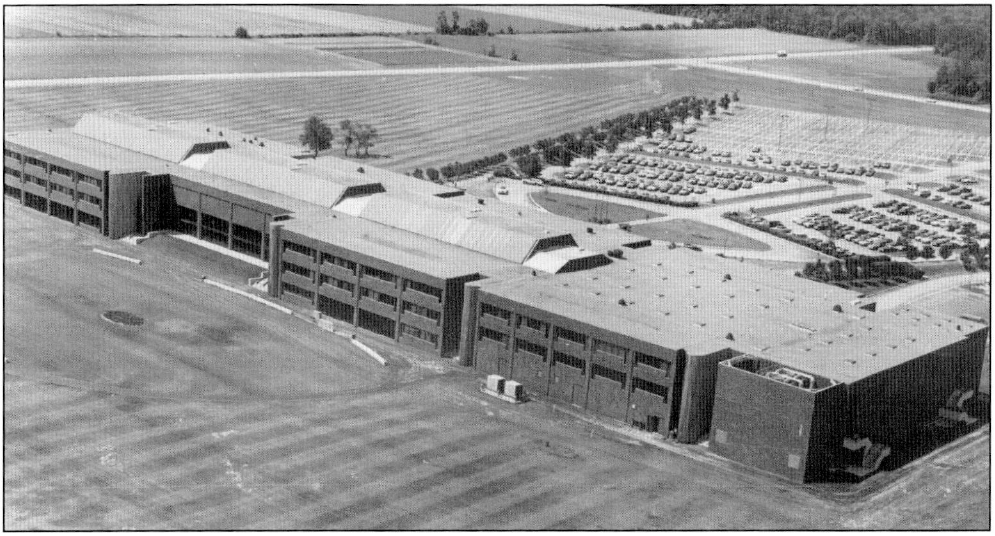

Genesee Community College received voter approval in 1965 and opened at its new campus on College Road in 1971.

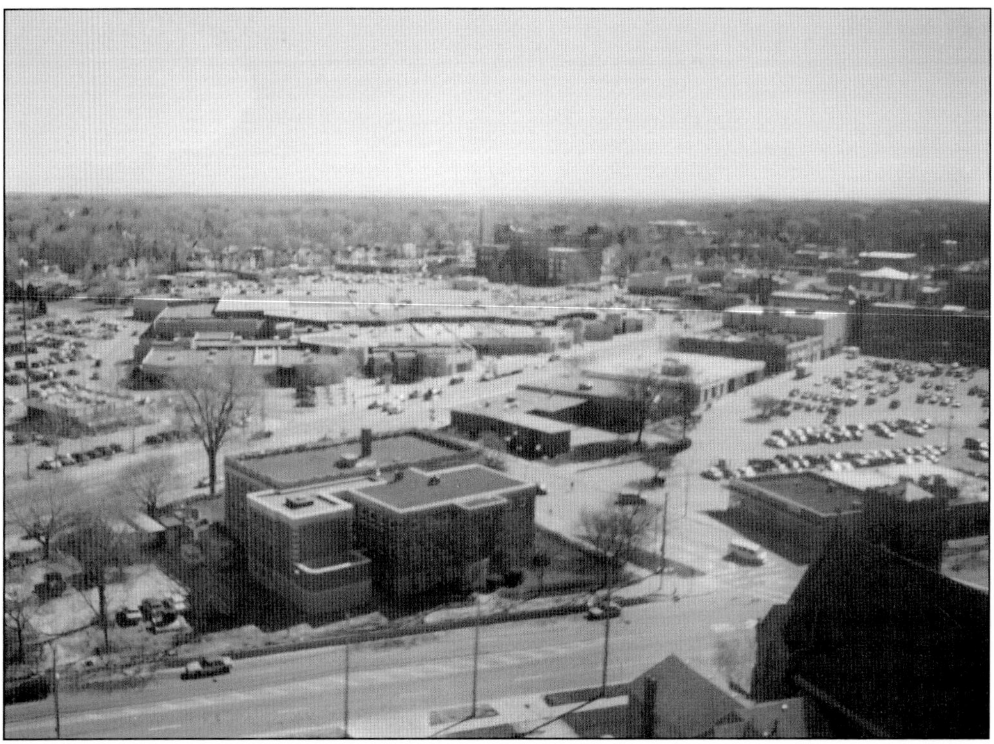

A groundbreaking ceremony was held in 1972 for the Genesee Country Mall.

Batavia's second woman police officer, Jane Wistner, became a full-time member of the force in 1975, after completing police training. She served until her retirement on December 30, 1992.

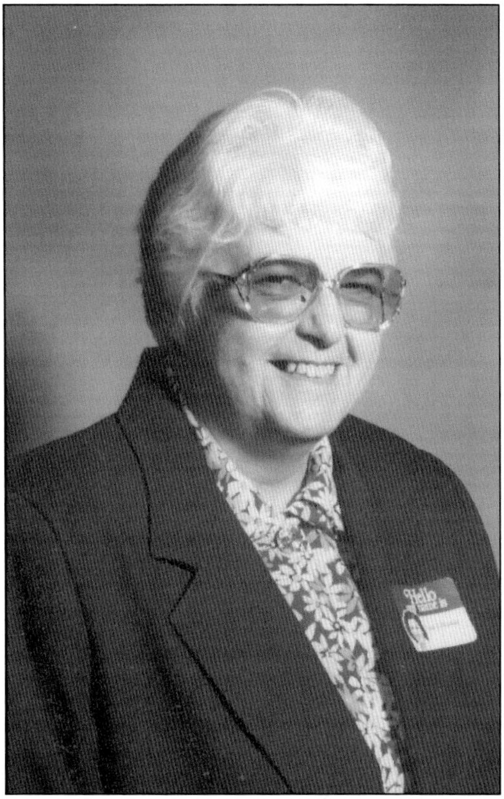

Doehler-Jarvis Division of National Lead Industries moved its aluminum work elsewhere in 1977. As a result, scores of the company's local employees lost their jobs.

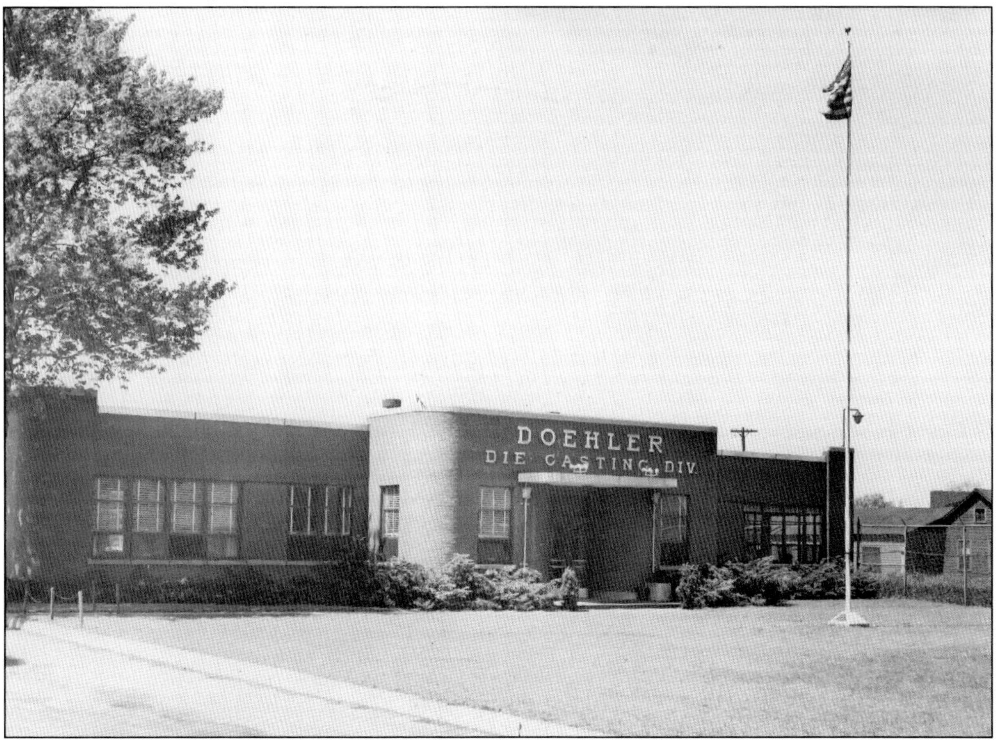

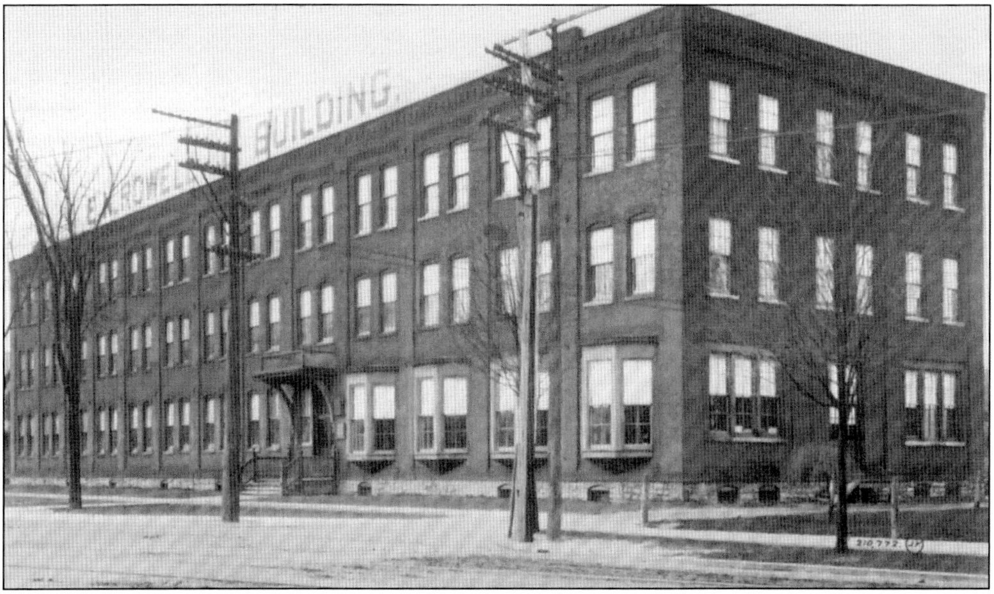

The E.N. Rowell Box Factory, once a thriving manufacturing plant, was razed in 1978.

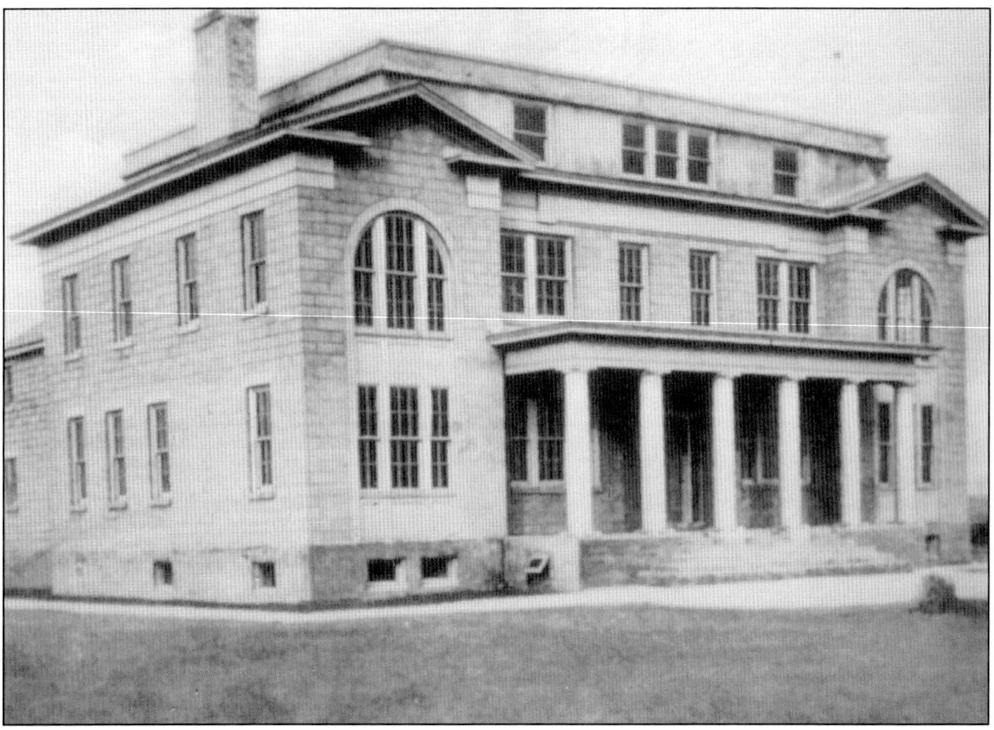

The New York State Troopers Barracks on East Main Street was razed in 1978. Richard Donk's used car dealership occupies the site today.

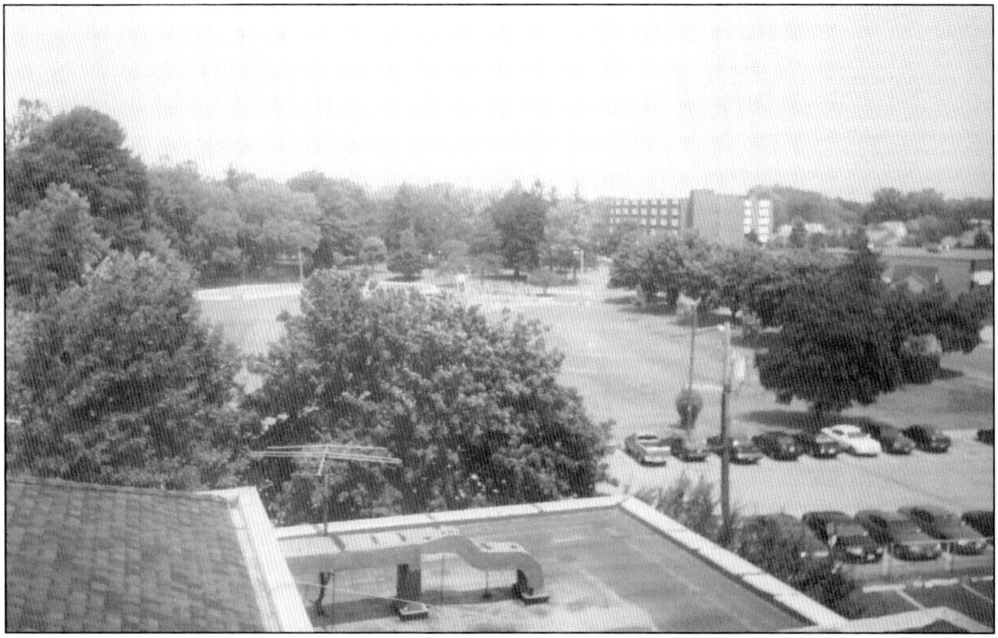

V.J. Gaulteri acquired a plot of land at 200 State Street on which to construct a high rise for elderly residents in 1980. In November of that year, work began on this 131 one-bedroom and two-bedroom-unit complex. That December, a lighted Christmas tree, a Gaulteri trademark, shone from the roof. The building, Washington Towers, was dedicated in March 1982.

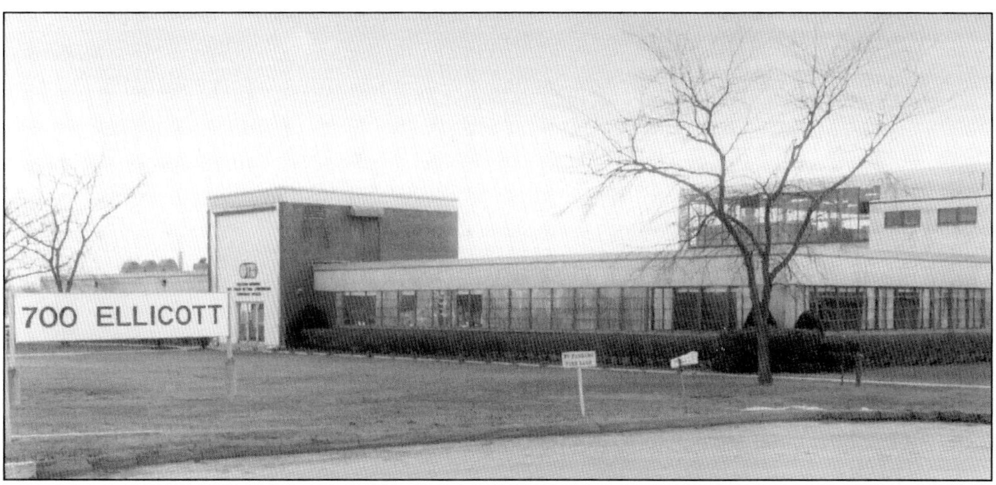

The R.E. Chapin Manufacturing Works Inc. moved from its Liberty Street complex to the former Sylvania plant at 700 Ellicott Street in 1981. The Liberty Street property was purchased by Jerry Reinhart, who developed it as the Batavia Industrial Center.

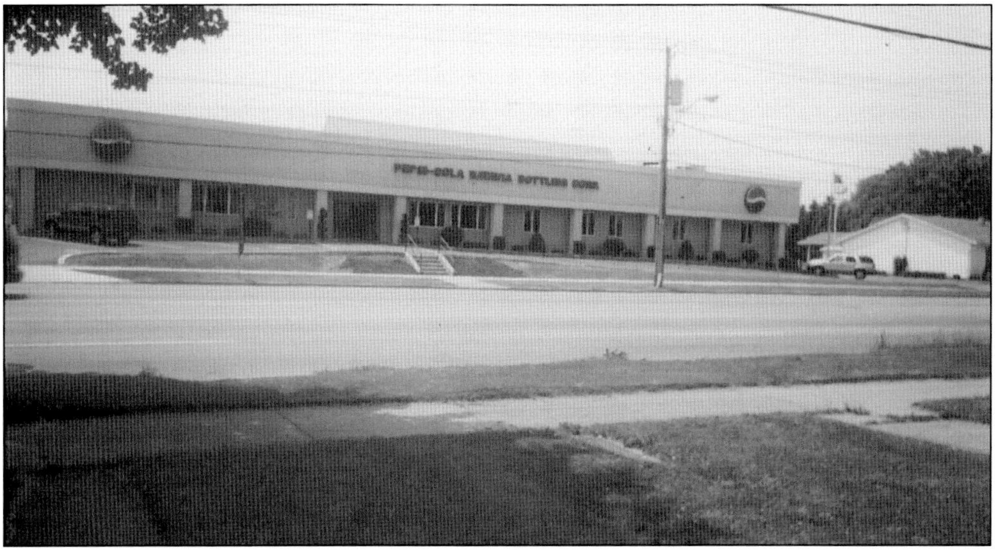

Pepsi-Cola celebrated its 100th anniversary in 1990 and gave its Batavia bottling plant a face-lift. Over the years, the plant has expanded and added a company called Loose Ends Vending, which supplies vending machine merchandise.

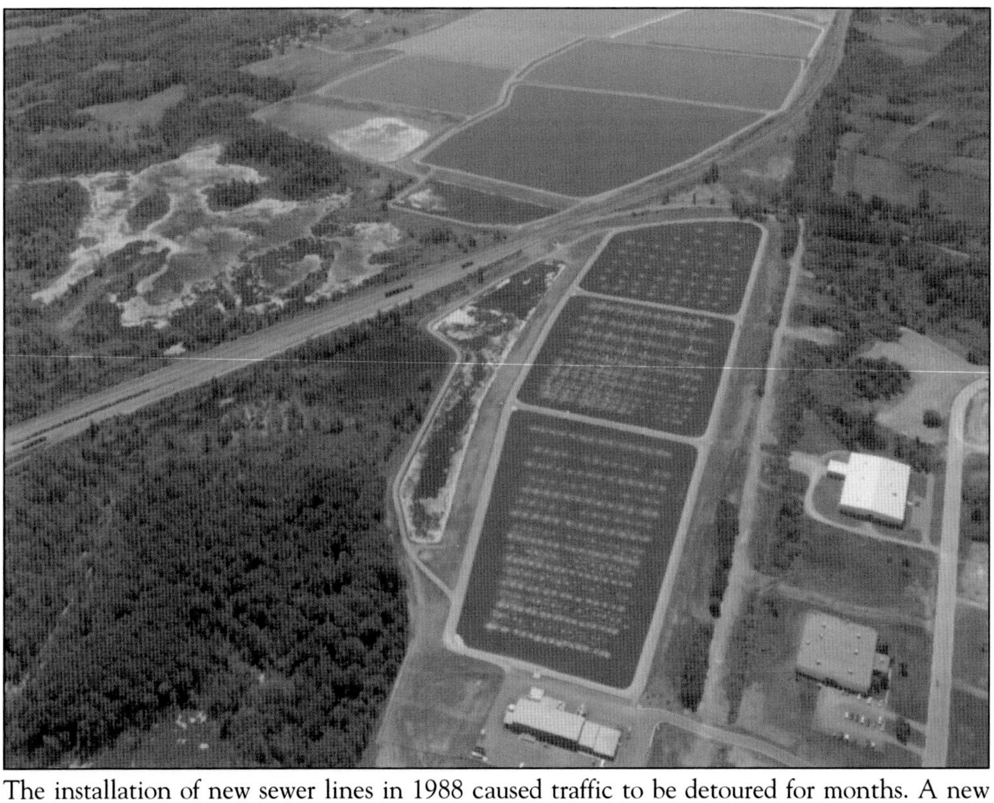

The installation of new sewer lines in 1988 caused traffic to be detoured for months. A new sewage treatment plant that was designed to last for decades was under construction.

Six

Agriculture and Fresh Ideas

Agriculture has long been the number one industry in Genesee County. This view shows one of the many abundant wheat fields in the area. Cornfields can also be seen throughout the county.

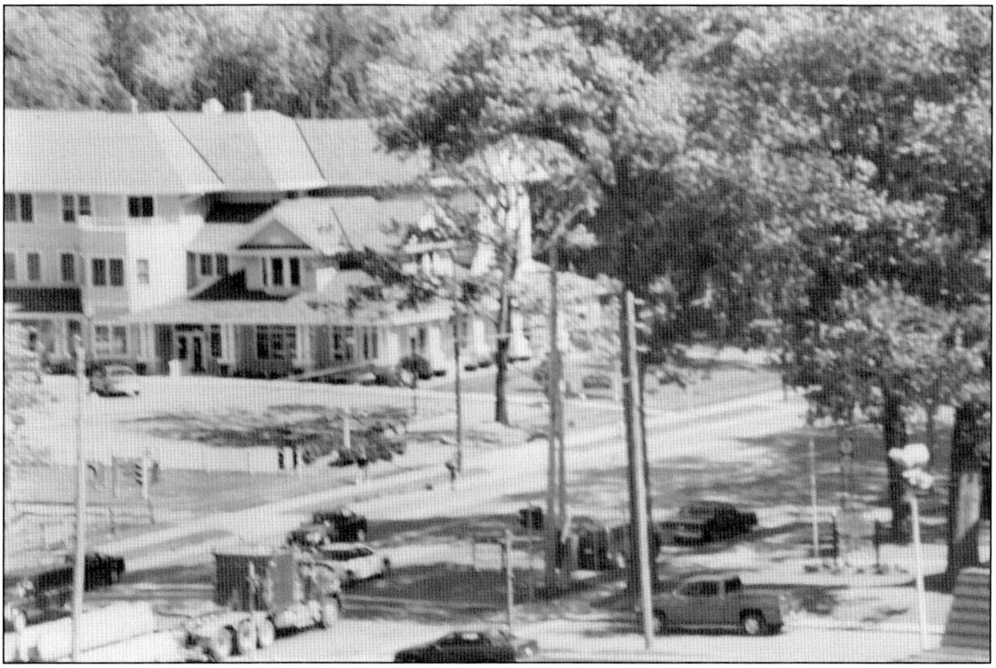

The Christian Science church (second building) was razed in 1993 to make way for the senior housing project that originally was called Trocaire Place. Recently purchased by Jerry Reinhart, the complex is now named the Victorian Manor and includes the Chardonnay Restaurant.

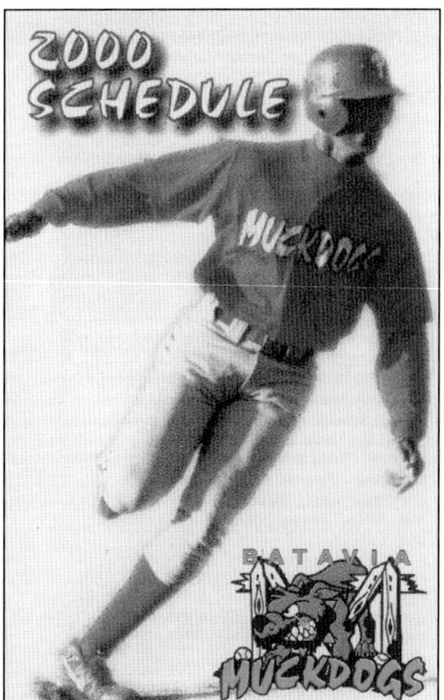

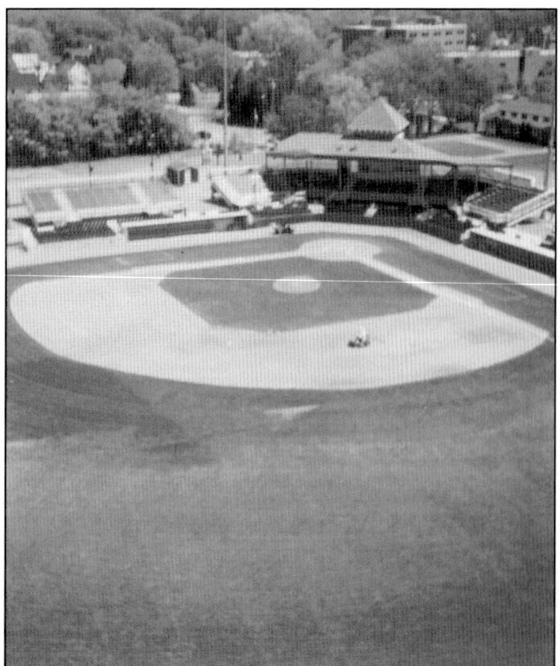

The new Dwyer Stadium, right, opened in 1996 on Bank Street as the home of the Batavia Clippers. The following year, the team was renamed the Batavia Muckdogs.

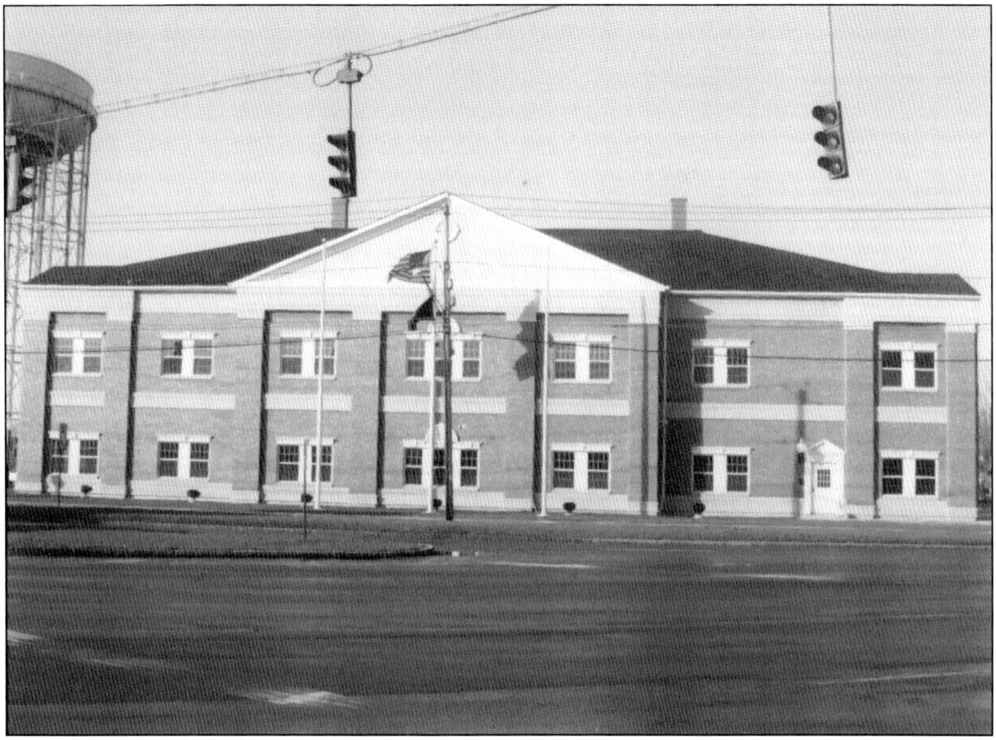

The new Genesee County courts facility was built in 1999 at the bend of the Tonawanda Creek. With the construction of this building, all courts were merged in one location.

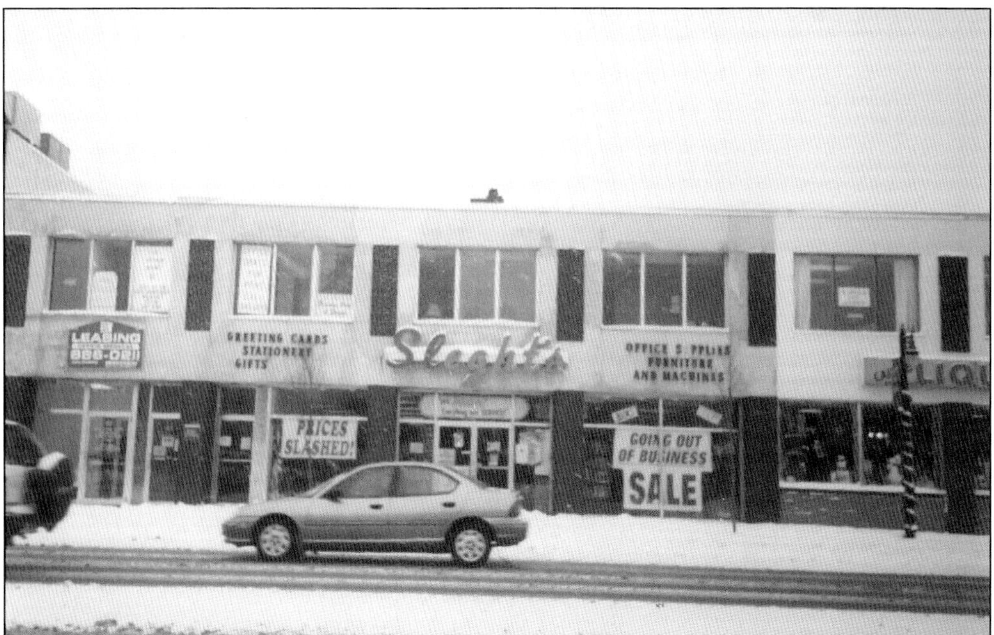

This photograph shows the oldest family-owned bookstore in downtown Batavia. Sleght's bookstore, owned and operated by Vincent March, announced in 1999 that it would be closing after 130 years in business.

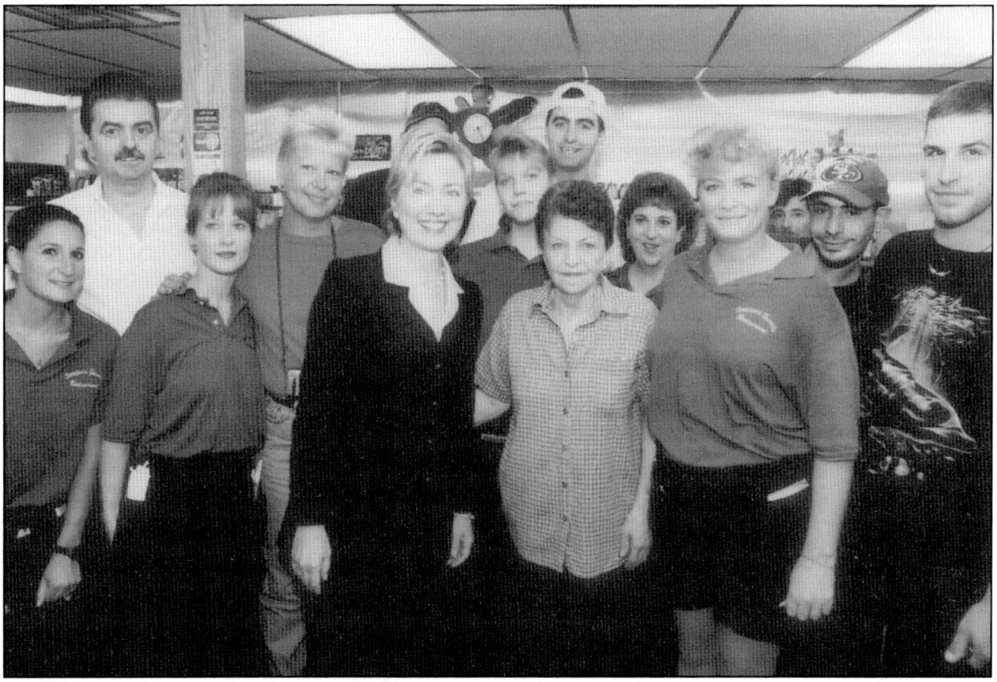

Hillary Rodham Clinton stopped in Batavia in 1999, during her campaign for the U.S. Senate seat from New York. This campaign stop was at Settler's Restaurant on Main Street.

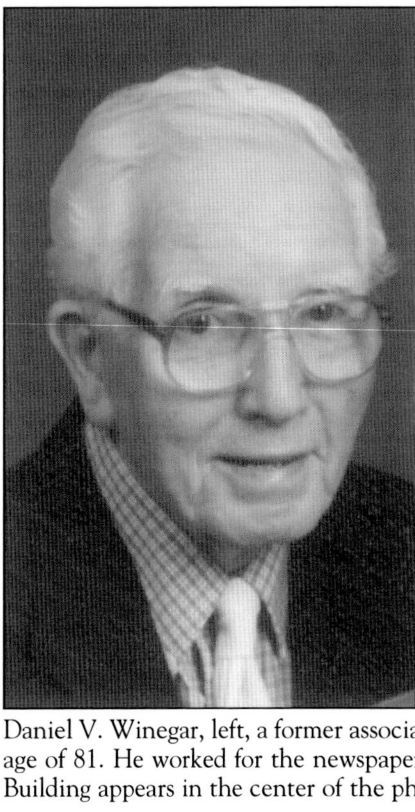

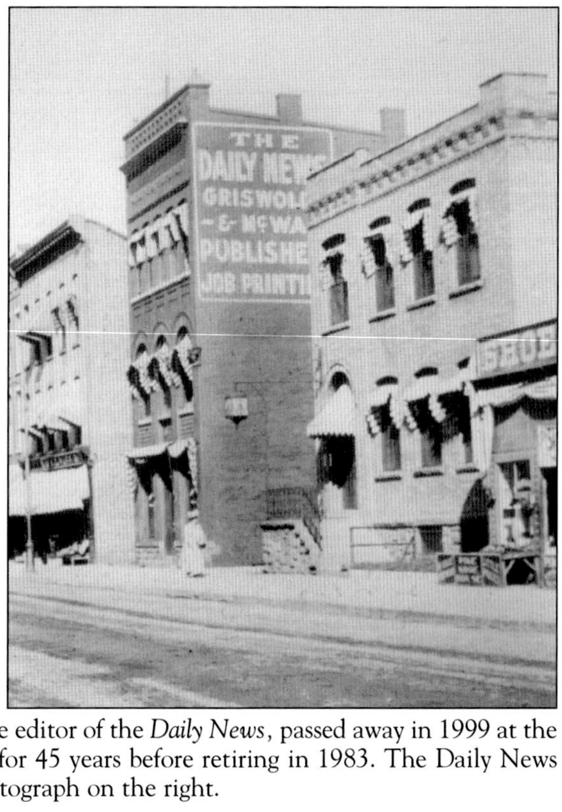

Daniel V. Winegar, left, a former associate editor of the *Daily News*, passed away in 1999 at the age of 81. He worked for the newspaper for 45 years before retiring in 1983. The Daily News Building appears in the center of the photograph on the right.

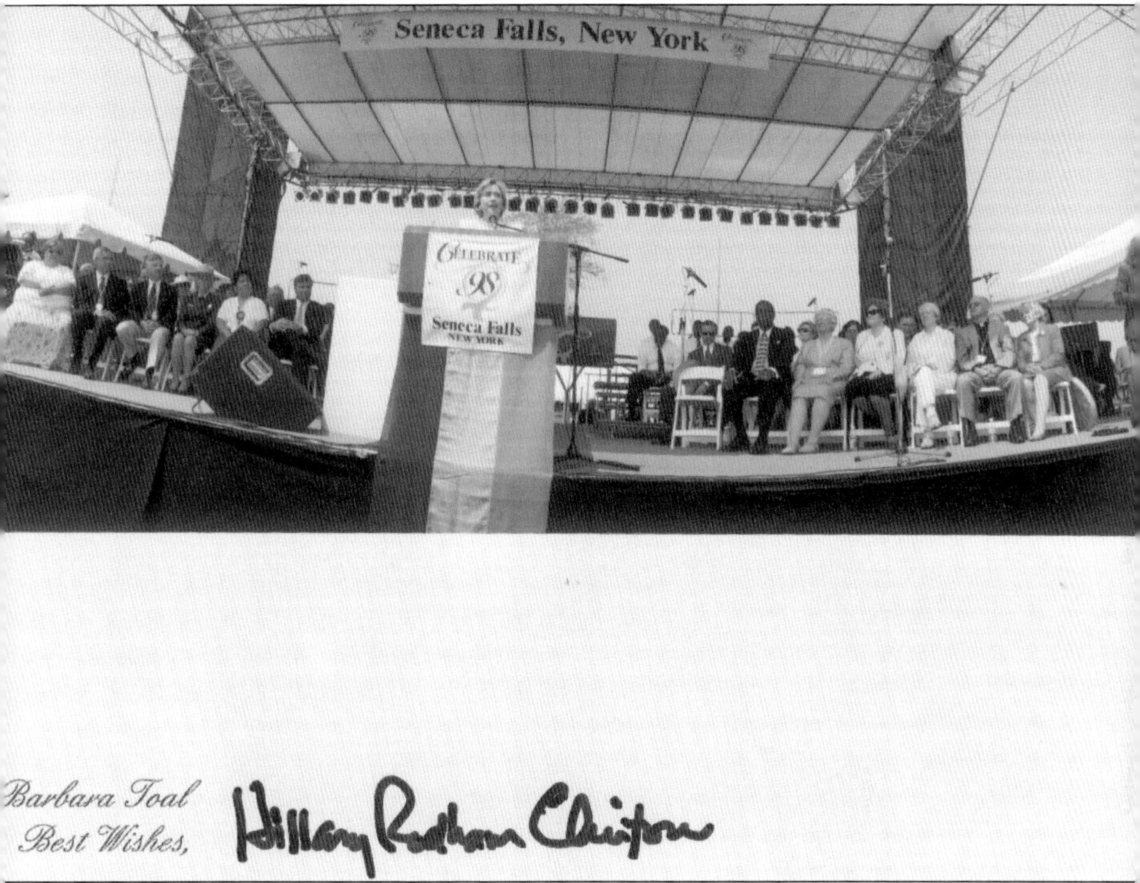

Hillary Rodham Clinton, center, spoke at Celebrate '98, the women's rights convention held in Seneca Falls 1998. This signed photograph offered best wishes to author Barbara Toal.

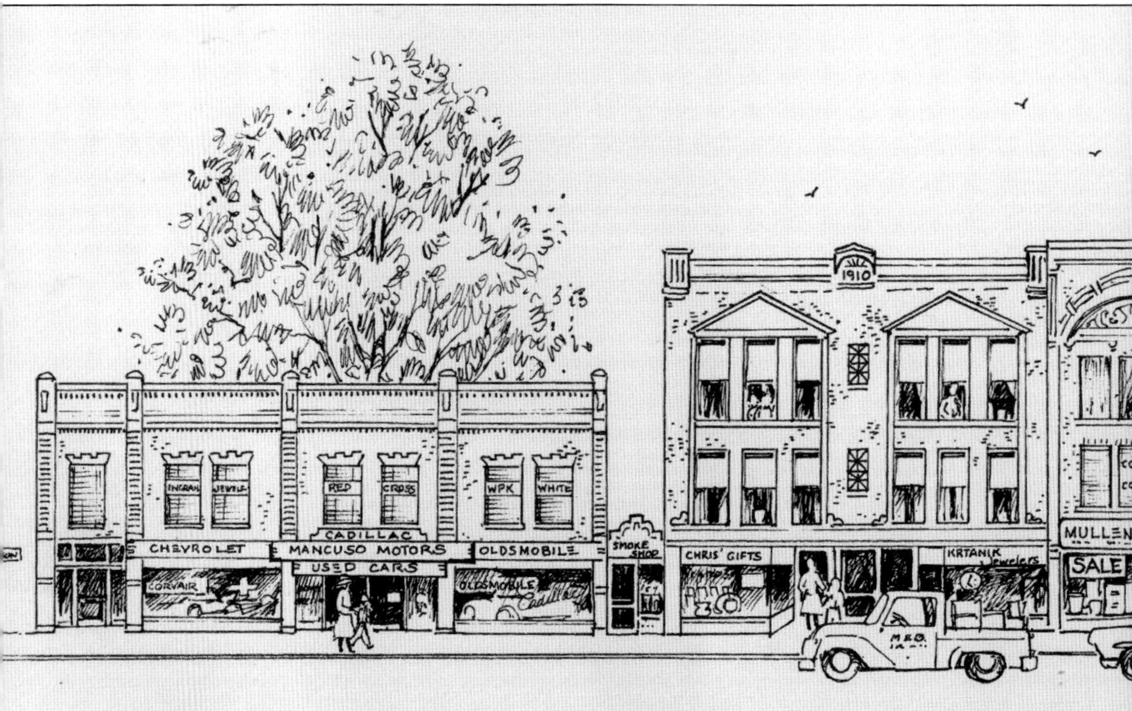

Local artist Patricia Burr depicts the downtown area as it appeared in the 1950s and 1960s. Above is the northwest section of Main Street. Below is the southwest central block between

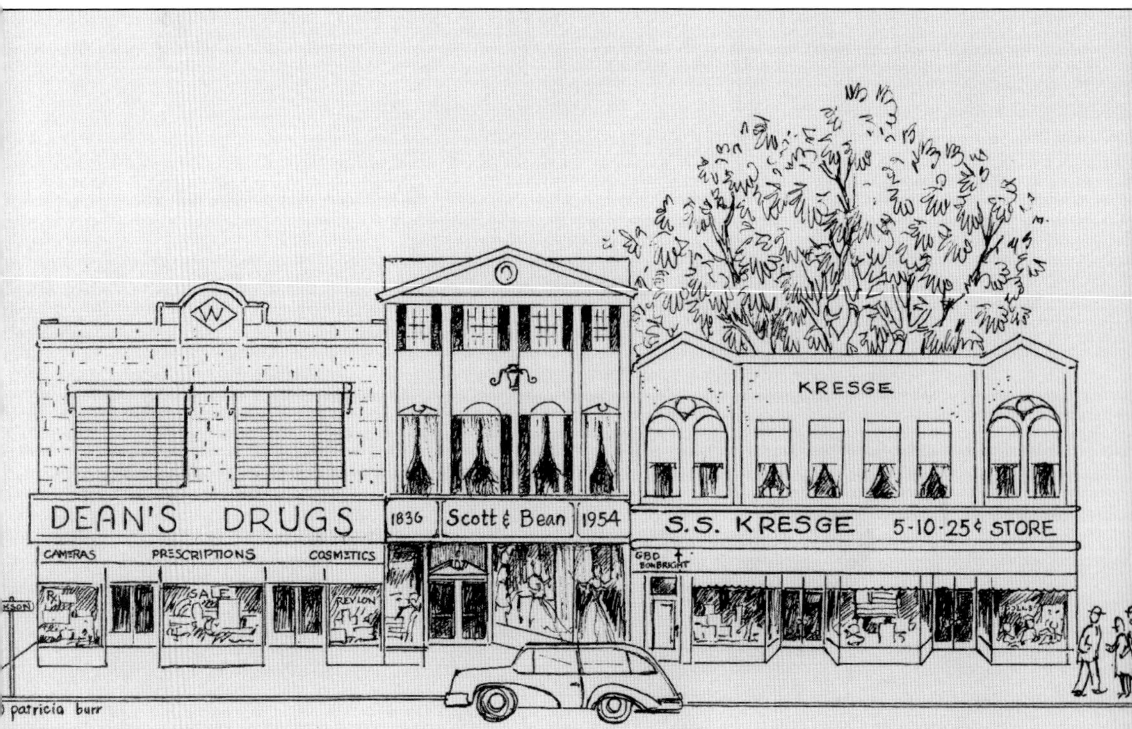

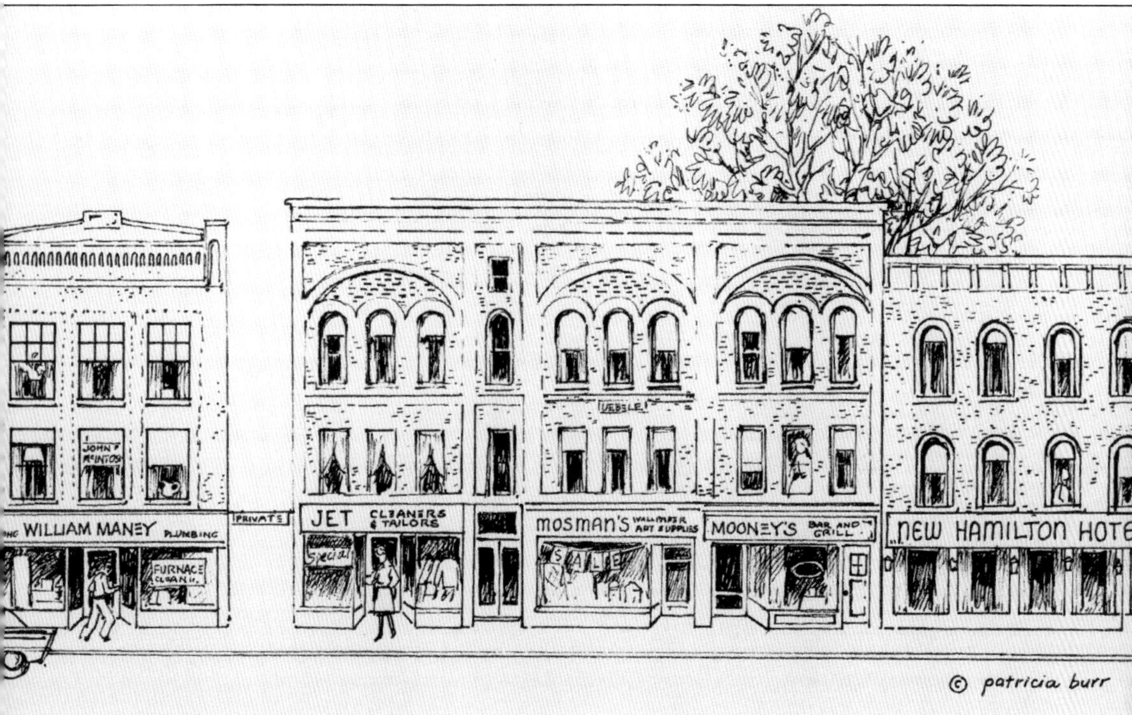

Jackson Street and Exchange Place.

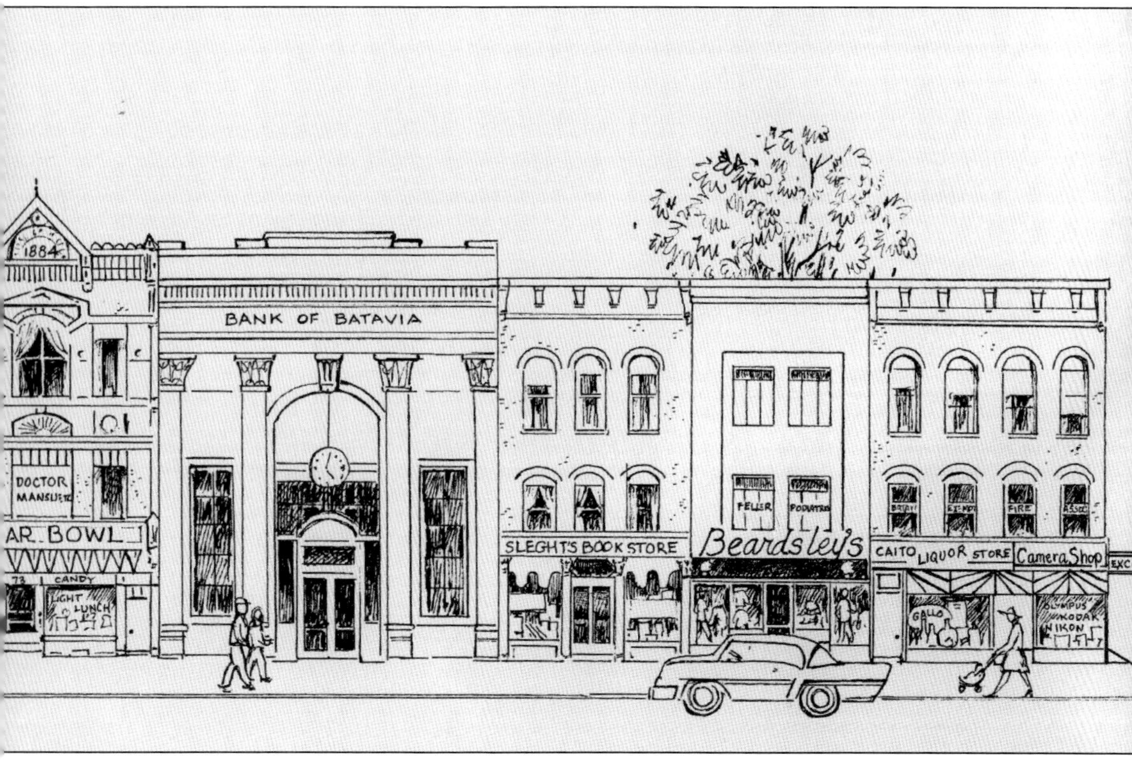

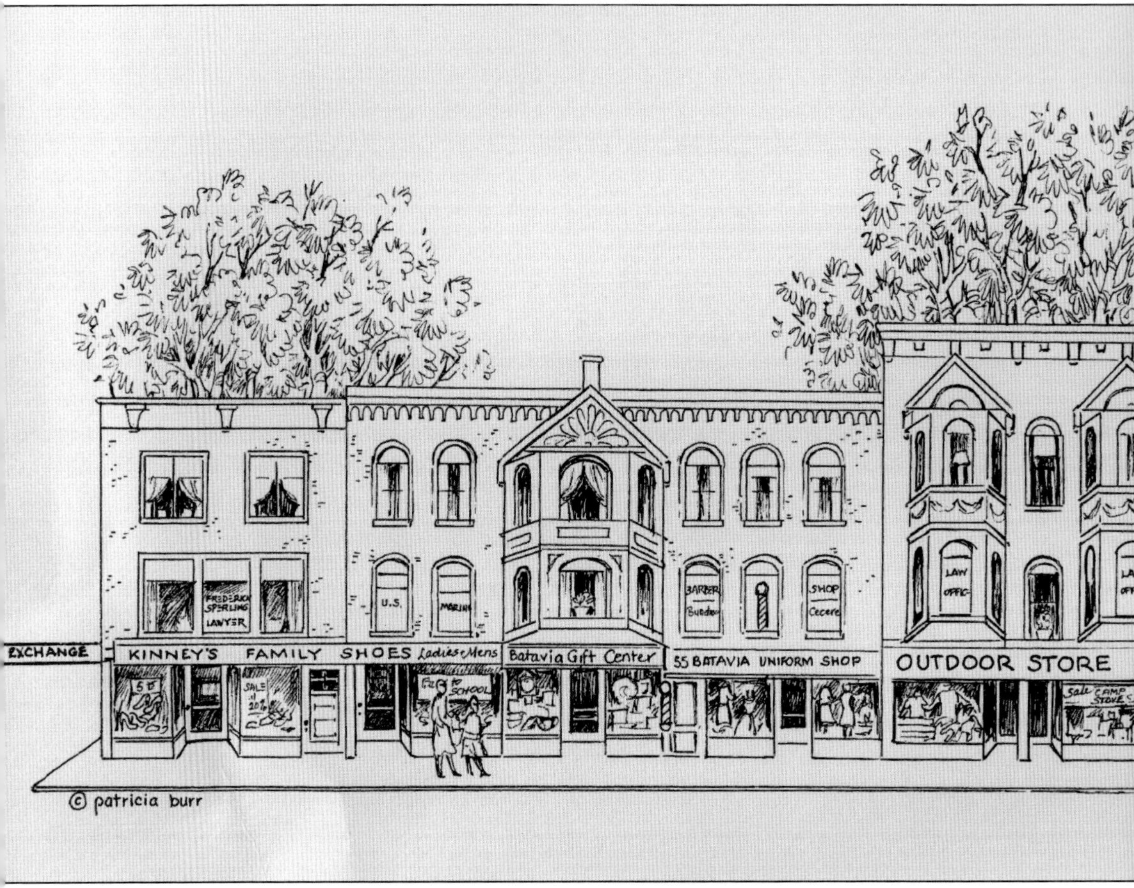

This drawing shows the downtown area in the southwest block from Exchange Place to Court

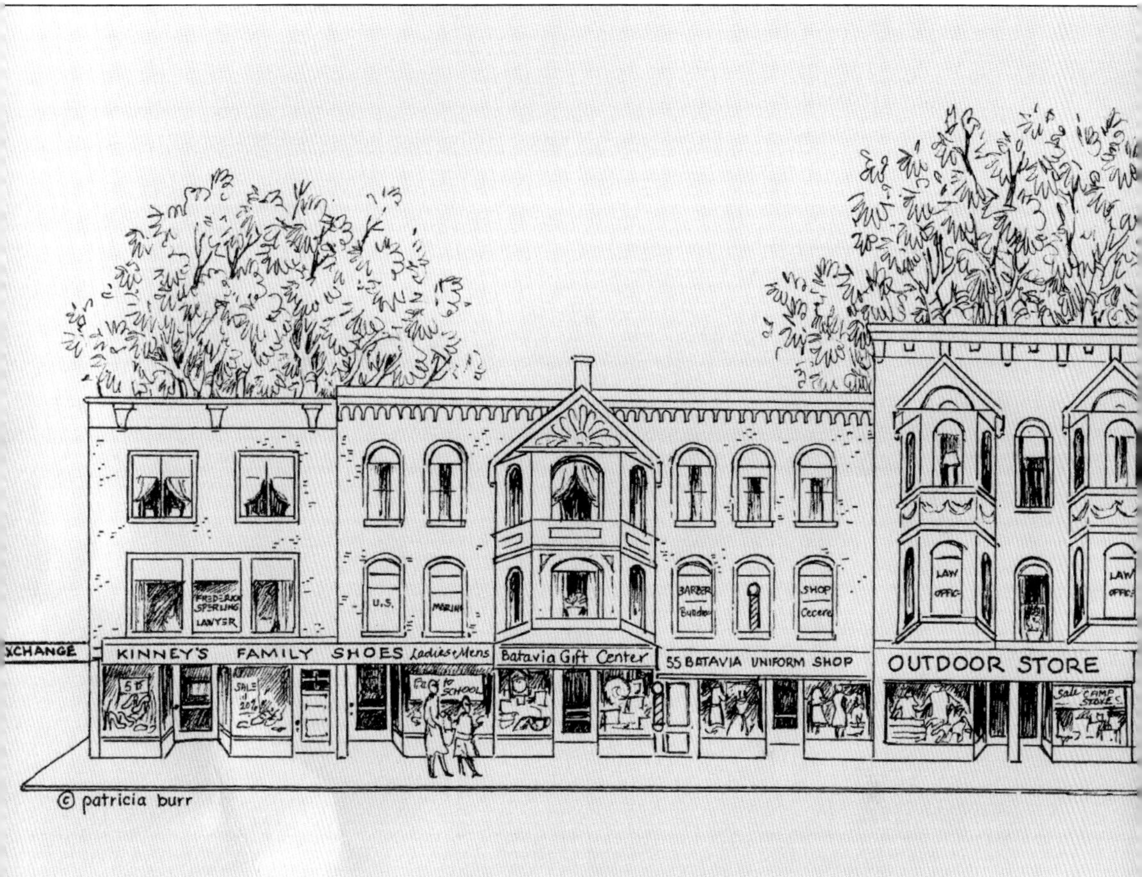

Street as it looked in the 1950s and 1960s. The drawing is by local artist Patricia Burr.

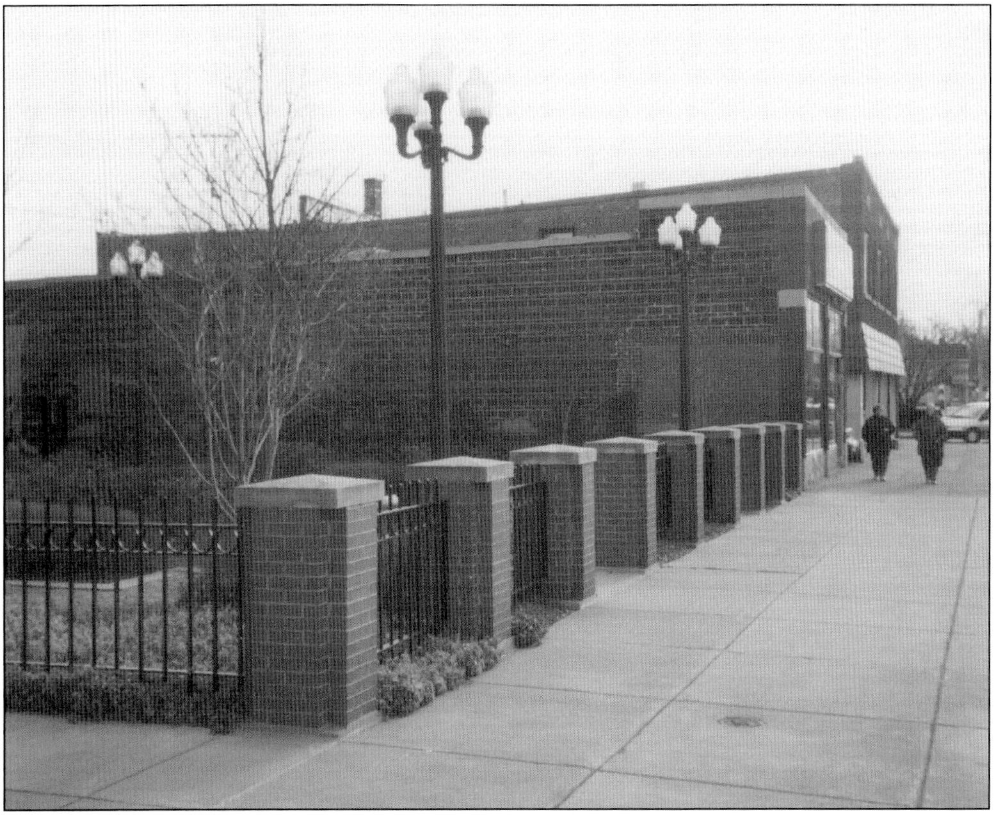

Jackson Street was being revitalized at the end of the 20th century. This photograph shows the area in front of the telephone company, south of the old Daily News Building.

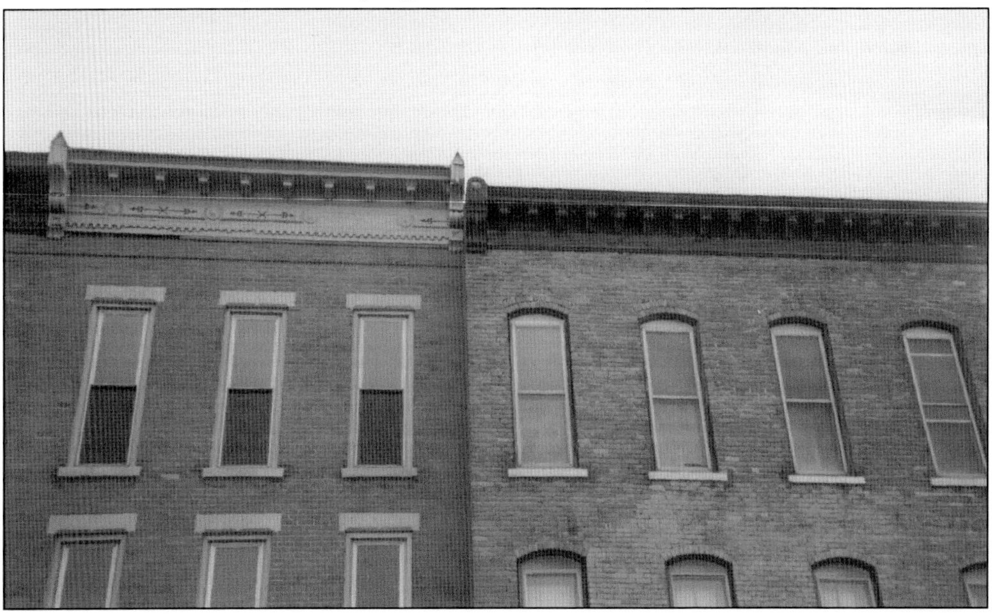

The cornices on these downtown buildings are examples of the Batavia Wood Working Company's products.

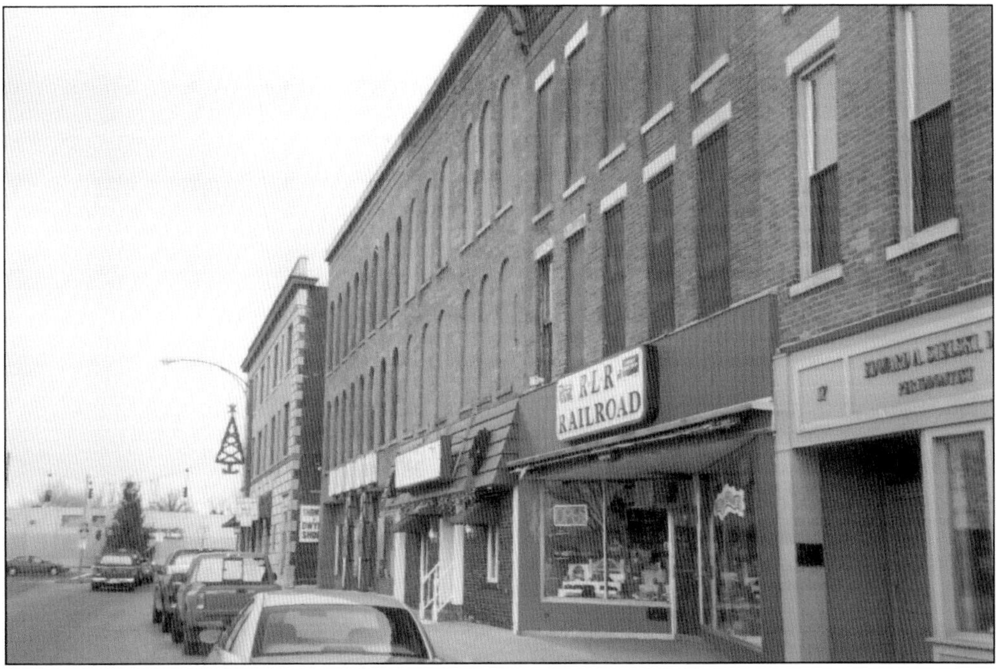

Another section of the block, above, shows some of the architectural restoration work that has been done. The photograph on the right focuses on an excellent example of architectural detail in the downtown area.

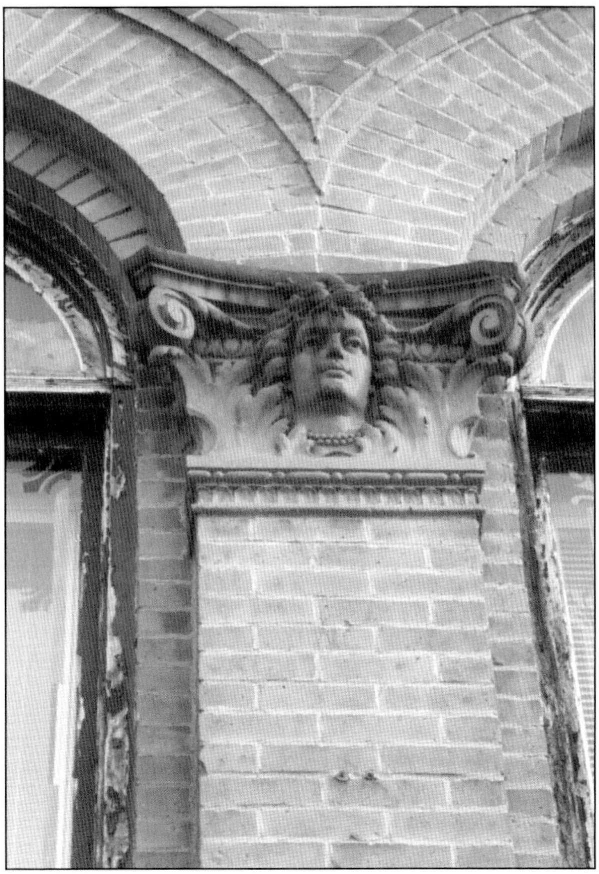

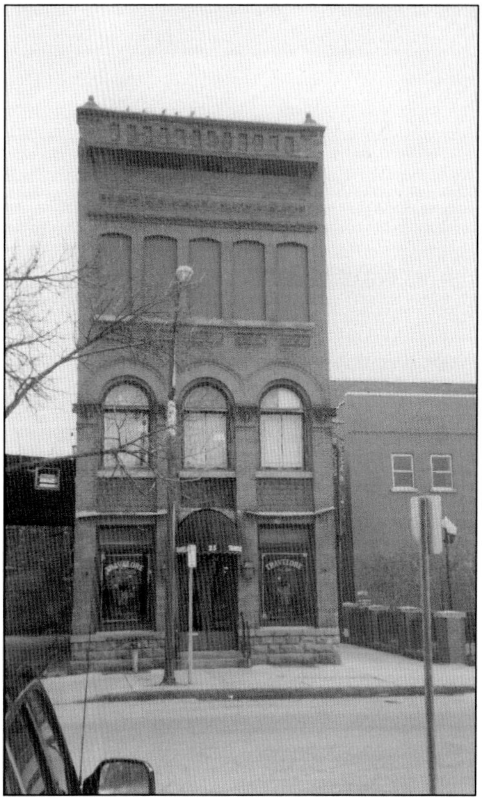

This building is part of the original Daily News Building. Today, it is the site of the the Travelore Travel Agency and other offices, which are located on the second floor.

This view shows the Travelore Building, just south of the entrance to the Jackson Square Alley.

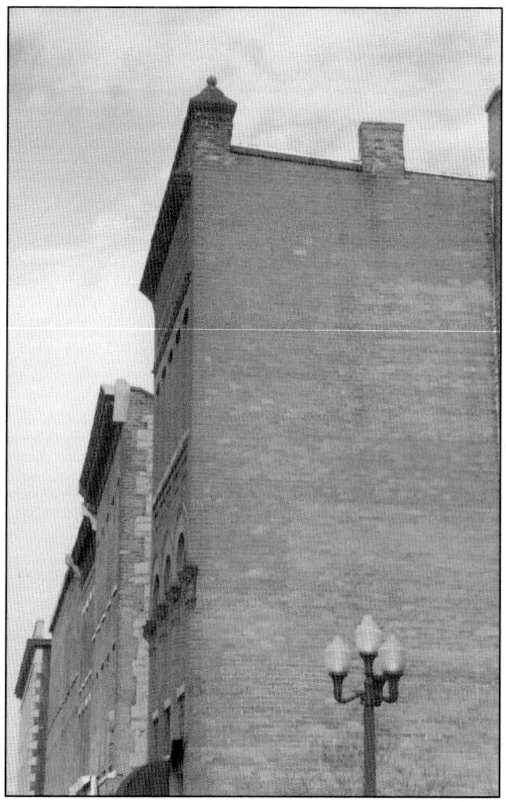

Seven

PROGRESS AND PRIDE

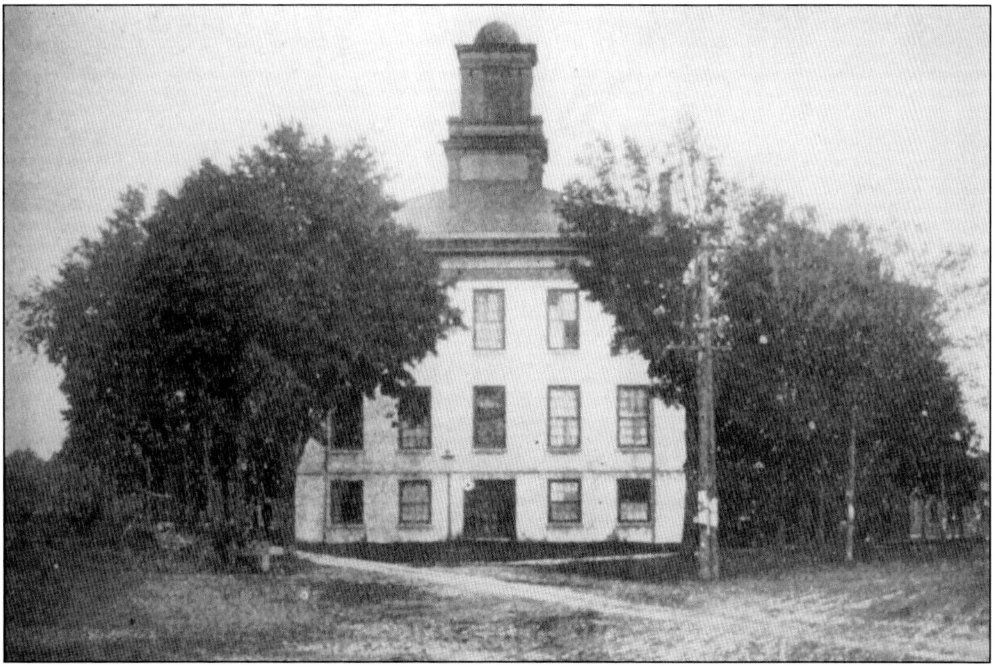

The courthouse was built at the fork in the road, where it still stands today (at Main and Ellicott Streets). However, in the early days the road was made of dirt. This is the first of several pictures of the courthouse at the fork in the road, presented here to show the progression from the first days up to today.

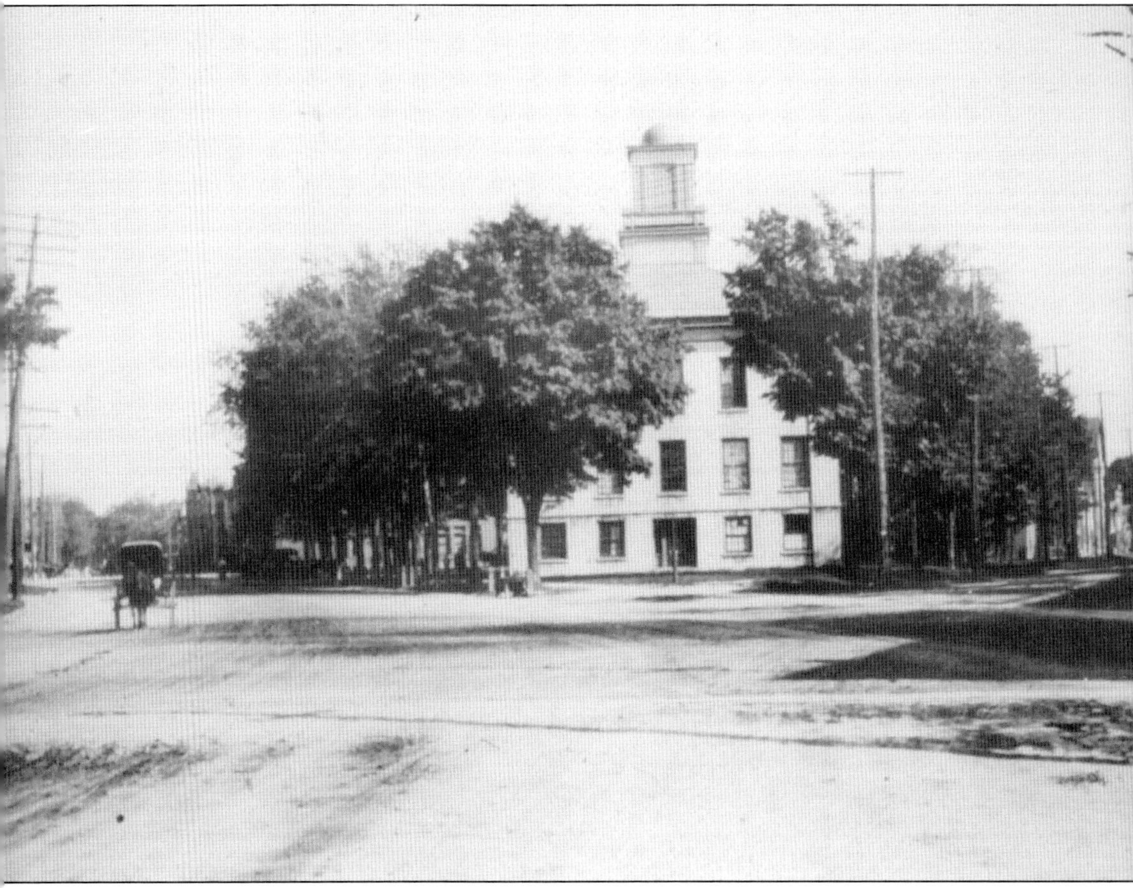

The courthouse is shown in the days of the horse and buggy, when dirt roads still ran through the towns and cities.

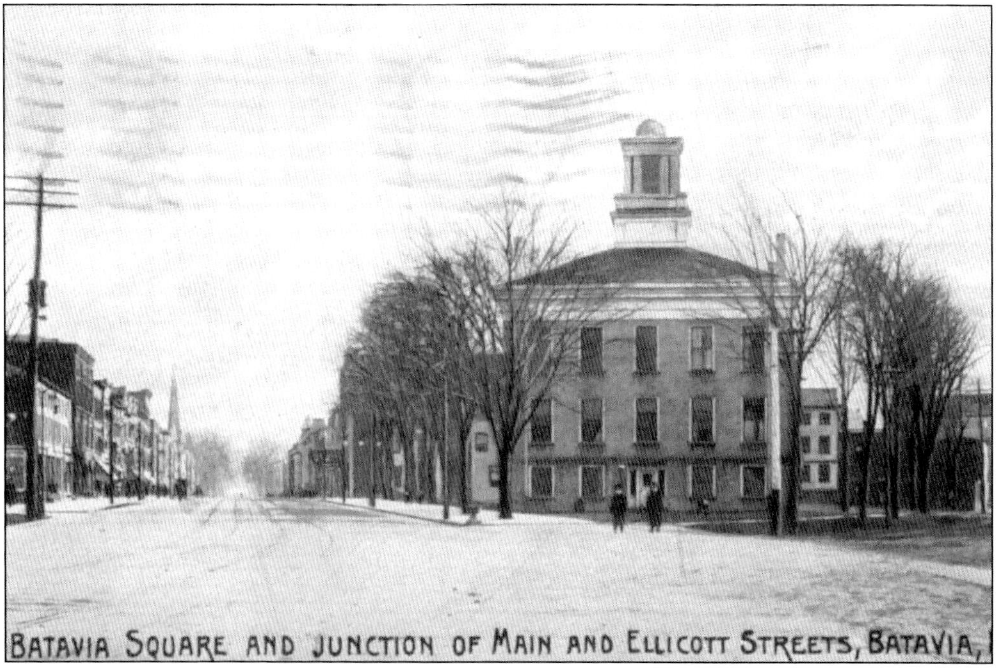

This view shows the courthouse in the first days of the trolley car. The postcard gives the location as "Batavia Square and the junction of Main and Ellicott Streets."

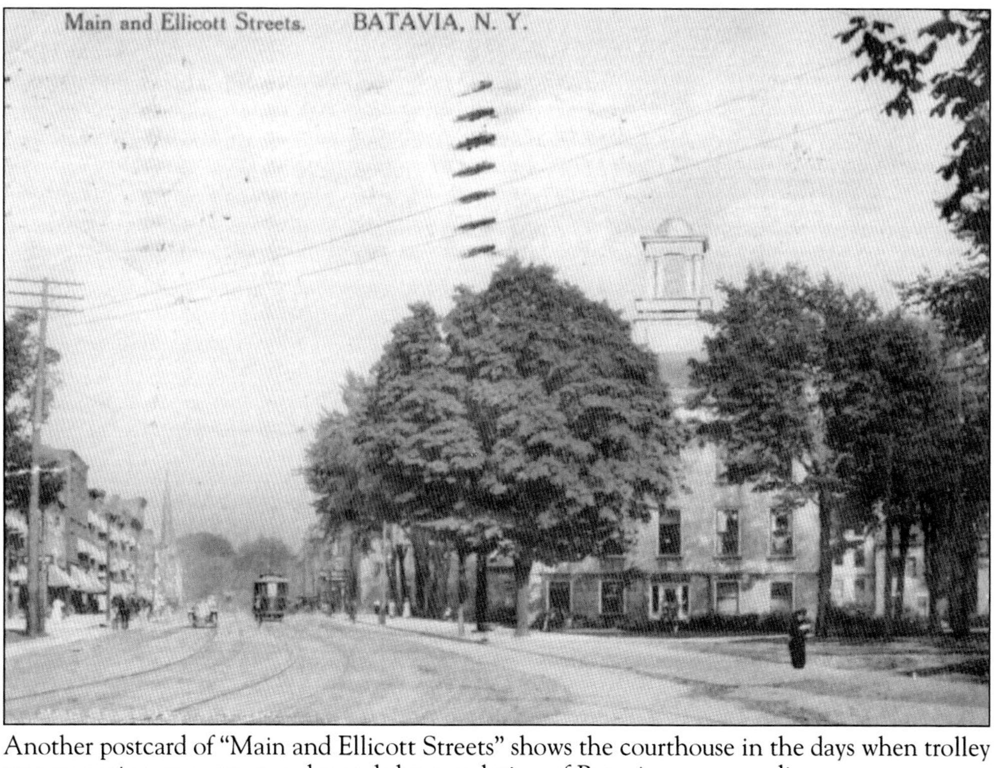

Another postcard of "Main and Ellicott Streets" shows the courthouse in the days when trolley transportation was very popular and the population of Batavia was expanding.

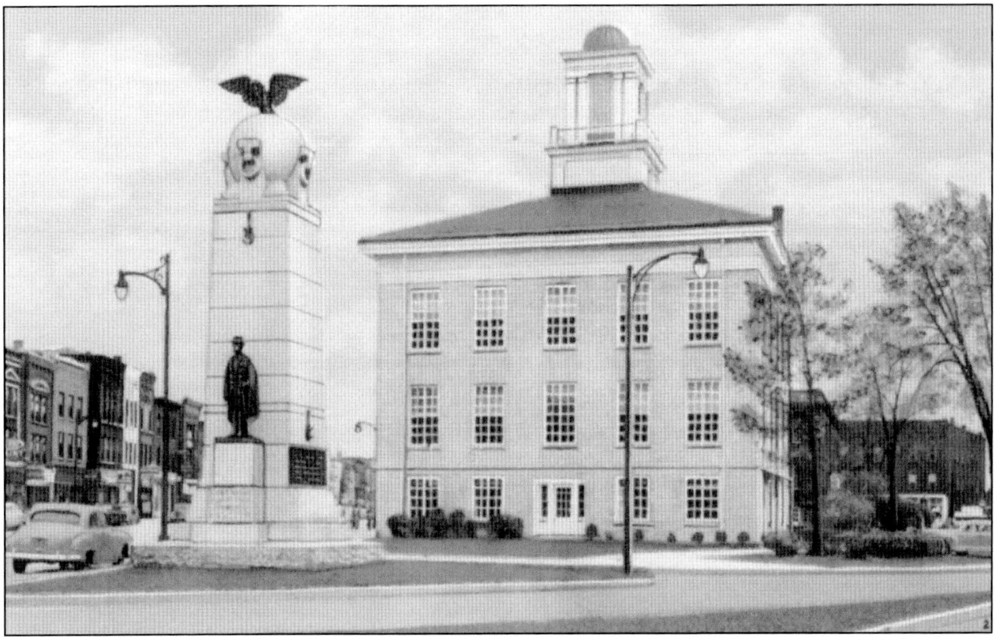

This is the same fork in the road where the courthouse stands. In the 1930s and 1940s, cars became very popular and the trolley became obsolete.

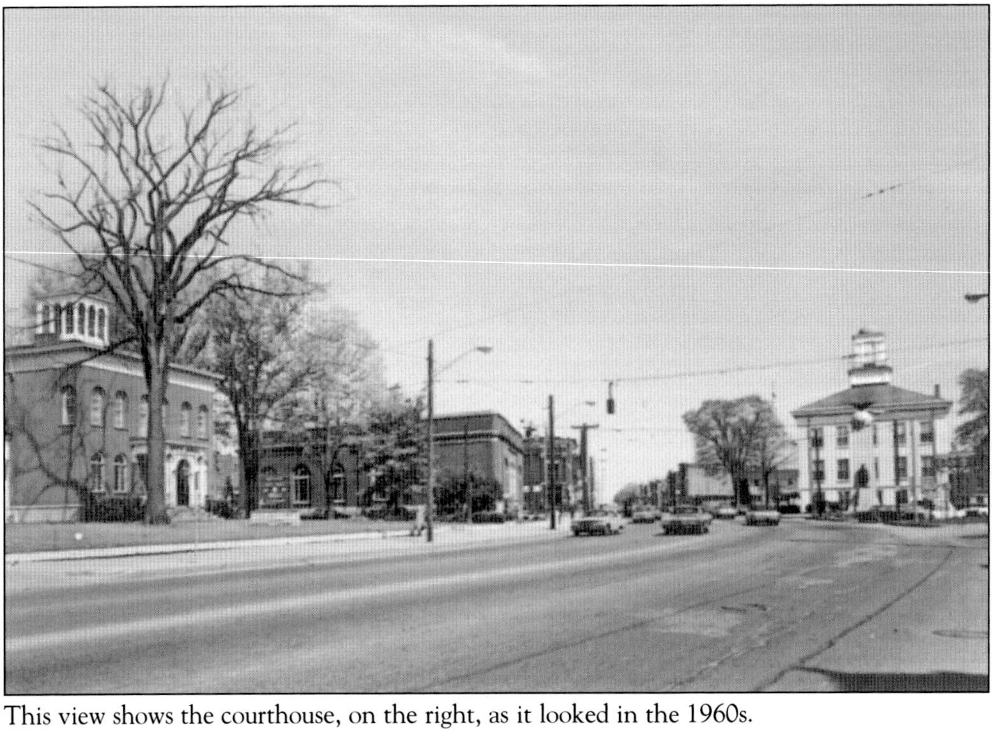

This view shows the courthouse, on the right, as it looked in the 1960s.

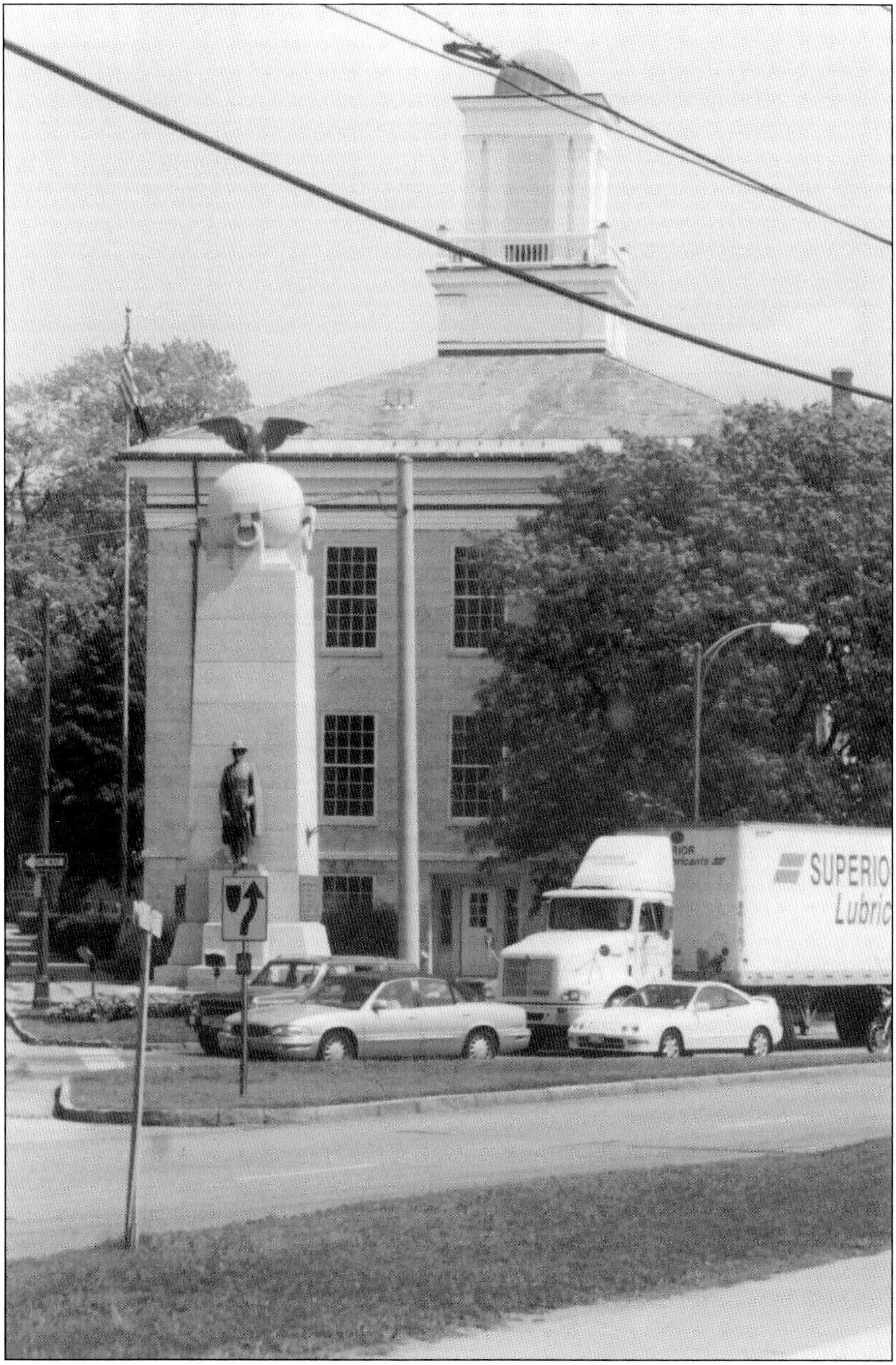

The last and most recent image of the courthouse shows how it appeared in the late 1990s.

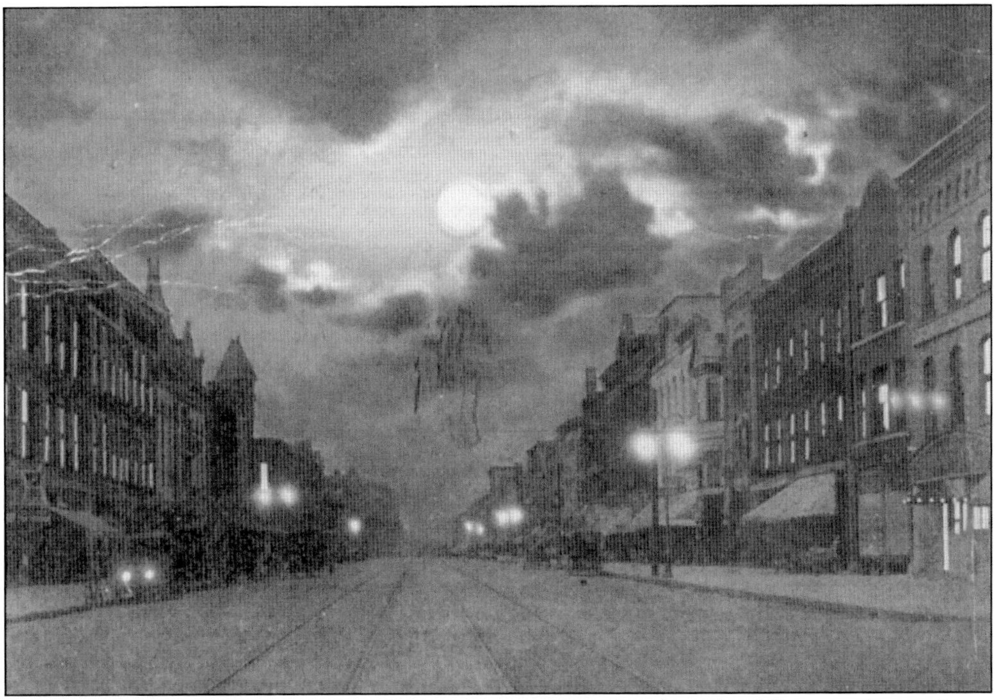

This view of Main Street was taken looking west on a night when the full moon far outshone the lights of the city.

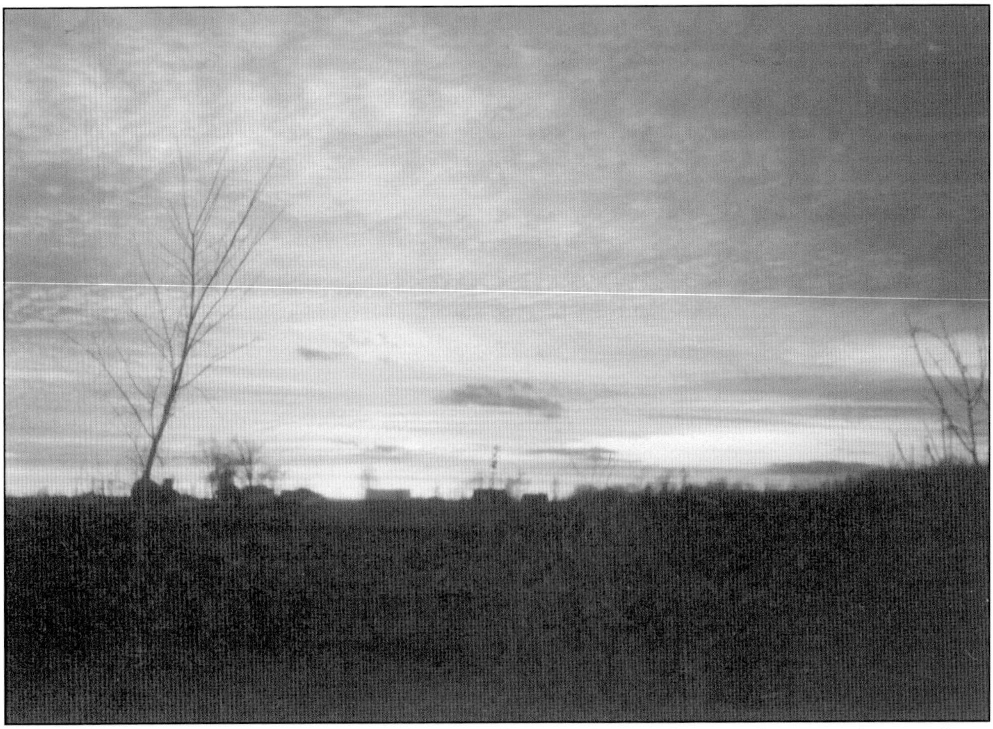

The farmlands of Genesee County are about to gleam in the sunshine at the start of a new day.

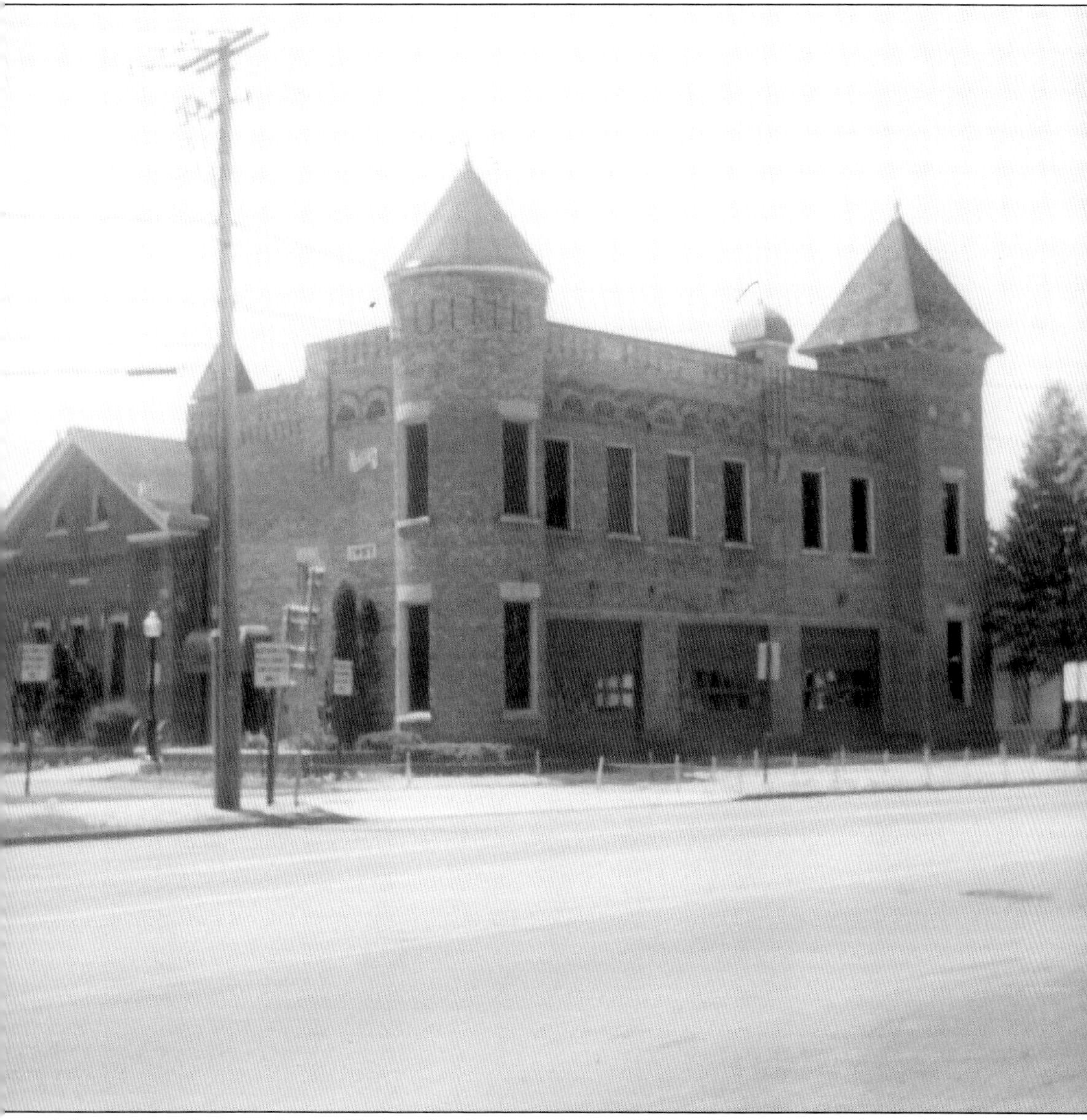

This is the old engine house. Today, the Genesee County History Department is located here.

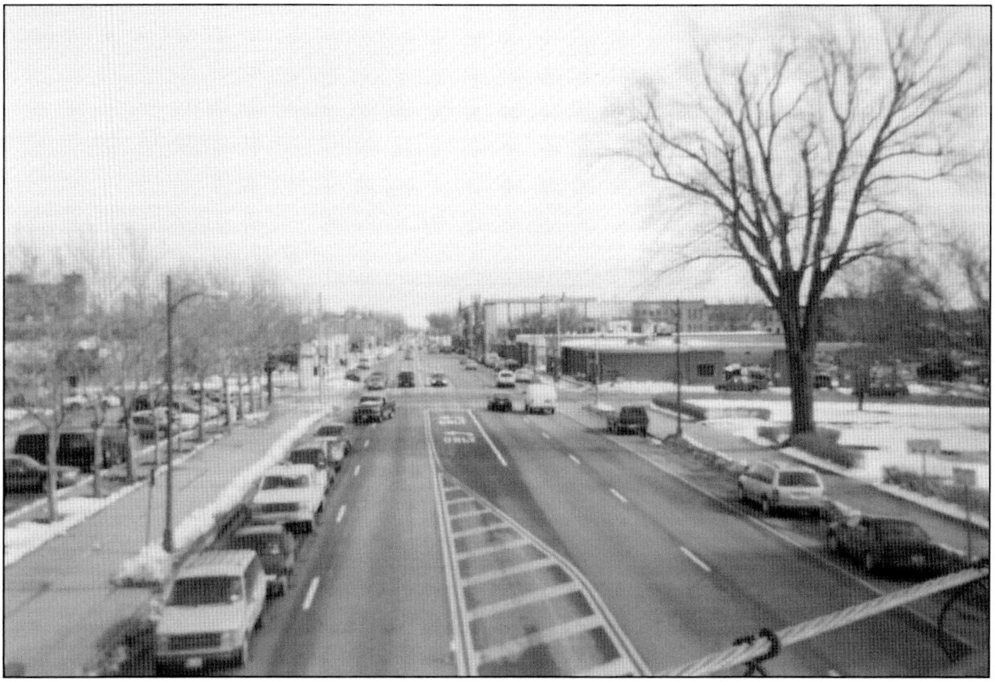

This view shows Main Street (Route 5) waiting for the proposed reconstruction and redevelopment of the road, scheduled for the year 2002.

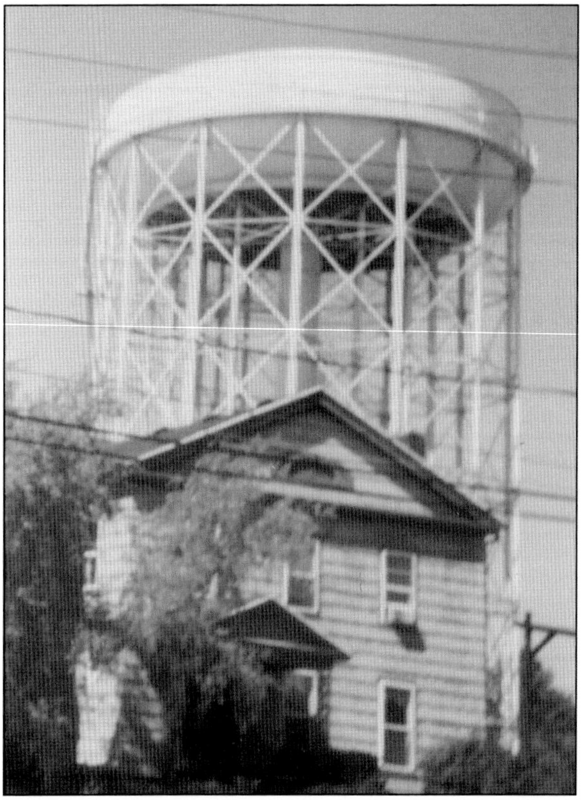

The water tower rises above the city—a city which has water issues on the public agenda.

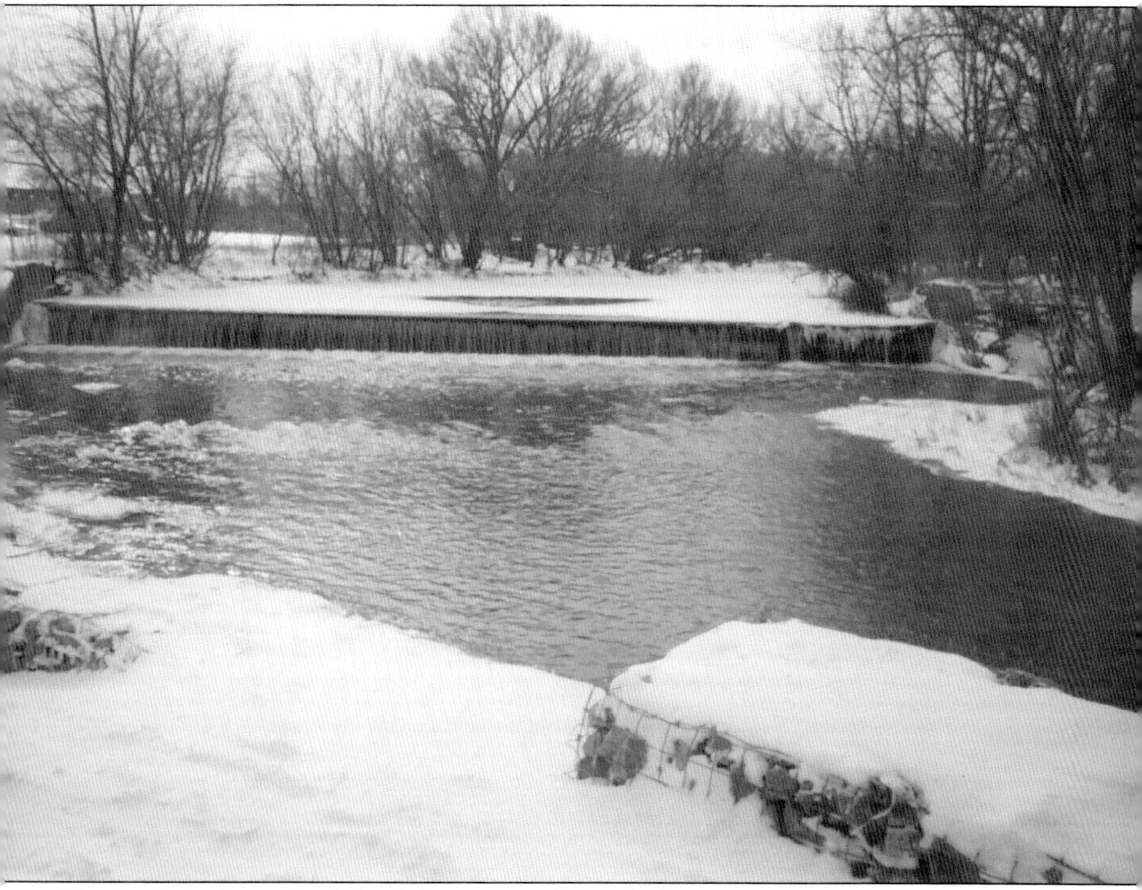

This lovely landscape lies behind the new courthouse facility. In this winter scene, the trees are bare, the ground is snow covered, and the Tonawanda Creek continues on its way.

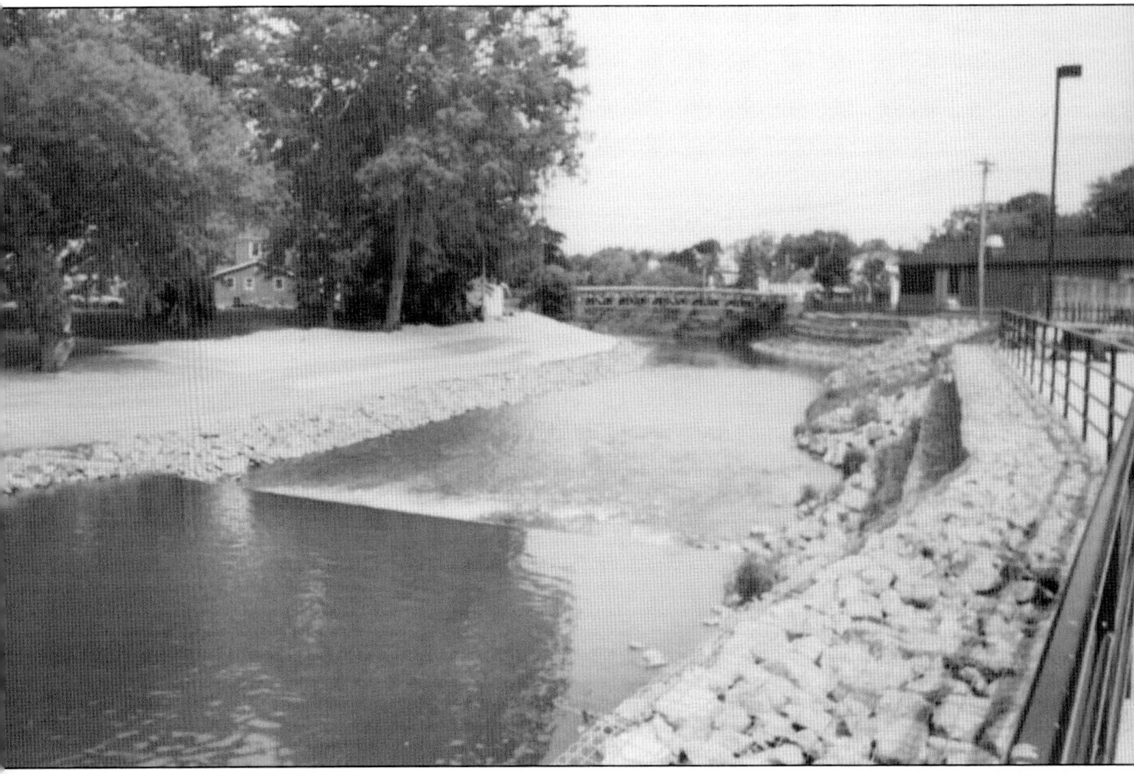

This view shows preservation work being done on the bed of the Tonawanda Creek by the Department of Environmental Conservation. The photograph was taken in 1999.

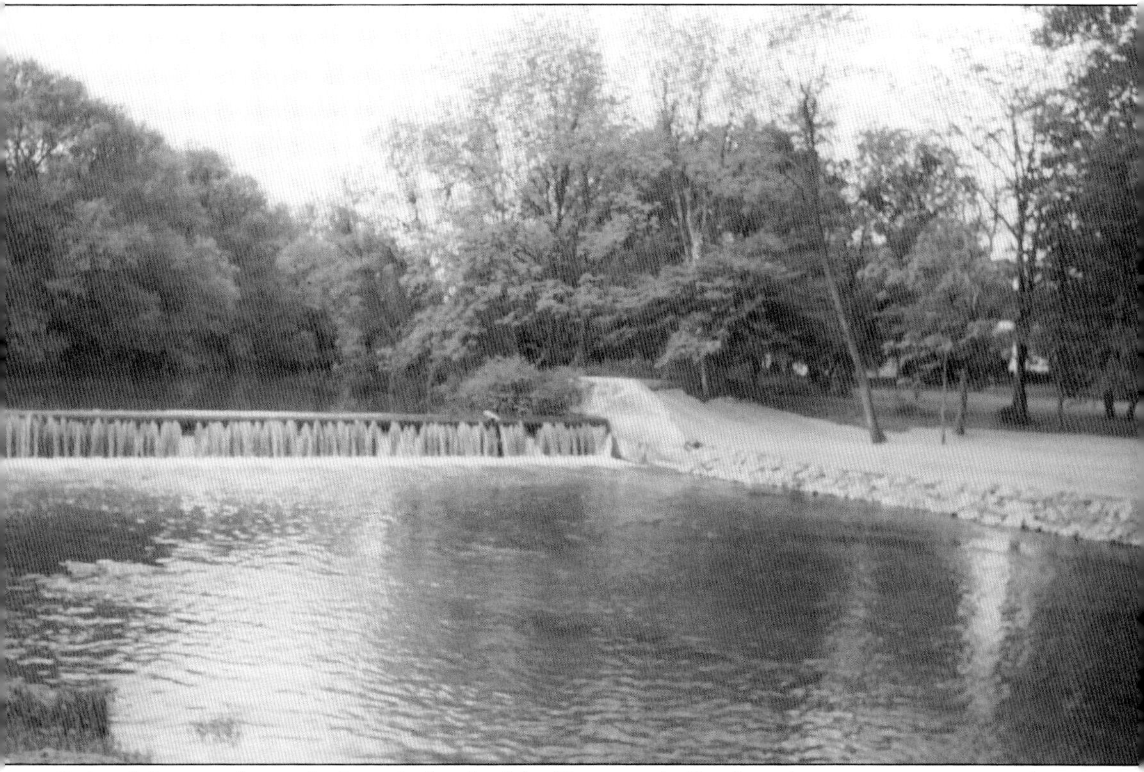

Behind the courthouse facility, the bank of the Tonawanda Creek underwent restoration work. The project was conducted by the Department of Environmental Conservation in 1999.

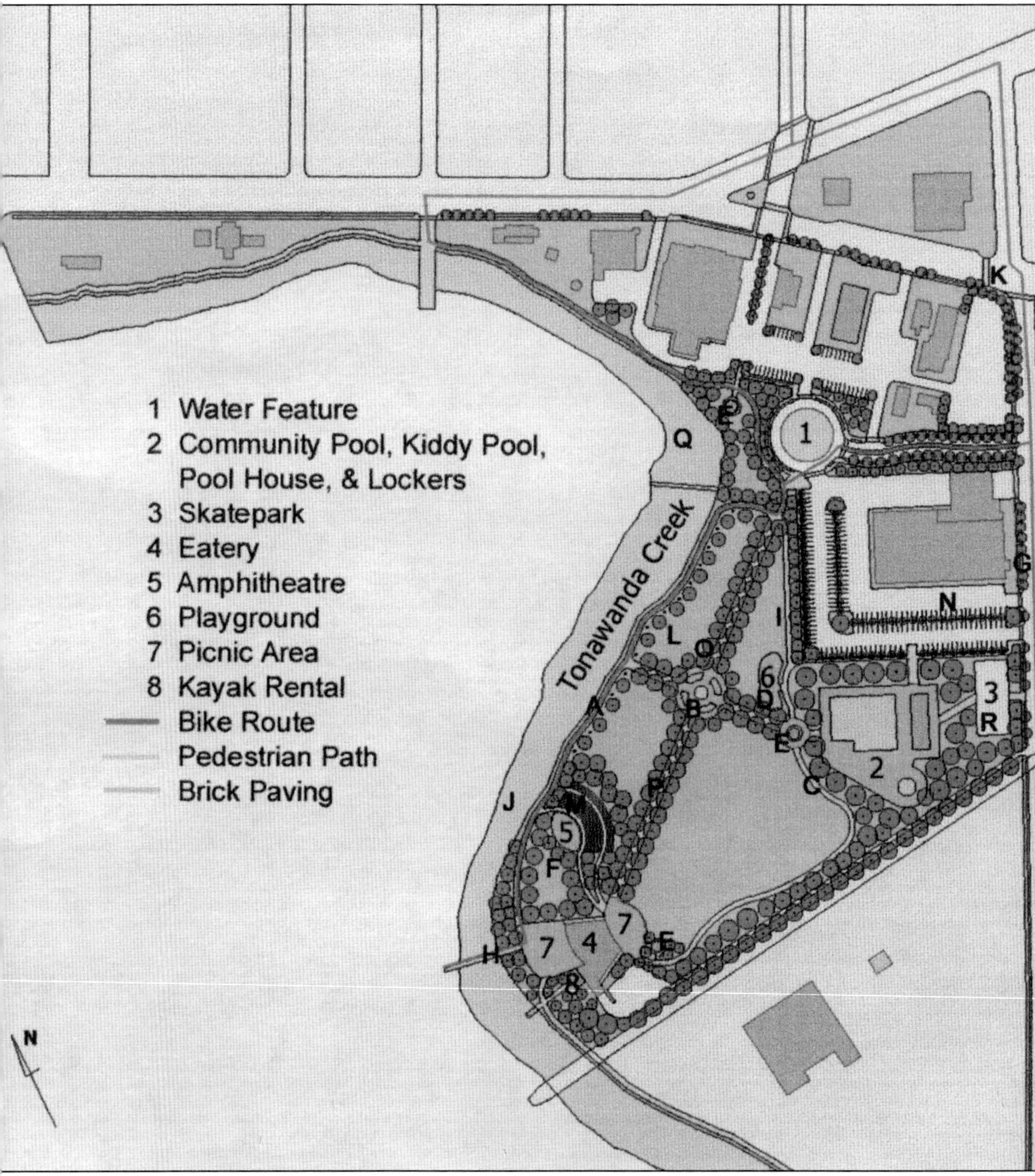

Recreational facilities abound in this plan for the proposed Batavia Creek Park. Drawn up in 1999, the plan includes walkways, bicycle paths, pools, a skating park, an amphitheater, a playground, and picnic areas.

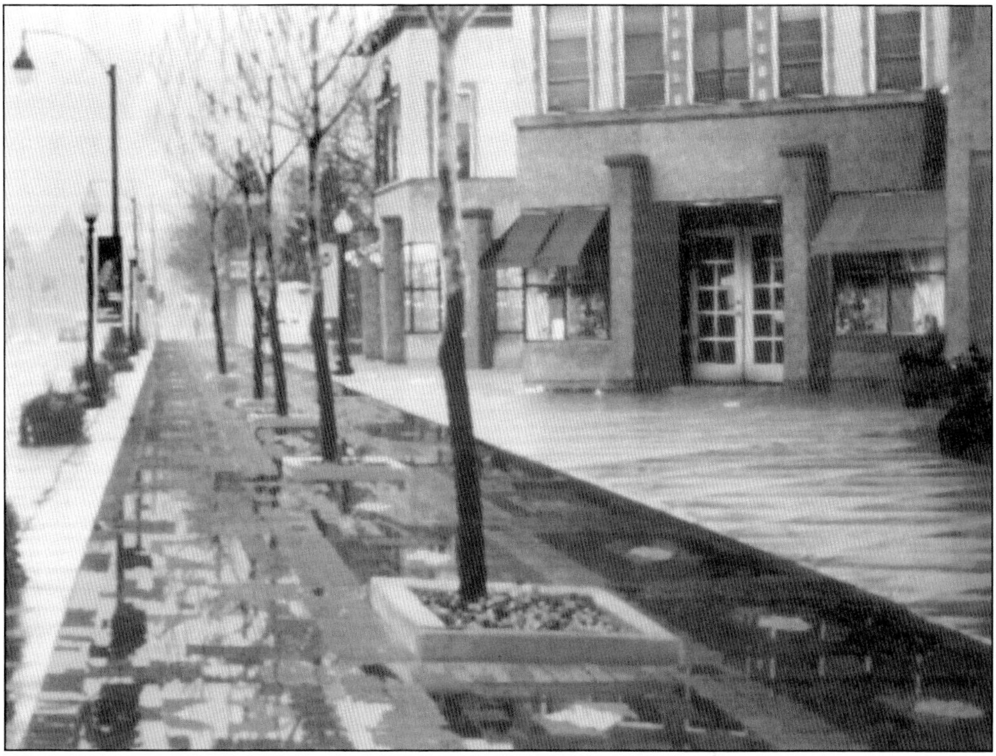

This view shows the Genesee Country Mall as it appeared near the end of the 20th century.

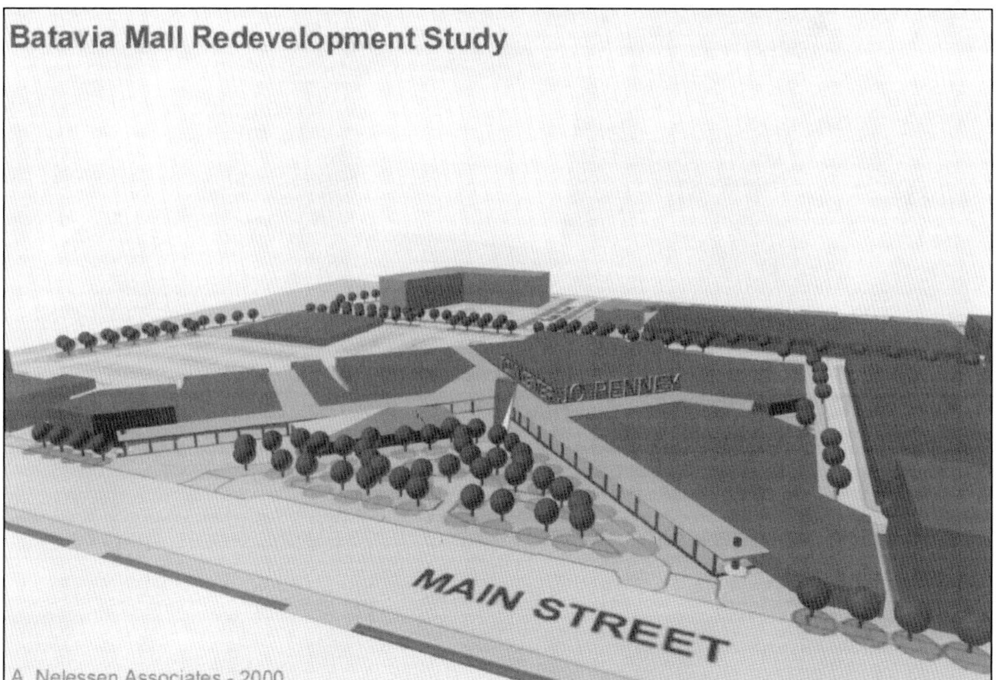

This model by A. Nelessen Associates was completed as part of the "Batavia Mall Redevelopment Study" for redesigning the Genesee Country Mall.

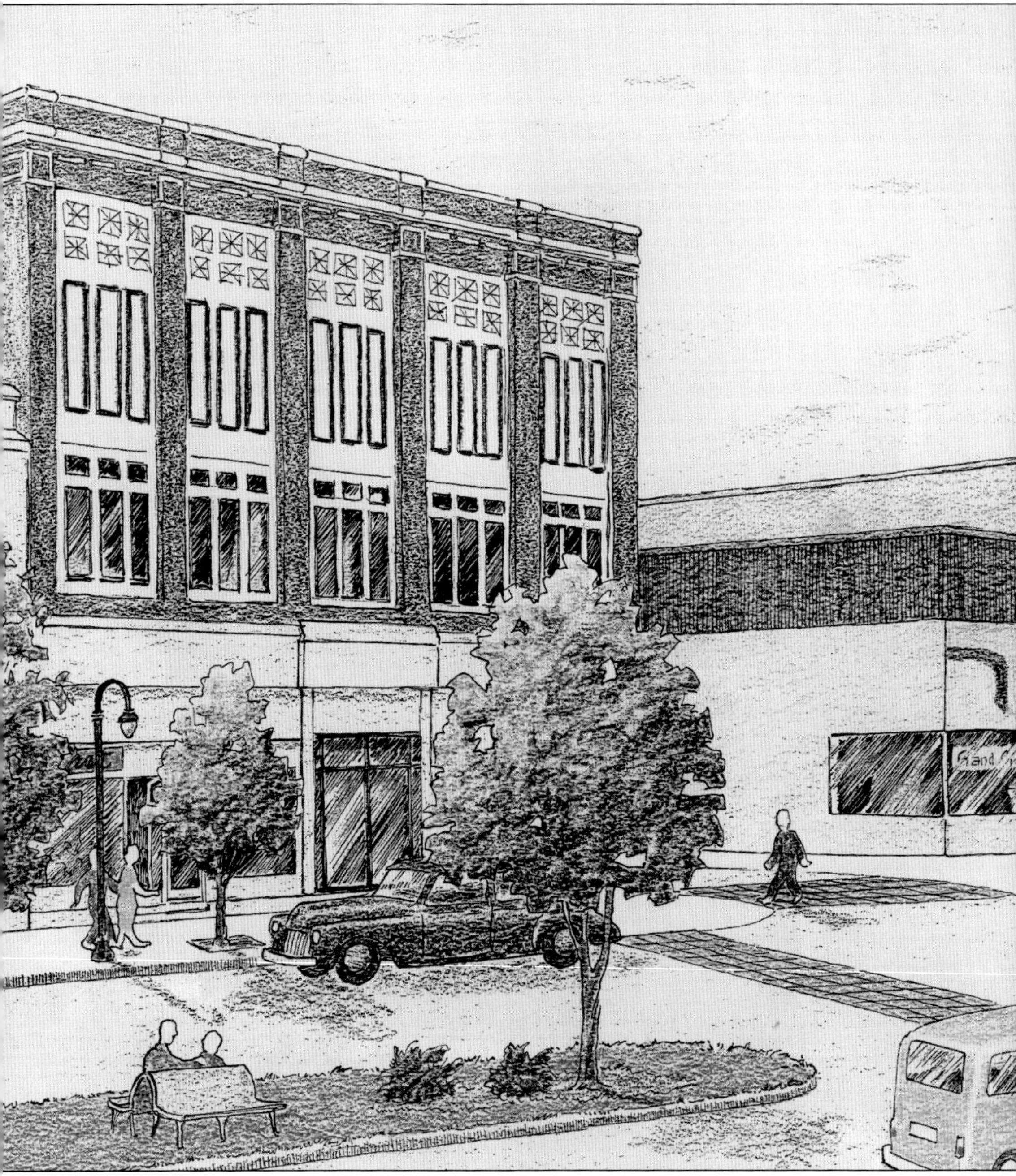

This sketch shows the proposed redevelopment of the south side of Main Street between Jackson Street and Center Street. The plan shows the area dressed up with pedestrian crosswalks, trees,

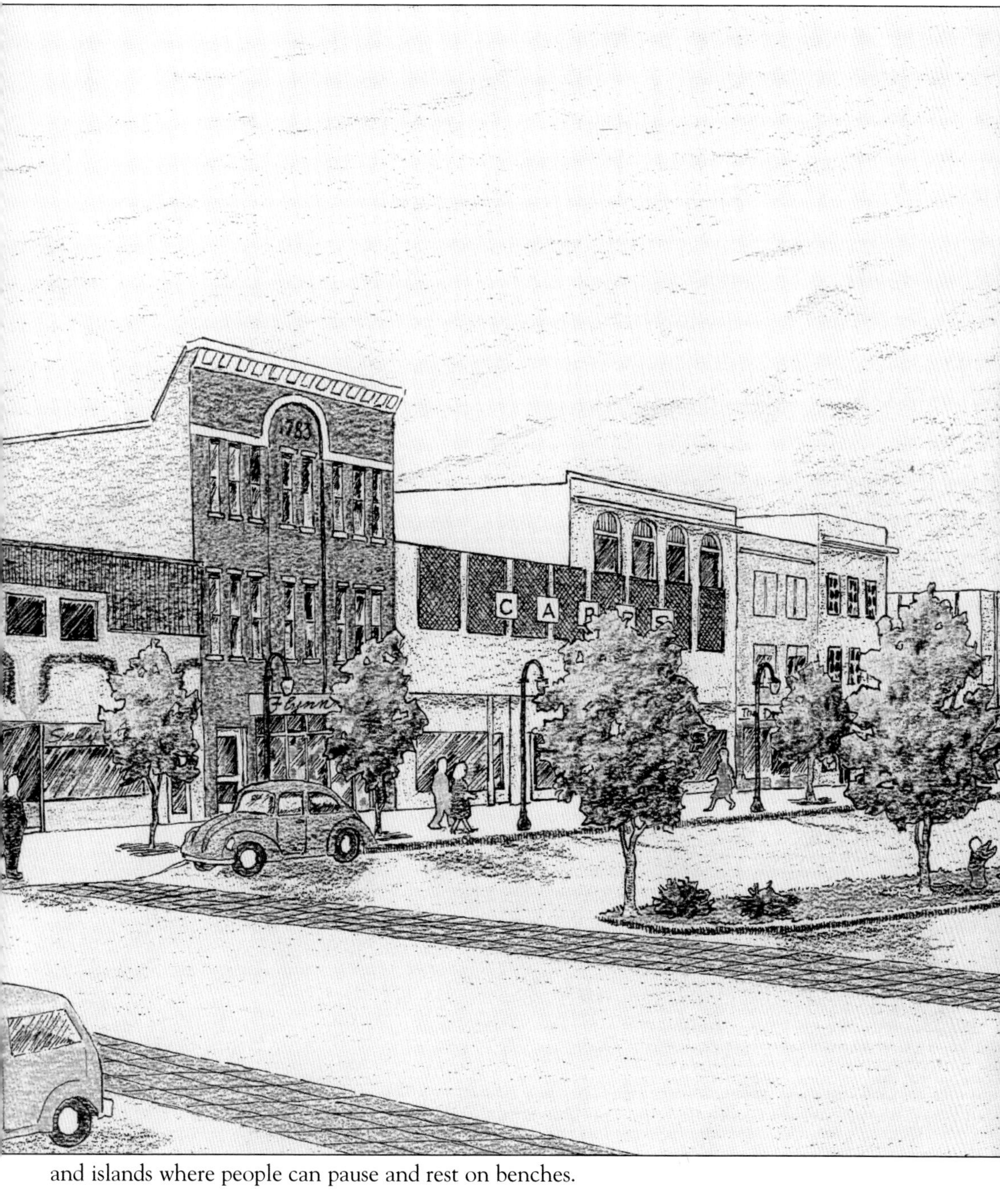

and islands where people can pause and rest on benches.

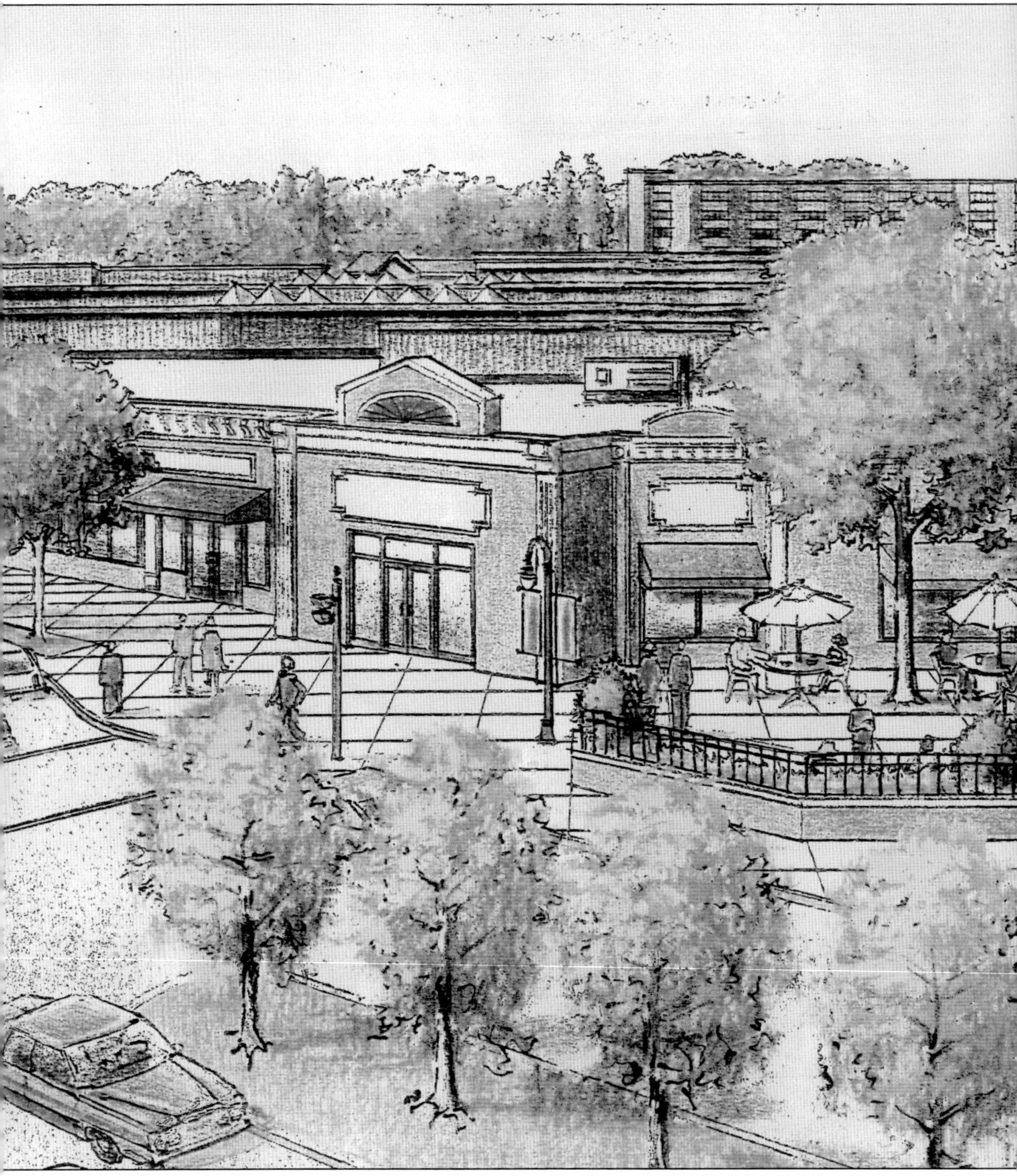

This drawing shows the proposed new design for the Genesee Country Mall. The plan includes a parklike area with trees and other plantings, streetlamps, benches, and umbrella-shaded tables

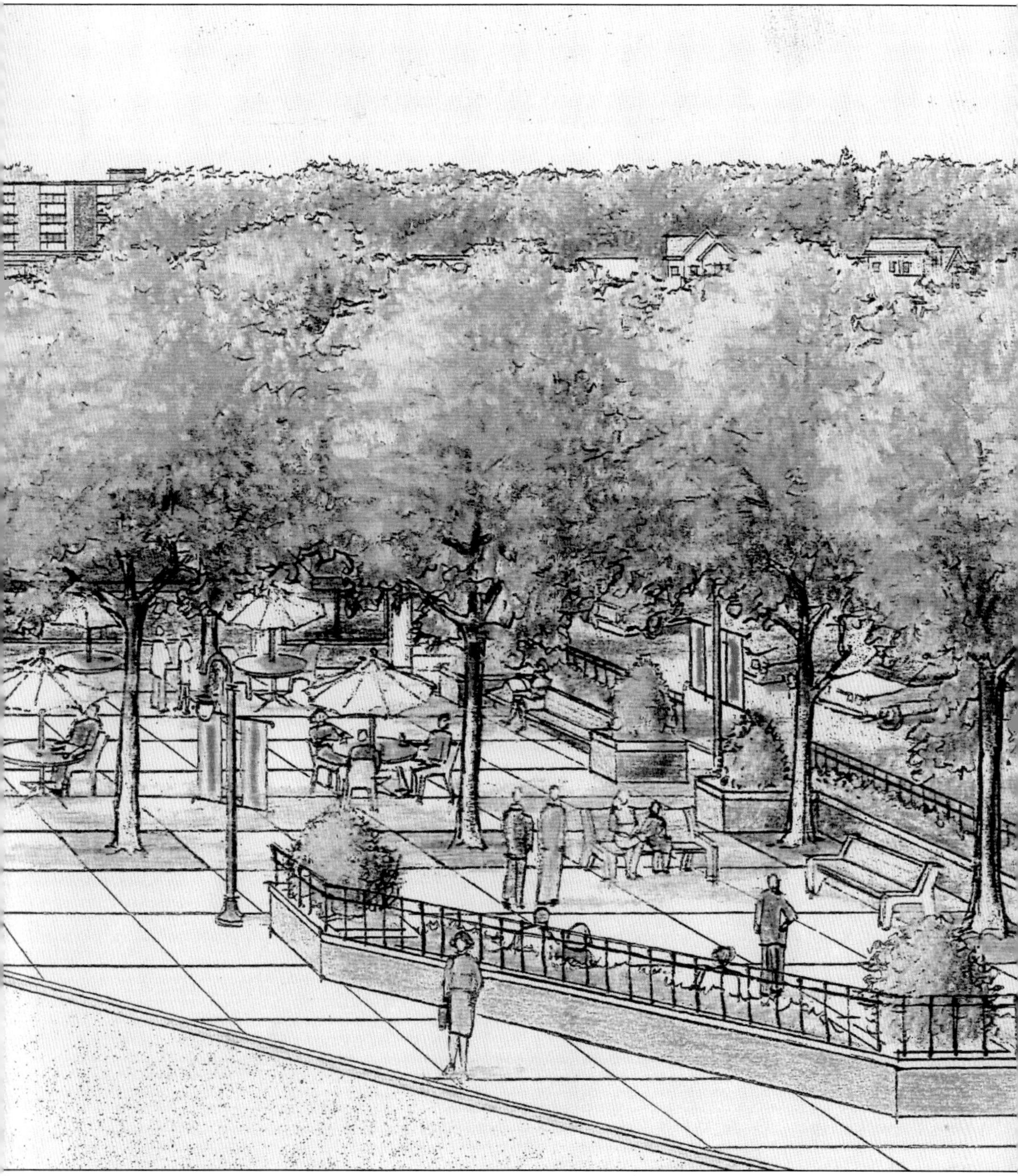

with chairs. The artist sketched the plan looking northwest from Bank Street.

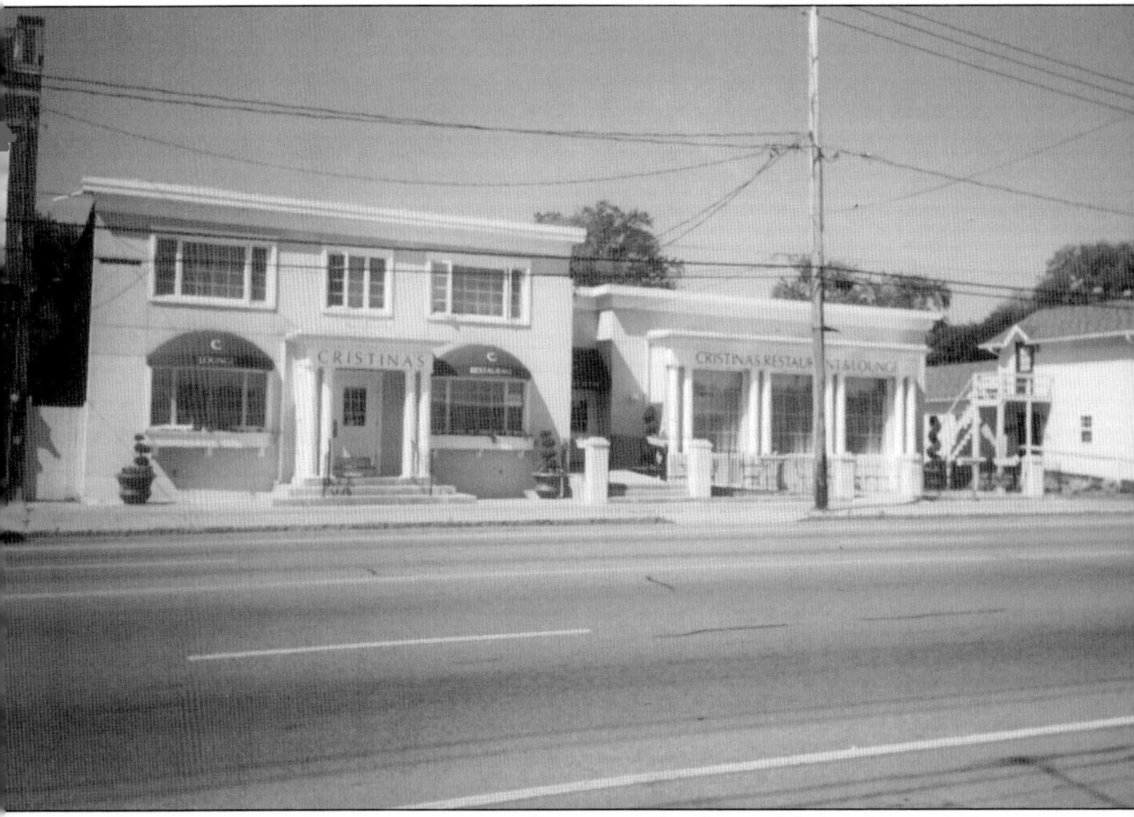

The former Ange's Restaurant was recently renovated and remodeled as Cristina's Restaurant. Owned by Charles Brumsted, the restaurant is located on Ellicott Street.

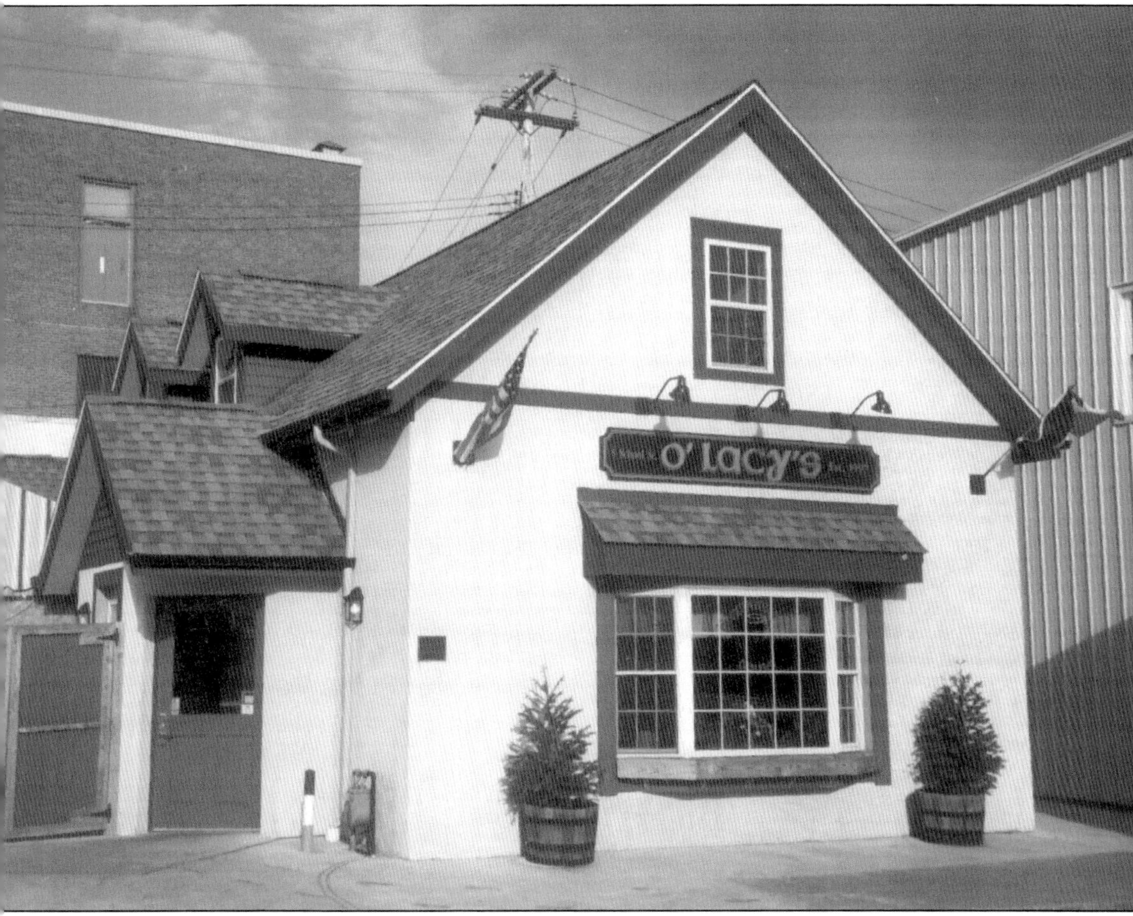

O'Lacy's Pub is a recent addition to the downtown area. Centrally located, it stands out from the buildings around it.

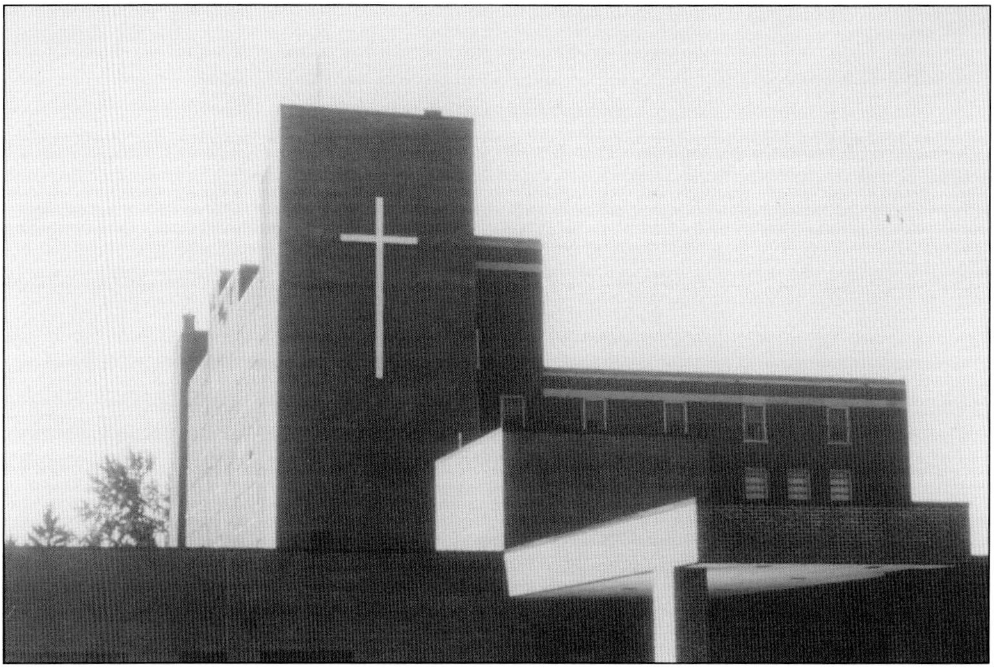

St. Jerome's Hospital and Genesee Memorial Hospital merged in 1999 to become the United Memorial Medical Center.

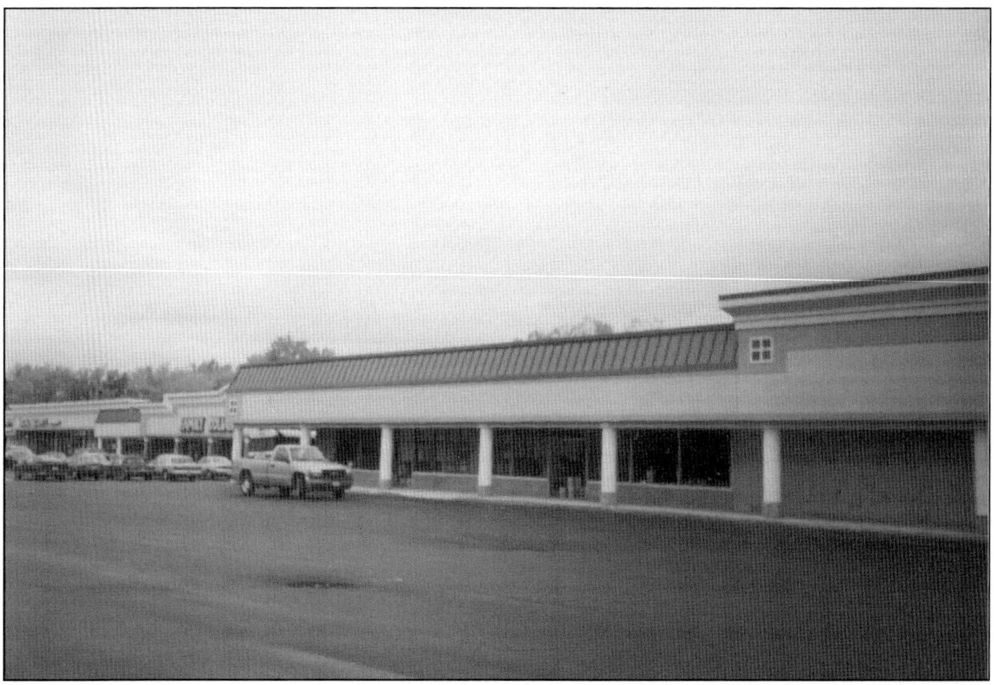

The Eastown Plaza was one of the shopping areas in Batavia for which a restoration project was planned and undertaken.

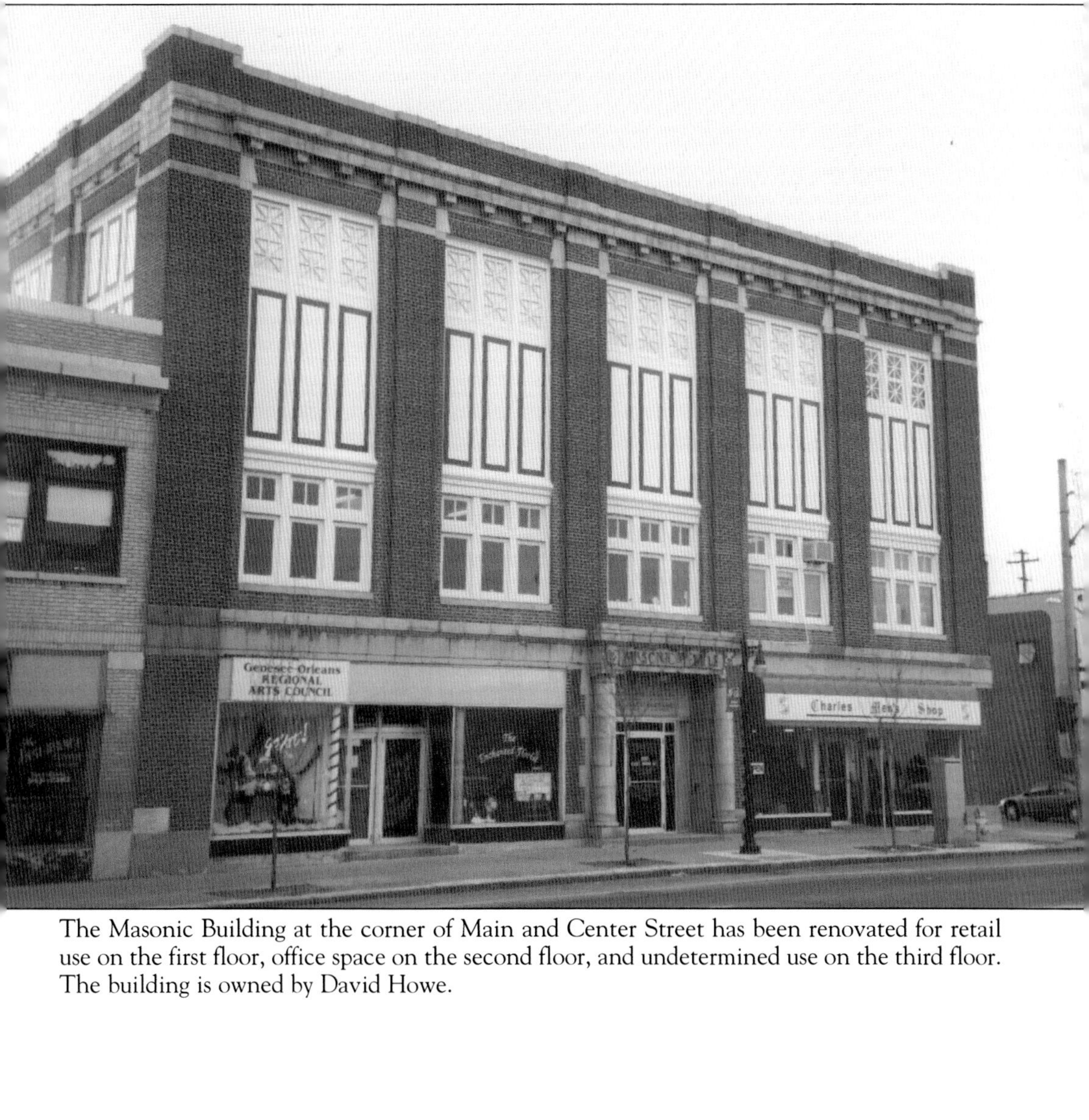

The Masonic Building at the corner of Main and Center Street has been renovated for retail use on the first floor, office space on the second floor, and undetermined use on the third floor. The building is owned by David Howe.

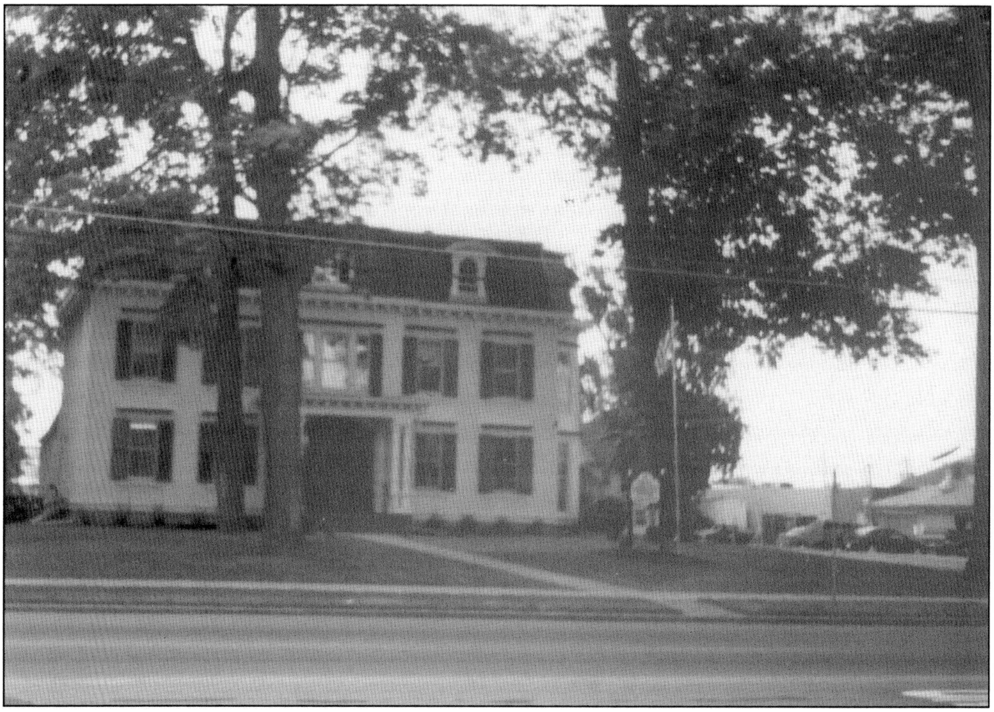

The office of the Genesee Cooperative Extension is located on a tree-shaded lot at the corner of Main Street and Masse Place.

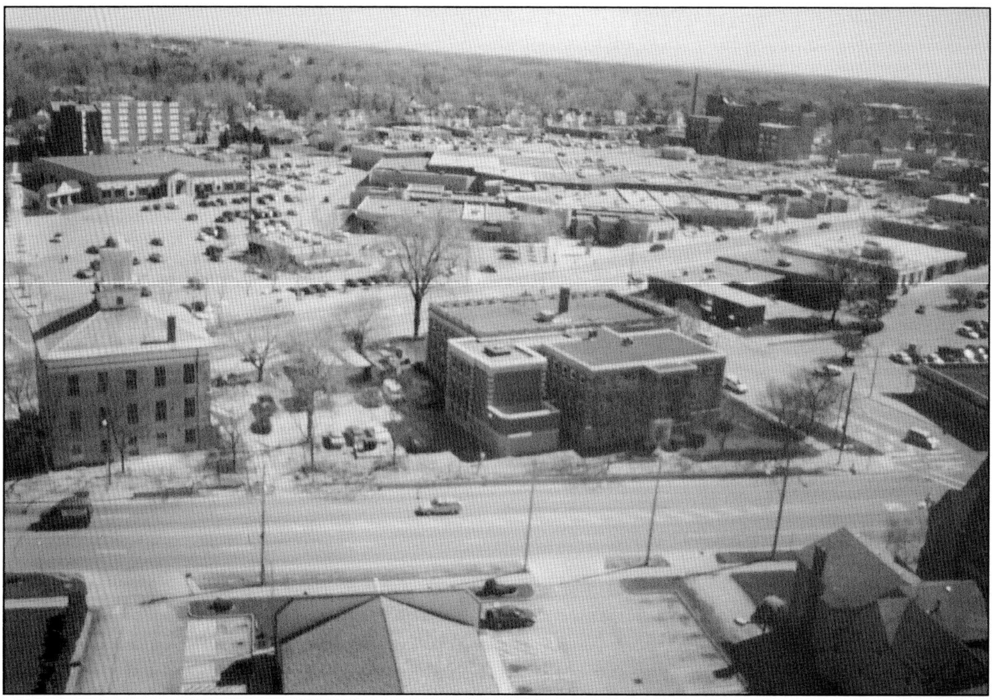

The newly restored County Building No. 1 is in the foreground, with the Genesee Country Mall directly behind it.

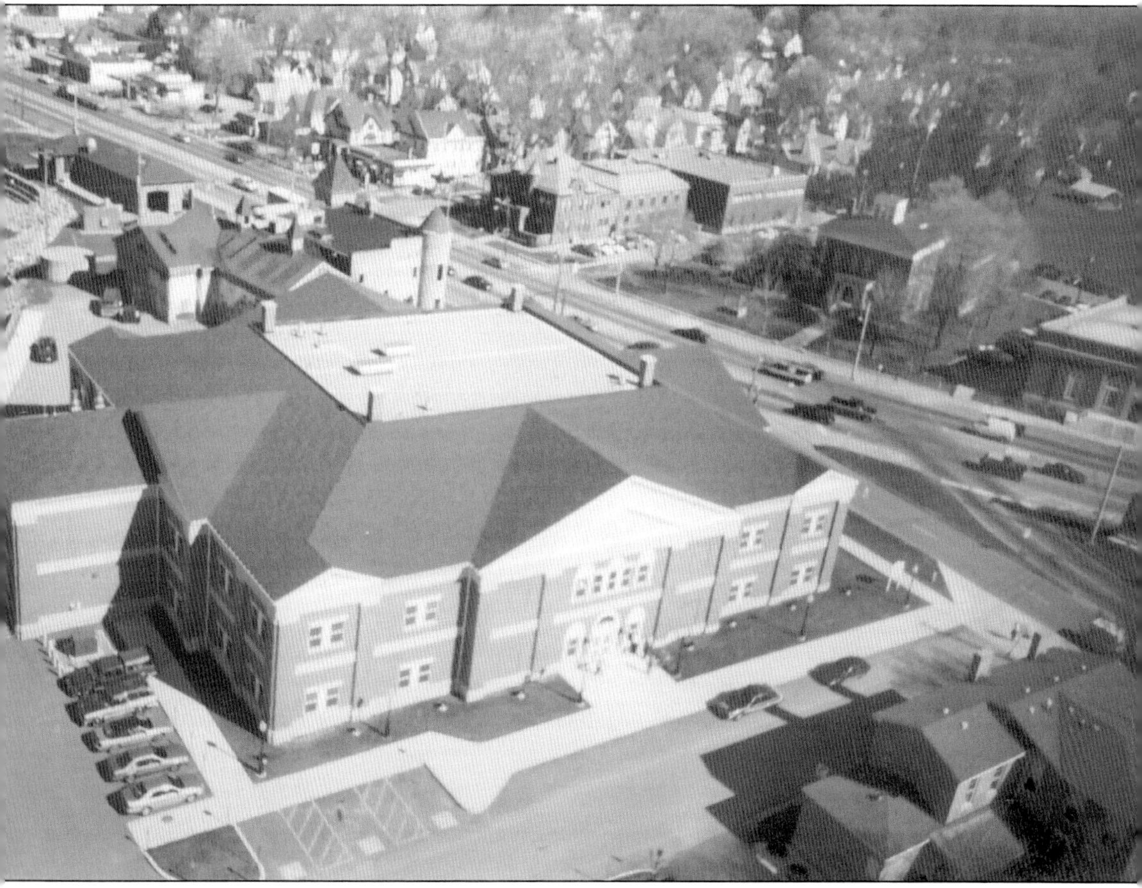

This is a bird's-eye view of the original Indian trails in modern times. Visible are the post office, the city hall, and the Genesee County Jail on the north side of Route 5, and the courts facility, the Genesee County History Department, and the central pump station on the south side.

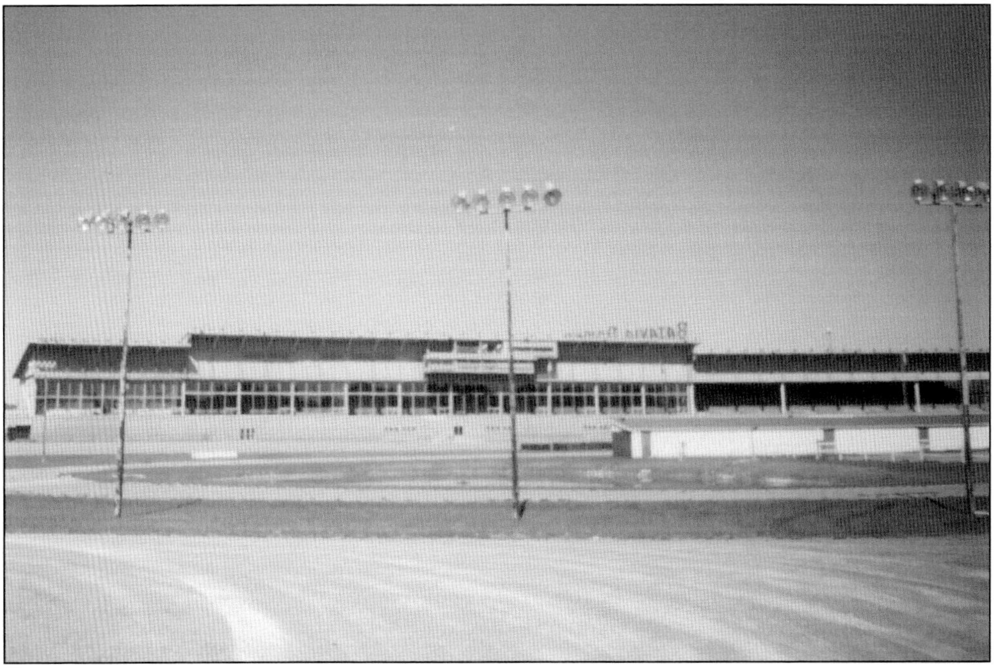

This above photograph shows Batavia Downs, which at the end of the 20th century was awaiting new plans from new owners, OTB. Below is a view of the racetrack at Batavia Downs.

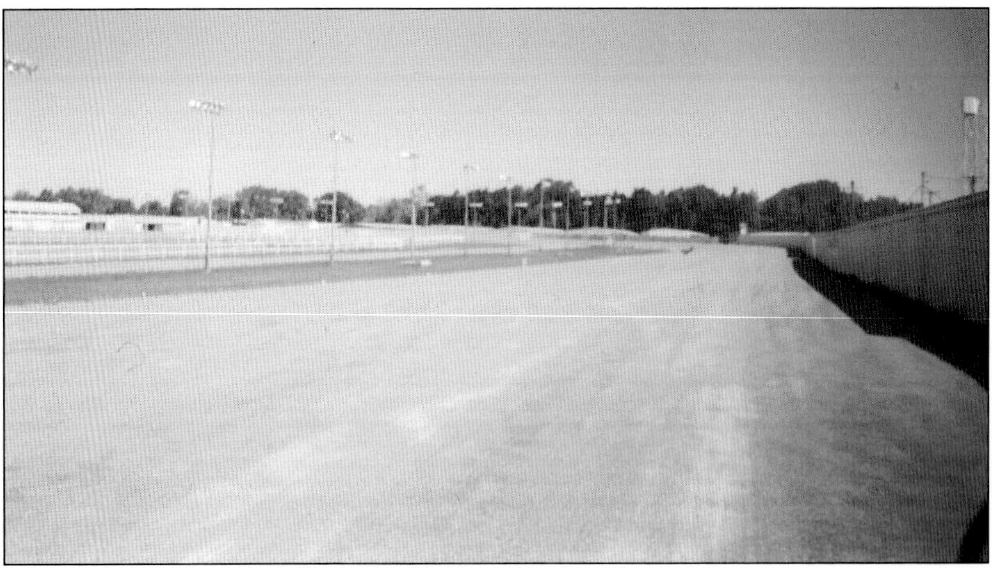

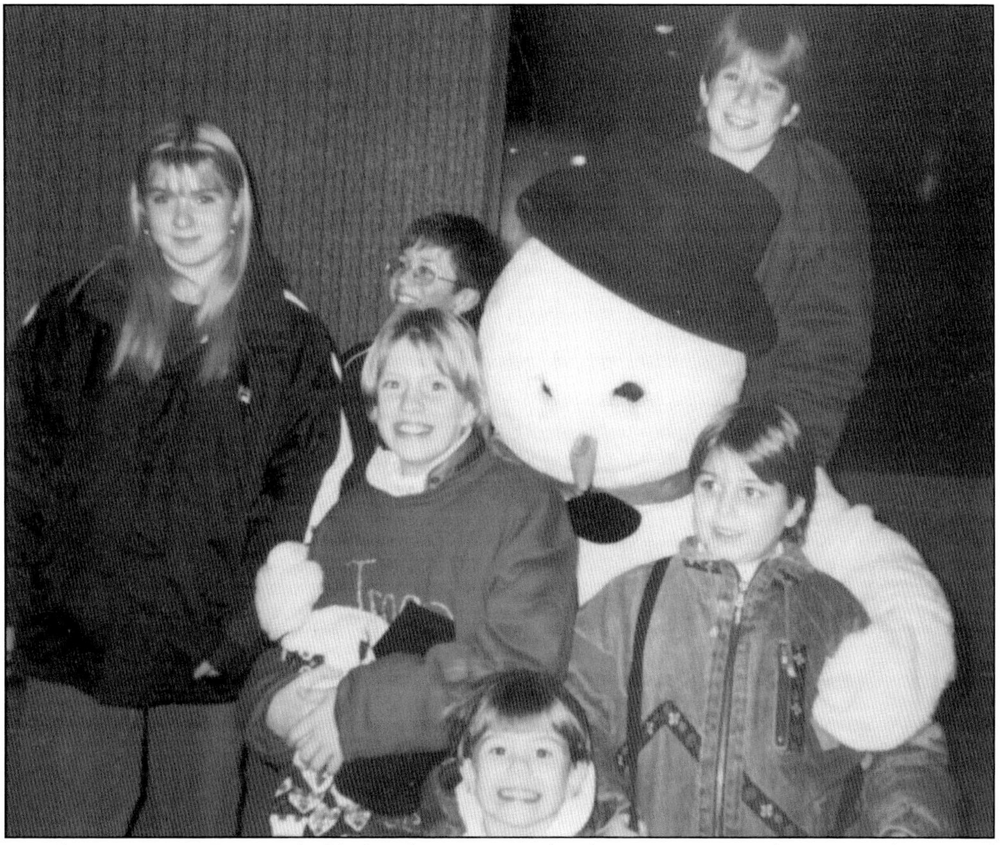

At Christmastime, Batavia holds family events in the downtown area. This one is the annual Christmas in the City, which offers the community a time to come together.

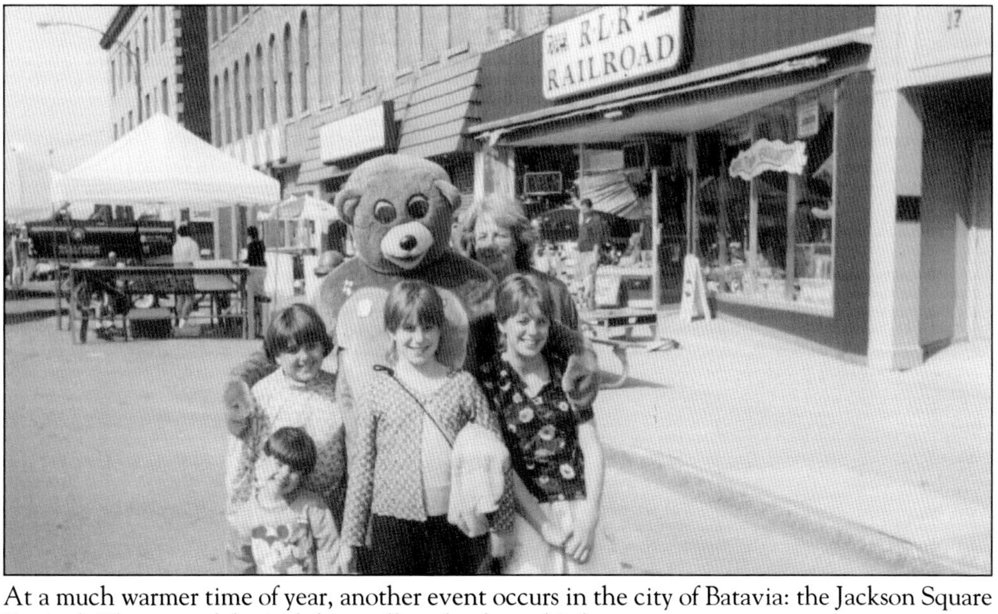

At a much warmer time of year, another event occurs in the city of Batavia: the Jackson Square Festival. The annual festival draws all smiles from this happy group.

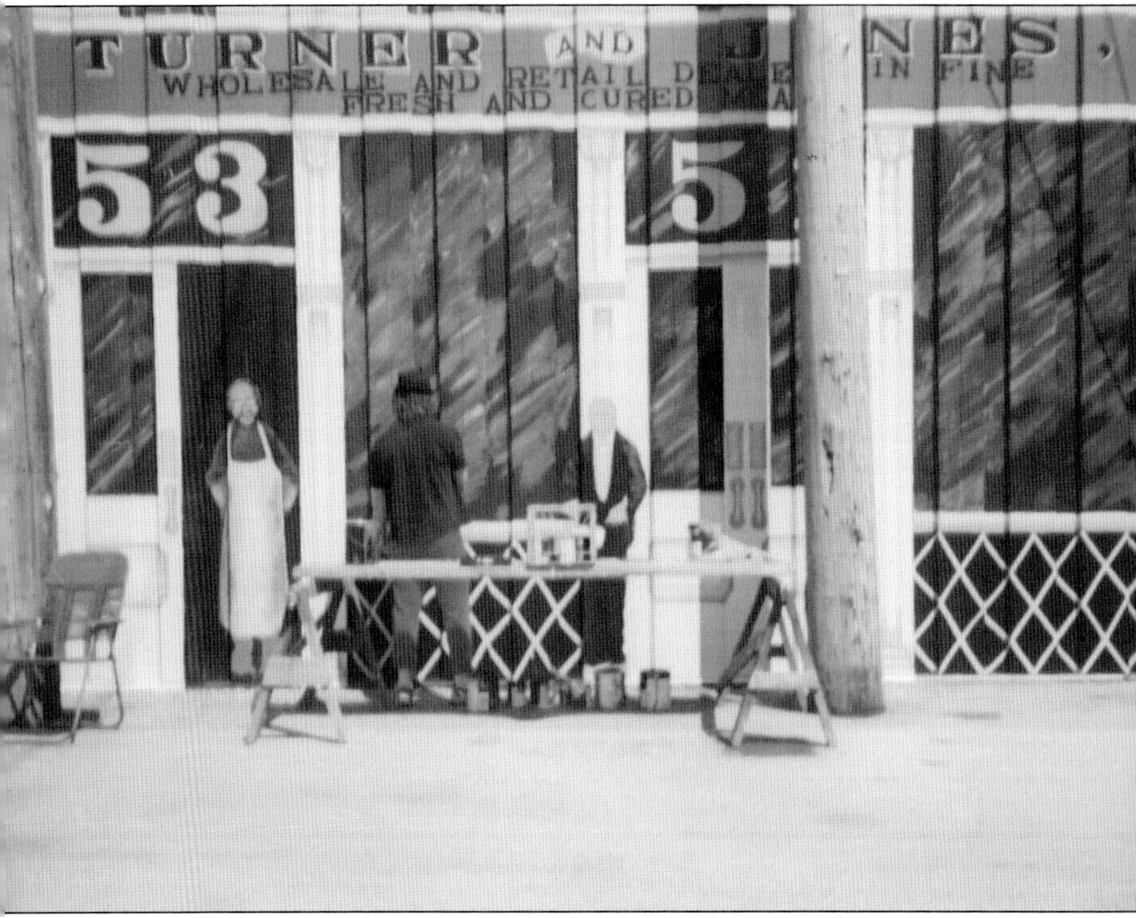

This area is named Jackson Square after the alley that is being spruced up by local artist Vincent Del Plato. The Batavia Improvement District Committee sponsored this cleanup project.

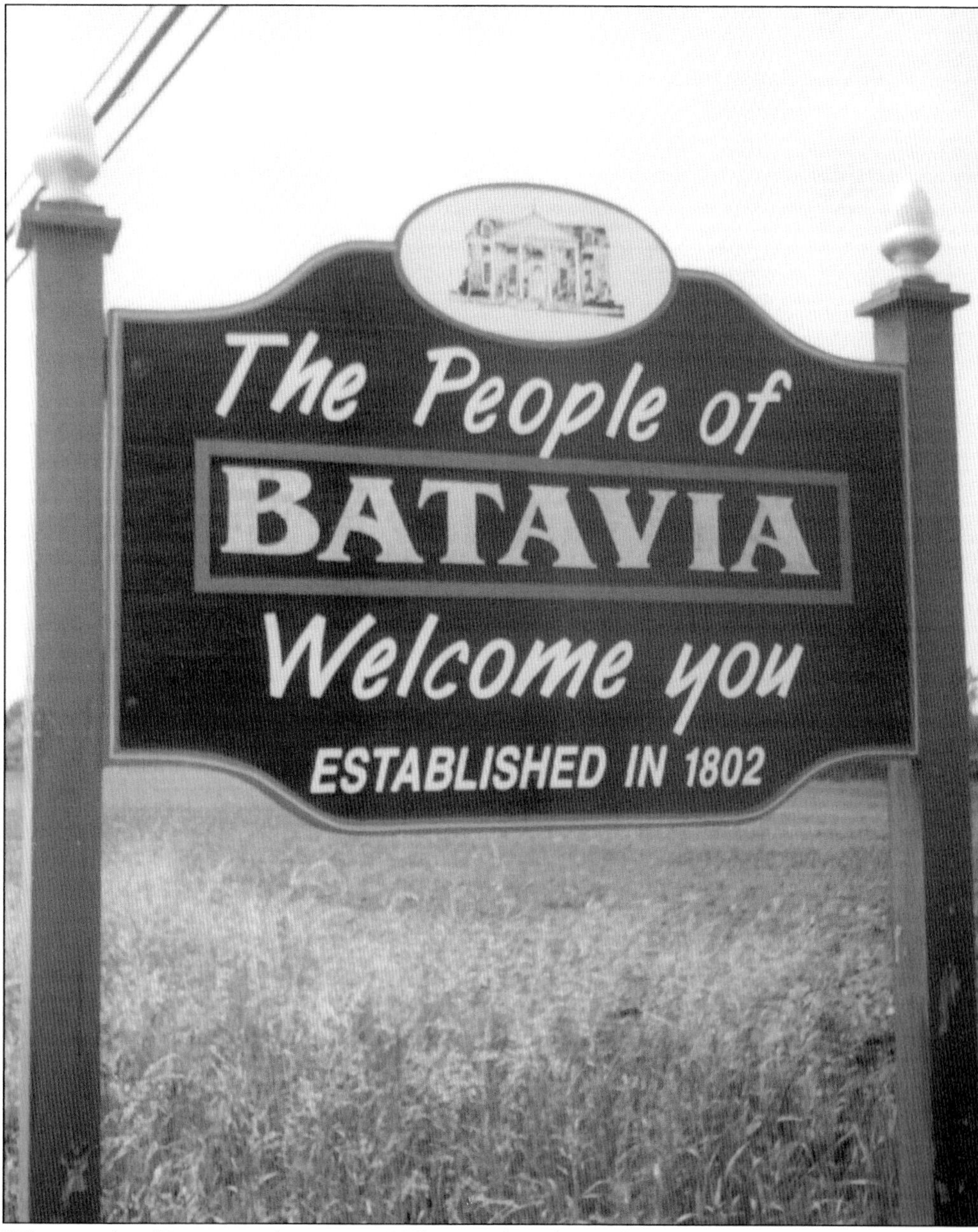

"The people of Batavia welcome you." This sign has the Holland Land Office Museum pictured at the top and the date that Batavia was established at the bottom. It greets everyone who enters the city limits from all major routes.

ACKNOWLEDGMENTS

First, I would like to thank all the citizens of Batavia who have opened up their homes, their collections, and their experiences so that I could add a personal touch to this pictorial history. Their memories, reminiscences, postcards, photographs, and personal histories are what have shaped and formed this book.

Thanks goes to Karl and Helen Bucholtz, Janet Cecere, Ruth McEvoy, Susan Conklin and all her staff at the Genesee County History Department.

I also extend thanks to Aunts Gladys Haworth and Ellen Price, Don Carmichael, Patricia Burr, Lester Wright, Walt Zelinski, Terry Peters, Jim Carney, the Holland Land Office Museum, Tom Rosica, Marlene Ackerman, and Phil Zipkin.

Also, I must thank my niece and nephews, Brianne and Ryan Toal and Shawn Wetmore, who helped me place the first picture with the text.

Finally, I could never have completed the book without the members of my extended "family," who encouraged me to forge ahead through countless hours at the library and at the computer: Christine Syracusa, Jessica Brantis, Rachel Brantis, Kaytlyn Warner, and Josette Warner. Thank you.

Any misrepresentations in this book are inadvertent and I accept all responsibility.

It is my hope that this work will provides future generations with some knowledge of, and some sense of value for, their local history.

I would like to dedicate this book to my mother and my father, who through the years taught me the value of community life; to my sister and brother for their support in all my endeavors; to the children of my brother and my sister; and to my late adopted son, Michael John Barbeau, a sorrowful loss that has renewed my appreciation of family and of history.